ANCIENT PHILOSOPHY

Ancient Philosophy

D M Singh

MD Publications Pvt Ltd
New Delhi
www.mdppl.com

Published by :

MD Publications Pvt Ltd
"MD House", 11, Darya Ganj,
New Delhi - 110 002
Phone : +91-11- 45355555
E-mail : contact@mdppl.com
Website: www.mdppl.com

ISBN : 978-81-7533-338-3

Published and Printed by Mr. Pranav Gupta on behalf of **MD Publications Pvt Ltd** at Repro India Limited.

PREFACE

Ancient philosophy is the philosophy of the Graeco-Roman world from the 6th century BC to the 6th century AD. It is usually divided into three periods: the pre-Socratic period, the period of Plato and Aristotle, and the post-Aristotelian period. A fourth period that is sometimes added includes the Neoplatonic and Christian philosophers of Late Antiquity. The most important of the ancient philosophers are Plato and Aristotle.

The main subjects of ancient philosophy are: understanding the fundamental causes and principles of the universe; explaining it in an economical way; the epistemological problem of reconciling the diversity and change of the natural universe, with the possibility of obtaining fixed and certain knowledge about it; questions about things that cannot be perceived by the senses, such as numbers, elements, universals, and gods. Socrates is said to have been the initiator of more focused study upon the human things including the analysis of patterns of reasoning and argument and the nature of the good life and the importance of understanding and knowledge in order to pursue it; the explication of the concept of justice, and its relation to various political systems. In this period the crucial features of the philosophical method were established: a critical approach to received or established views, and the appeal to reason and argumentation.

While there are ancient relations between the Indian Vedas and the Iranian Avesta, the two main families of the Indo-Iranian philosophical traditions were characterized by fundamental differences in their implications for the human being's position in society and their view on the role of man in the universe. The first charter of human rights by Cyrus the Great as understood in the Cyrus cylinder is often seen as a reflection of the questions and thoughts expressed by Zarathustra and developed in Zoroastrian schools of thought. Indian philosophy begins with the Vedas where questions related to laws of nature, the origin of the universe and the place of man in it are asked.

In the Vedic view, creation is ascribed to the self-consciousness of the primeval being. This leads to the inquiry into the one being that underlies the diversity of empirical phenomena and the origin of all things. Cosmic order is termed rta and causal law by karma. Nature is taken to have three qualities sattva, rajas, and tamas.

I am very grateful to Mr. Pranav Gupta, Director of MD Publications Pvt Ltd, New Delhi, for his kind cooperation and support for this book.

D M Singh

CONTENTS

1

Ancient Philosophy and Its Impact

Introduction

Socrates is talking to a friend, Aristippus, who believes in going for what you want when you want it and not deferring your gratifications. Socrates objects that as a policy this may be dangerous; if you are unable to control your desires you may end up at the mercy of people who can, and who use their superior self-mastery to compete with you successfully and to gain control over your life. Aristippus doubts this. He can, he says, lead a life which is devoted to self-gratification and yet manage to avoid being dominated by others; and this is the way to happiness.

Socrates disagrees. It isn't, he thinks, just a matter of evading what others can do to you. It's a matter of how you regard your own life. To make the point he tells Prodicus' story of how the demi-god Heracles, at the start of adult life, came to a crossroads. Two women came along, each urging him to take one of the opposing ways. One was self-consciously fashionable.

The Sophists

'Sophists' is the term used for a number of intellectuals in the fifth century BC who, while they did not form a unified intellectual tradition, represented a new departure. They travelled around various cities, teaching for money a variety of intellectual skills, the most saleable being skills in rhetoric and argument which would give the Learner an advantage in public life. Although only some of their concerns fit into the philosophical tradition, they have remained on its edge because Plato immortalized them in many of his dialogues as pompous incompetent fools, a foil to his own hero Socrates. Plato's depiction is gleefully unfair, but we Lack enough independent evidence to counter it in any detail.

The most famous sophists were Hippias of Elis, Prodicus of Cos, Thrasymachus of Chalcedon and Protagoras of Abdera. Hippias was famous for the Large number of his accomplishments and Prodicus for his study of Language. Thrasymachus is portrayed in the *Republic* as holding an account of justice which aggressively reduces it to the interest of the stronger. Protagoras is the only one who held an important philosophical thesis, namely relativism, the view that for a belief to be true is just for it to appear true to the person who holds it. Plato refutes this view in his dialogue *Theaetetus*.

Plato despises the sophists for many reasons. He rejects their views, particulary relativism, and he thinks that teaching intellectual skills for money debases these by turning them into commodities, valued for what they do for you rather than respected for their own sake. He also thinks that, just because they do not take it seriously, the sophists are in fact incompetent at philosophical argument. In his presentation of them, of course, they certainly are bold and made-up; she ran ahead of him and urged him to take the easy road of satisfying desires and going through life doing what he wanted, deliberating only as to how to do so with least effort. My friends, she said, call me Happiness, though my enemies call me Vice (or Pleasure). The other woman, solemn and modest in manner, appealed by her words rather than her appearance, and urged him to follow her, Virtue, even though her way was one of effort and frequent frustration rather than easy success. What I offer, she said, is worth while but requires work and self-denial; vice and pleasure offer an easy road to happiness, but the initial appeal fades and leaves you with nothing worth having, whereas virtue is the way to achievement and respect, which forms real happiness.

The Choice of Heracles forms a frequent subject in western art. The version illustrated here, by Paolo de Matteis, was commissioned in 1712 by the philosopher Anthony Ashley Cooper, third earl of Shaftesbury, to provide an illustration for his own book on virtue. It and many similar depictions reinforce something that makes a modern reader uncomfortable: moral choice is depicted as two females competing for a man. Moreover, even though one point is that what matters is reality, not appearance, this point is itself expressed in terms of one female being, on due consideration, more attractive than the other.

But apart from this, we may feel puzzled as to why this story, which seems to us over-obvious, should be famous. Clearly, we may think, if you are asked to choose between virtue and vice, you should choose virtue, but that's the easy part; the hard part is working out what virtue is, and depicting it as a modest maiden rather than a shameless floozy not only is a sexist way of presenting it, but doesn't help us much. If we think this, it is probably because much twentieth century ethical thinking has made the ancient ethical framework unfamiliar. But this is a comparatively recent development, and one now rapidly being reversed, as virtue becomes more familiar in both philosophical and political discourse. We are now, it turns out, in quite a good position to appreciate the claims of Virtue on Heracles.

Virtue and Vice are offering Heracles differing roads to happiness. Prodicus was one of the first philosophers to make explicit something important; we are all, in our lives, aiming at happiness. We find the thought also in the slightly later philosophers Democritus and Plato; the latter stresses that it would be ludicrous to deny that happiness is our overall goal in life, the destination on everyone's road.

But Prodicus also made a mark by emphasizing something else. When you are starting out on adult life, aiming at happiness, and doing so consciously, you will be faced with a *choice*. You can't have it all; you can't go through life gratifying your desires and still hope to achieve anything worthwhile or to live a life that you or others can respect. Recognizing explicitly that your aim in life is happiness brings with it the realization that you have to reflect on and order your life in one way rather than another. Life presents you with the alternatives; you have to make the decisions. Centuries later Cicero, aware of much sophisticated discussion, still thought that the story said something profound about everybody's life and their attitude to it.

Happiness and Pleasure

In the different tellings of the story the shameless floozy is indifferently Vice or Pleasure. In our traditions of moral philosophy it may seem strange that pleasure is the bad, rejected way of getting happiness. John Stuart Mill, a major founder of the Utilitarian tradition, actually defined happiness as pleasure and the absence of pain, but even if we do not see happiness as actually constituted by pleasure it still seems somewhat odd to see happiness as achieved by virtue *as opposed to* pleasure. Here we can see that ancient ethical thought gives a different conceptual role to happiness.

Happiness in ancient ethical thought is not a matter of feeling good or being pleased; it is not a feeling or emotion at all. It is your life as a whole which is said to be happy or not, and so discussions of happiness are discussions of the happy life. It is our bad luck that for us what is happy are not just lives, but also moments and fleeting experiences; modern discussions of happiness tend to get confused very rapidly because such different things are being considered. In ancient ethics happiness enters ethical discussion by a very different route from the 'feel-good' one.

Sometimes you step back from your routines of daily life and think about your life as a whole. You may be forced to do this by a crisis, or it might be that passing a stage in your life, such as becoming an adult rather than an adolescent — as in the Heracles story makes you think about what you are doing in your life overall, what your values are and what matters most to you. For the ancients this is the beginning of ethical thinking, the entry point for ethical reflection. Once you become self-aware, you have to face choices, and deal with the fact that certain values, and courses of action, exclude others. You have to ask how all your concerns fit together, or fail to fit. What you are looking for, all ancient thinkers assume, is how to make sense of your life as a whole, by bringing your concerns under the heading of your final aim or goal, your *telos*. For someone who fails to unify her concerns in any overall way is radically in denial about the way all her projects are hers, fit together in *her* life.

What can you say about the way your life is tending, the values you are expressing in your life? At first, probably not much. It is only after thinking through some ethical theories that you will have much of an explicit idea as to what values are unifying your life. But there is one thing that you can say, even before venturing on to theory: as philosophers from Prodicus on agree, and as is most famously set forth by Aristotle, everyone agrees that their final end is happiness, and that what people seek in everything they do is to live a happy life.

Why is this supposed to be so obvious? It would not be obvious at all if happiness were introduced via the notion of pleasure or feeling good. But happiness answers to *formal* properties that our final end has. That is, the happy life has to meet certain demands before we can even start asking what its content is; any candidate for being the content virtue, pleasure or whatever has to meet these demands. The overall end which unifies all your concerns has to be *complete*: everything you do or go for is sought for the sake of it, while it is not sought for the sake of anything further. It also has to be *self-sufficient*: it does not leave out any element in your life that has value as part of living well. These are common-sense points, though they have powerful implications. And on the level of common sense or intuition, happiness is the only aim, plausible as an aim in your life as a whole, which is complete and self-sufficient. We do other things in order to be happy, but it makes no sense to be happy for some further reason. And once we are living happily we lack nothing further to be living well. These points are obvious with the ancient conception of happiness. But, as Aristotle immediately points out, they do not settle very much, for great disagreement remains as to how happiness should be specified, and the different schools of thought about ethics take off from here.

One point is clear right from the start, however. Happiness is having a happy life it applies to your life overall. Pleasure, however, is more naturally taken to be something episodic, something you can feel now and not later. It is something you experience as we perform the activities which make up your life. You can be enjoying a meal, a conversation, even life one moment and not the next; but you cannot, in the ancient way of thinking, be happy one moment and not the next, since happiness applies to your life as a whole.

Hence we can see why Pleasure's role in Prodicus' story is to provide an obviously faulty road to happiness. Pleasure fixes us on the here and now, the present desire which asks to be satisfied; and this gets in the way of the self-control and rational overall reflection which is required by a life devoted to things that are worth while. Pleasure is short-term, while happiness is long-term. So, in complete opposition to the modern way of looking at the matter, it looks as though pleasure is not even in the running to be a candidate for happiness. How could your life as a whole be focused on a short-term reward like pleasure? Someone who does this is making a big mistake, giving in to the present satisfaction at the cost of a proper concern for the rest of his life.

In fact hedonism, the view that pleasure is our ethical end, is always on the defensive in ancient ethics. Opponents like to make it appear as though this is because there is something inherently unworthy about humans going for pleasure, but this is edifying rhetoric. The problem is rather that pleasure is defective as an aim that could structure a person's entire life. We can see this in the two major hedonist theories.

Aristippus founded a school called Cyrenaics after their home at Cyrene in North Africa. It was not a very unified school, but they all held that our final end namely what we seek in everything we do is pleasure, and by pleasure they uncompromisingly meant what we experience when we enjoy or feel good about some experience. Pleasure is a movement, not a settled state (and so is pain). Pleasures do not differ from one another, and one pleasure is not more pleasant than another; that is, pleasure is taken to be a single kind of experience which is always the same whatever the circumstances which produce it. We have access to pleasure only by our direct experience of it, and we have knowledge only of our experiences, not of the objects which produce them. Hence past pleasures, which have vanished, and future pleasures, which are still to come, cannot be compared with the present pleasure which we experience, and the Cyrenaics sometimes speak as though only the present exists; certainly the present is all that matters, and our lives should be so shaped as to get present pleasure.

Kinds of Hedonism

Aristippus of Cyrene in North Africa (c. 435-355BC) went to Athens and was an associate of Socrates. Evidence about his Life is unreliable, consisting mainly of anecdotes showing him Living a colourful Life devoted to gratification, with no care for his dignity or for other people. However, he cared enough about his daughter, Arete, to teach her his ideas, and she passed them on to her son, Aristippus the Younger, who may be the source of the systematic philosophy attributed to the school of Cyrene.

Epicurus of Athens (341-270 BC) developed his own version of hedonism in a way that he represented as self-taught, although he did have some philosophical education. Around 307 he set up a philosophical school in Athens. Unlike the schools of Plato, Aristotle and the Stoics, it was not one which met in a public place and in which teaching prominently included argument and debate. Epicurus' school was called the Garden after its home, and his teaching put a premium on Learning and memorizing the words of Epicurus and other founding members. Discussion took place orally and in writing throughout the school's history, but Epicureans regarded Epicurus as a saviour from unhappiness and a shining Light in a way that philosophers from other schools found too deferential. Epicurus' main contribution was his hedonistic ethics; in his philosophy of nature he took over the views of the earlier Atomist Democritus, developing a world-view in which, unusually in ancient philosophy, there is no room for providence or teleology of any kind, and the gods, though they exist, take no interest in the world or in human beings.

This might sound like a suicidal strategy for living your life, one that is bound to favour short-term production of intense present pleasure from, for example, sex and drugs, with no thought for your future. In fact the Cyrenaics do not have to hold this; they only have to hold that reflection on and concern for your life as a whole has value only insofar as it tends to produce present pleasure. This means that overall reflection about your life can have value only instrumentally, as a means to something else. This thought seems to have been found deeply unpersuasive; at any rate the Cyrenaics were never more than an eccentric school in ancient ethical thought.

Epicurus seems to have learned from their failure, and he makes an effort to present pleasure as a candidate for happiness that meets the overall demands, thus making his theory more acceptable and mainstream. Your concern with your whole life, he thinks, is not just a means to enjoyment of the present; rather, it matters to you in its own right, as people commonly think. However, the happy life is, in fact, a life of pleasure.

We can see from the moves already made that this is going to sound strange: how can focusing on short-term gratifications also be a long term concern with what matters overall in your life? Epicurus has to deny that pleasure is always short-term enjoyment. There are two kinds of pleasure, he insists, and while one of them is the kind of enjoyment that people get from activities such as eating, drinking, sex and the like, and is a 'movement', there is also another, 'static' kind, and *this* is what we should be seeking as the right way of achieving the happy life. Static pleasure is the absence of bodily pain and mental trouble; it is the state where you are functioning without impediment or discomfort. Epicurus boldly claims that this state is the highest pleasure that we can achieve-that is, you achieve happiness not by doing things that make you feel good, but by so ordering your life that you achieve this condition of painlessness and tranquillity. Unsurprisingly, doing this involves 'sober reasoning', which scrutinizes your life carefully and rejects activities which will result overall in impingements on your tranquillity. Hence short-term gratification and success is rejected if the results will lead to a less balanced and undisturbed plan of life overall. The Epicurean happy life, then, far from being a wild pursuit of fun experience, turns out to be a cautious and risk-aversive strategy for maintaining tranquillity. Critics did not tire of pointing out that, even if this is an acceptable idea of living happily, it is a peculiar conception of the most *pleasant* way we could live.

We can see why, given the ancient framework for ethics, hedonism is at a disadvantage. Hedonists seem condemned to giving an implausible account either of happiness, as with Aristippus, or of pleasure, as with Epicurus.

Our modern conception of happiness is frequently understood in terms of pleasure and desire-satisfaction (something aided by the wide and confused way we use 'happy'), and this can make it hard at first to see the appeal of ancient theories of happiness. If happiness is just getting what you want, then the ideas in the Choice of Heracles make no sense. However, our ideas about happiness derive from many sources and also contain elements more congenial to eudaimonism. We think of a happy life as involving achievement and success, for example, rather than just getting what you want. Theories of happiness as desire-satisfaction systematically run into problems once we face them with thoughts about our life as a whole.

Happiness and Virtue

Until recently, though, the really alien idea in the Choice of Heracles would have been thought to be the role of Virtue. In modern ethical thought, until quite recently, virtue had become something of a joke concept, one that could be understood only historically and could not be seriously used in ethical thinking. In the last decade, however, 'virtue ethics' has had a spectacular comeback. Once again, however, we find that there is not a perfect match between our notion of virtue and the ancient one, and so some explanation and comparison is needed.

A minimal conception of ancient virtue is that of having a systematic concern to do the morally right thing. All that this assumes is that we have some grip on the idea of doing what is morally right, as opposed to what is wrong. We do not have to start with an elaborate theory as to what is morally right; our account of this is deepened as the account of virtue develops.

Virtue is a richer notion than this, but already it is distinguished from non-moral concerns the idea, for example, that virtue is a sort of non-moral 'excellence'. (Unfortunately, a misguided attempt to 'modernize' ancient ethical texts has led some translators to render the Greek word *arete* by 'excellence' rather than the supposedly old-fashioned 'virtue', thus obscuring the point that the texts are about morality. This is especially unfortunate now that modern moral philosophers are recognizing the moral import of virtue.)

Someone wanting to be prepared to do the morally right thing, not just occasionally but systematically, will have to have developed self-mastery and strength of mind to overcome the (very many) incentives we have to do something else. Hence it is not surprising that Virtue tells Heracles that her way is difficult and often unpleasant and frustrating. It is fine to do the morally right thing, but the virtuous person has to do a lot more than that. She has to develop a disposition, a firm state, of doing the morally right thing. And to get to that point she has to have developed two things, a firm understanding of morality and the willingness to act on it. Neither is easy or rapidly developed, and by the time someone is virtuous he will have made himself be a certain kind of person. Hence there is a connexion between virtue and your life as a whole: becoming virtuous is becoming a person with a certain kind of *character*, and this requires reflecting in a thoughtful way about your life as a whole and the kind of person you aspire to be, as well as having the motivation to follow through on this. Neither is going to happen if you simply go along satisfying your desires and never developing the ability to think and act in the long term.

The modern conception of virtue is in many ways weaker than this. A virtue is often thought of as a kind of habit of acting in a certain way; this makes the virtues look like separate habits which grow up in locally isolated ways, since it certainly seems that you can develop a habit of generous giving without having a habit of acting bravely. In the ancient way of looking at it, isolated habits of action have to be unified by your understanding of what is morally appropriate, since it could hardly be the case that morality made one set of requirements for generosity and another, quite unrelated set for courage. In ancient ethics the point is not to have localized virtues but to be virtuous, to have the unified understanding which grounds all the virtues and is called practical wisdom or *phronesis*.

The ancient conception of virtue, moreover, is one in which practical wisdom takes the form of practical reasoning which is integrated with the motivation to do it. There are many ancient theories as to the relation of reason and emotion; but all agree that in the virtuous person emotion and feeling are not, or are no longer, fighting against reason. The person who understands what the moral action requires, but has to battle down contrary motivation in order to do it, is not yet virtuous, but only self-controlled. Virtue requires that the person's motivation go along with her understanding.

Virtue, then, is a pretty demanding idea, in the ancient way of looking at it. It's not hard to see why critics of Epicurus' hedonism charged that he could not account for virtue. If pleasure is what we should be going for as our overall aim, then it is hard to see why we should care about the claims of morality except as means to gaining pleasure or avoiding pain. Epicurus denies that he is committed to this, but his critics seem to have the better of him here.

Most pressing, in ancient ethical debates, is the issue of the place of virtue in happiness. Virtue is the right pathway to the happy life, but this leaves many options open. Happiness is our overall aim, the goal for whose sake we do and seek everything else, while we don't seek to be happy for any further reason. Being a virtuous person will matter for this, but surely, we may think, common sense requires that other things matter too for example, having a reasonable amount of money and other necessities, achieving success and so on. How could a happy life be a completely poverty-stricken and unsuccessful one?

Aristotle, who among ancient philosophers sticks most closely to common sense, agrees that this reaction of ours is an important one. Happiness, he holds, does require some amount of 'external goods' like money and success. On their own, no amount of such goods could make you happy, since whether or not you have them is not primarily up to you, and he thinks that, once you have begun to reflect ethically on your life, happiness must come from your own reflection on and organization of your life, and cannot just lie in external goods that circumstances can give and take away. Aristotle, however, fights shy of the idea that you can make yourself happy by making yourself virtuous. If that were so, he says, then a virtuous person would be happy even if he met with great and undeserved misfortunes, such as being tortured on the rack and that would be hopelessly absurd.

Aristotle's conclusion tends to sound reasonable to us, since we have almost certainly never thought that being a virtuous or moral person is sufficient for having a happy life; so we can miss the point that in terms of the ancient theories it is a very unsatisfactory position to be in. He has to hold that the kind of person you are matters for having a happy life more than having money, status and so on, which matter only a certain amount; but he cannot say just how much they matter, since he is unwilling to say that a person who loses just that amount of money, status or whatever, is bound to be unhappy. Often he stresses that what is significant for living a happy life is not the goods you have but the use you make of them; just as the shoemaker does the best he can with whatever leather he has, and people who have suffered misfortunes do the best they can with what circumstances allow them. Hence he is unwilling to allow that a virtuous person who at the end of his life falls into great misfortune (such as Priam, the good king of Troy who lives to see his sons killed and city destroyed) must be considered to have lost their happiness. On the other hand, he wants to skirt what he sees as the ridiculous conclusion that the virtuous person is, just by being virtuous, happy whatever bad things happen to him. Hence he can allow neither that Priam after the fall of Troy is happy, nor that he is unhappy; he is torn between the common-sense view that of course he isn't happy, and the more theoretical idea that he has not lost his happiness, since happiness has to come from what you have made of your life, not from what other people do to you. So Aristotle's position is not really coherent an irony, since he is the ancient philosopher most popular with and appealed to by modern authors developing theories of 'virtue ethics'.

Plato and the Stoics, more willing than Aristotle to discount ordinary views, defend the view that being virtuous is sufficient for a happy life. We can see that this is not, in the framework of ancient ethical thinking, the disastrously high-minded but implausible claim that it would seem if brought out without preface nowadays, but it may still seem unrealistic.

They think, however, that Aristotle makes a mistake in allowing that external evils subtract from the contribution to happiness that virtue makes. In fact, they think, virtue has a quite different kind of value. The Stoics put this point dramatically by saying that virtue is the only thing that *is* good, whereas health, money and so on should be called 'indifferent', although if we naturally go for something, such as health, it is a 'preferred indifferent'. They were not afraid to make themselves sound somewhat ridiculous by inventing new terminology disallowing straightforward computation that includes both virtue and external goods. In this respect they anticipate some of Kant's ideas about moral and non-moral value.

But is it just high-minded assertion that virtue is what matters most? Among the ways this is defended is the view, widespread in ancient ethics, that virtue is a kind of understanding of moral value (an understanding which, as we have seen, includes and is not opposed to affect and positive motivation), one that can be seen as an expertise or skill, exercised on the materials provided by the circumstances of your life. Just as a product or a work of art can be produced skilfully even with limited or inferior materials (something clearest in the performing arts) so a life can be well, and so happily lived even though the circumstances the person had to work on were inferior or positively bad. Aristotle comes near this idea when he compares the person in misfortune to the shoemaker doing the best he can with inferior leather; but he is too impressed by the idea that the product will be inferior to appreciate the point that the exercise of skill, the actual performance of the expert, may well be as impressive (or more so) in reduced circumstances as in good ones. The idea that virtue is a skill and that external advantages are its material makes prominent the idea that you make your own life; whatever you have to work with, the moral quality of your life comes from the way you live it, the choices you make and their implications for your character.

This idea is strikingly egalitarian, and accounts for the Stoic position that happiness is attainable not just by those well-provided by life with money, good looks and status, but also by those who have bad luck: slaves, the conquered, people in limited social positions, like most women in the ancient world. It is notable that two of our major Stoic texts from the period of the Roman empire come from Marcus Aurelius, an Emperor, and from Epictetus, a freed slave. Stoicism was available equally to both of them as a philosophy to live by.

But if external goods do not contribute to our happiness, why should we even bother with them? The Stoic position here is subtle and hard to Can you be happy on the rack?

'The happy man needs the goods of the body and external goods, i.e. those of fortune. In order that he may not be impeded. Those who say that the victim on the rack or the man who falls into great misfortunes is happy if he is good are, whether they mean to or not, talking nonsense.'

' Aristotle's works on this, the *Nicomachean Ethics* and others, have ideas about virtue which are petty and grovelling and vulgar. thcy dare to grab from virtuc the diadem and royal sceptre which she holds inalienably from Zeus. They do not permit her to make us happy, but put her on a Level with money, status, noble birth, health, beauty and other things which are common to virtue and vice. Just as any of these without virtue is not sufficient to render its possessor happy, so virtue without these, they say, is in the same way insufficient to make its possessor happy. How, then, is the value of virtue not destroyed and overthrown?'

Atticus, second century AD Platonist express briefly, but important here is the idea that we should make moral decisions from where we are. When you start to think about virtue, you are not a blank slate; you already have a given nature with needs for food, security, and so on, and also a social position: you already have a family, a nation, a job, and so on. It would be absurd, flouting human nature, to try to sacrifice or ignore these facts in the name of virtue; rather, we should aim to deal virtuously with them, always remembering that the demands of virtue trump them. Again, there are many affinities with Kant's moral thinking.

Virtue, Ancient and Modern

'Virtue ethics' has recently moved to the foreground of contemporary moral thinking, and with it an engagement with ancient ethical theories (unfortunately with a disproportionate emphasis on Aristotle). A common worry, which threatens to isolate the ancients from us, is that the development of a virtue is the development of a habit of doing the morally right thing but what that is, is given by what virtuous people in your society do. Virtues develop within cultures and traditions; noticing this obvious enough point sometimes produces the charge that eudaimonist ethics is essentially conservative. Aristotle delineates the virtues recognized in *his* society; but these are the virtues of a privileged élite – free adult Greek males — and have dubious moral relevance beyond that, or to potential social improvements.

This common charge misses the point. Of course we begin by emulating the people we recognize as virtuous in our society; hence, unsurprisingly, virtues differ between cultures. But this is all prior to the beginning of ethical thought; ancient ethics begins at the point when the individual starts to reflect about her life as a whole, and make decisions which recognize the necessity of choosing between options, as Heracles does. The ancient ethical agent takes charge of his life; as practical reasoning develops he becomes ever more in control of it, and ever more responsible for the quality of it. Of course the result is different now from what it was in ancient Greece. How could it not be? The options are different. What is the same is the difference that is made when the agent stops drifting along in her life and taking for granted the social pressures on it, and starts to think ethically about it and the form it takes.

Ancient ethical thought is attractive because, among other things, it unites two concerns which are hard to find together in other traditions. One is a sense of the demands of morality, the recognition that morality makes a huge difference to all of your life.

2

Desire's Hunger and Plato's Ideas

Introduction

Plato's sexual reforms also have great significance in the history of sexual morality in Western culture. In a transmuted form, his ideas influenced the sexual prescriptions of the Jewish Platonist Philo and Christian Platonist church fathers, such as Clement. Plato's dream to break and bridle Greek sexual mores finally gained authoritative power in this Alexandrian religious venue, which was itself undergoing a turbulent, and at times violent, transition between the times of Philo and Clement, for this was when Christianity in Alexandria was developing partly from, and partly in opposition to, Judaism in Alexandria. In this venue, however, Plato's ideas succeeded only in a limited way and on religious terms distant from his own. He would have needed an interpreter to understand how the problems that he associates with uncontrolled sexual desire were written into the Tenth Commandment that Philo and Clement produced. My concern in this chapter, however, is to elucidate Plato's principles of sexual and reproductive conduct along with their underlying motivations and ambitious social aims.

These features include the impulse for genital stimulation, which Plato thinks has a strong proclivity to become corrupt, the related impulse to reproduce, and the broader social practices a populace must follow to behave with appropriate sexual and procreative decorum. Plato aims to minimize and preferably to eliminate what he regards as ingrained customs of sexual unrestraint that have myriad harmful effects on the individual and society. In their place he seeks to install civic mores that are motivated by and consistent with the virtue of sexual moderation that he formulates in the *Republic, Laws,* and other dialogues.

To Plato's mind, of course, human erotic experience goes well beyond the irrational sexual appetite and the desire to reproduce. He appreciates that persons become aroused for reasons beyond the sexually appetitive, as shown in his explorations of the Platonic love for the beauty of the body, for the beauty of the soul, and for the form of Beauty itself. Though Plato is well disposed toward Platonic eros, he does not try to mandate its attainment among his prospective guardians and citizens. In the *Republic* and *Laws,* he writes like a sex educator, legislator, and philosophical city founder, not, as in the *Symposium* and *Phaedrus,* like a transcendental prose poet on fire for Beauty. My study follows suit. I concentrate on Plato's sexual regulations, the conception of genital and reproductive urges that informs them, and the broader nexus of customs he would establish to control those urges. Platonic eros is relevant here mainly for the forceful distinctions he makes between it and the appetitive desire for genital pleasure and procreation.

Attributing Ideas to Plato

Plato allows us access to his ideas in his middle and later writings, even though he wrote dialogues with many voices rather than treatises in his own voice. Here I am concerned strictly with the middle and later works, such as the *Republic* and *Laws,* because these dialogues contain his ideas about sexual desire and sexual reform. In these writings, the primary dialectician offers a number of coherent ideas, including principles of sexual conduct, that Plato seriously maintained at the time he wrote them. This is not to suggest, however, that Plato doctrinally adhered in perpetuity to those ideas, used them to construct a grand system, or tried to contain the full compass of his thought in his writings. I mean only that Plato supported the favored dialectician's ideas for some time and is to be held responsible, as author, for being their promulgator. This main figure in the drama, who is often, but not always, Socrates, presents a set of ideas that diverges greatly from the more Socratic set in Plato's early dialogues, especially the aporetic writings. Vlastos and other scholars have inferred that the later set is Plato's and worth studying as such. Aristotle corroborates that this traditional hermeneutic of the middle and later writings is correct, and he explicitly states that Socrates in the *Republic* and the Athenian stranger in the *Laws* reflect Plato's views. To doubt Aristotle's reliability about which ideas are Plato's would be skepticism taken to an extreme, for he was a member of the Academy for twenty years, during the middle period, and he was by and large an intelligent respondent to Plato's thought. Since the favored dialectician in the middle and later dialogues presents sexual principles that belong reliably enough to their author, I call them Plato's here.

Human Desire for Sexual Activity and its Pleasures

Plato considers sexual desire to be a kind of physical appetite for sexual relations, just as hunger and thirst are physical appetites for food and drink. Sexual desire, hunger, and thirst are the three core appetites. "For human beings all things depend on a threefold need and appetite. He reiterates this position more informally elsewhere by grouping sexual desire into this trio of appetites. The body has its "appetites and pleasures," which include "whatever one drinks, eats, and uses for sexual activity," and philosophers give them low priority among their main concerns in life. Persons who suffer from "appetitive licentiousness" (ékolasðoñíåíáa) reveal this condition by "getting drunk, stuffing themselves, and indulging in sexual activity. " Plato in the middle and late dialogues thus both explicitly and implicitly indicates that he considers sexual desire to be a core physical appetite along with hunger and thirst.

The Platonic physical appetites aim for the specific pleasures that come from sating a bodily want. The appetitive aspect of the soul, given its craving for sexual relations, food, and drink, is "comrade of satieties (plhrðëíñþ-óåùísevn) and its pleasures". As Plato sees it, persons stimulated by the appetites more precisely want the replenishment provided by, say, having recently finished a beverage rather than wanting its other pleasant aspects, such as finding it enticing to look at and refreshing to drink in and swallow. Hence the physical appetites in human experience are inseparable from the pleasures that accompany replenishment. The pleasant feelings that occur from eating when one is hungry or drinking when one is thirsty are paradigmatic instances of such pleasures. Plato similarly considers sexual activity to be sufficiently like eating and drinking to class it with them. To our minds the sexual appetite might seem a somewhat unusual member of the trio. Human beings do not die from sexual abstinence as they do from being deprived of water and food, and it is questionable whether lovers feel full from engaging in mutually stimulating sexual relations, even though they may feel satisfied or spent and not want another immediate round of lovemaking. Plato, however, nowhere sees need to explain why his appetitive schema applies as readily to human sexual desire as it does to hunger and thirst. He clearly thinks that just as persons want and feel pleasure from consuming food or drink when hungry or thirsty, so too sexual pleasure is a genuinely consuming passion. Human beings naturally want to sate this appetite on a regular basis when they become sexually depleted, and they enjoy doing so.

The desire for sexual replenishment and its pleasure is an inherent part of human nature in Plato's view. He describes it as "innate", though it manifests itself not at birth but later in life. Plato differentiates sexual desire in this respect from its counterpart appetites. "For human beings [the appetites for] food and drink arise immediately once they are born. The third, sexual desire, arises last". The sexual appetite starts to become active quite early in life as Plato sees it, for he would sternly regulate "the sexual behavior of male and female children, as well as that of women for men and men for women". Once awakened, its periodic craving eventually diminishes, but not until persons are well advanced in years.

Plato has theological and physiological reasons for considering the sexual appetite to be inherent in human anatomy. First, the gods instilled the sexual appetite into human nature when they created mortals in accordance with the demiurge's specifications. Second, sexual desire is a function of specific bodily organs, such as the liver and genitals. Third, in the *Republic* and in later dialogues the three physical appetites also belong to the irrationally appetitive part of the embodied soul. The sexual appetite is accordingly an inherent part of the human body in Plato's view, and the force of this embedded design of the gods is felt throughout most of one's lifetime.

The sexual appetite has a wide-ranging palate according to Plato. It is "ready to try everything" of a sexually pleasurable sort, be the pleasures homoerotic, heterosexual, or some other pattern. Men, for instance, sate this appetite with males as well as females. The sexual appetite, further, develops an elaborate taste for the illicit if it is not properly controlled. When it is particularly intense and left to its own devices, such as happens when people sleep, it stimulates them to dream with bold craving for sexual relations with any animate being, be it animal or human, mortal or immortal. All are on the fantasy menu, especially if the desired target is off limits, such as a god or goddess or a man's own mother. The main requirement of the sexual appetite, then, is an indiscriminate pleasurable friction from diverse sources, rather like a cat ready to rub up against any leg, be it a person's, a table's, or a chair's. Most alluring to the undisciplined sexual appetite, however, is the leg that is forbidden.

Plato nonetheless maintains that the sexual appetite of most people is driven in turn by an urge for the pleasures of reproductive intercourse. In the human physiology of the *Timaeus,* the sexual appetite of women is ruled by a procreative imperative. Their wombs are "an inner animal with a yearning for reproduction." The sexual appetite of most men is also under the sway of the procreative imperative. Semen, which Plato locates in the spinal marrow, wants to come to fruition in human form. Semen prior to emission is willful in this manner because it is already partly alive and seeks to become a complete human animal. It "breathes" within the marrow and instigates a "life-giving" or "reproductive sexual appetite". Thus, even though the sexual appetite seeks pleasurable rubbing quite apart from any reproductive goal, women's wombs and the semen in the male spinal cord direct this appetite toward procreation for the vast majority of human beings, male and female alike.

The procreative imperative is nonetheless not an absolute master. Some men and women have a more pronounced homoerotic directive than a reproductive one. The recognition that Plato gives to homoeroticism, however, is limited to sexual love between males that eventually accords greater value to intellectual pursuits than to genital pleasures. The primary sexual directive that persons experience, as he puts it, depends on whether their inclination is motivated mainly by the immortal soul or the perishable body. Some men, whose stimulus is the soul, turn toward like-minded younger males. Though they are sexually involved at first, their intellectual engagement with each other gradually makes sexual pleasure less interesting and less frequent. Males in this relationship produce metaphorical progeny that Plato finds more worthy and enduring than children, such as poetry, philosophy, and law codes. Other men, the vast majority, have a stimulus that is more the body, and they turn toward women to reproduce children. Plato does not consider the male homoerotic drive that remains vigorously sexual and does not fit his model of Platonic eros. He is also at best oblique in acknowledging that some women too have a homoerotic inclination, and he accords this relationship no intellectual honor whatsoever. Plato's thoughts about homoeroticism are useful, despite their obvious limitations, as they show that he finds the reproductive imperative to be far from universally dominant.

Plato claims that the appetites for the pleasures of sexual activity, food, and drink are irrational. He defends this position through his much questioned argument about distinct sources of motivation in the human soul, namely, physical appetition, spirit, and reason. Conflicting desires about whether to have a particular drink, for instance, indicate to him that there is a struggle between the appetitive and rational forces in the soul. Such conflict reveals "the presence in the soul of that which urges and that which restrains from drinking. That which restrains is something different from that which urges". The restraining force is "reason". Physical appetition, by contrast, is "irrational", on the grounds that the conflict would not occur if the physical appetites were rational. Thus, for Plato the appetites are irrational given his conception of what happens in the human psyche when one both wants and does not want to have a drink, eat food, or engage in sexual activity.

Plato further maintains that the irrational physical appetites function in an antirational, and not merely arational, way. Since the appetites for food, drink, and sexual activity have no access to reason, they cannot know when enough is enough. They are aggressive in their ignorance, which leads them, contrary to reason, to strive always to exceed the limits of healthy appetition, to provoke human agents to consume or indulge far more than they should. Hunger, for instance, inevitably leads to gluttony unless reason hems it in and controls it. Were it not for the wise restraining power of reason's rule, human beings would end up in a ruinously excessive appetitive condition, rather like the legendary wine-drinking and pleasure-seeking Sardanapallus or the destructively voracious Erysichthon.

"The innate physical appetite for pleasures [of replenishment] irrationally draws one toward [such] pleasures. If it prevails in us its name is licentious violence. 'Licentious violence' is polyvalent. [For example,] when the physical appetite prevails over better reason in relation to food and dominates among the appetites, it is gluttony [and the person is gluttonous] and as for the names of the sibling appetites, the appetite that gains sway is clearly the suitable term to apply to the person," such as "drunkard" for persons with an excessive passion for wine. Plato underscores the antirationality of the three sibling appetites with a number of natural and political metaphors. The appetites are a wild animal or an unruly, lawless mob that is incorrigibly persistent in its desire to rebel against reason's limits. When they gain the upper hand, the soul experiences a kind of civil war or tyrannical overthrow, an appetitive coup. The appetites, then, inherently try to storm the citadel of reason because they really do want to eat cake, big slices of it. Although Plato's metaphors are vivid, his position is not compelling. He does not justify why he shifts from arguing that the physical appetites are irrational to asserting that they are imperiously antirational, with the use of suggestive imagery displacing argument. Plato's conception of the physical appetites seems more grotesque than plausible, for it suggests that a sex-mad version of the Monty Python glutton evinces the human appetitive condition its purest unregulated form. This seems dubious. Plato is nonetheless earnest be careful to control your appetites, or the explosive glutton will be you. Human reason must remain vigilant to prevent the appetites from wreaking havoc and driving persons into destructive excess.

Among the three appetites, in Plato's view, the sexual appetite has the strongest and most incorrigible propensity to excess. From later childhood through old age it stimulates the "greatest and sharpest need (xreðoñíåíáa)" and "the fiercest and most intense" feelings of appetitive pleasure. The sexual appetite is also especially "tyrannical" in its impulse to overthrow reason. As Sophocles maintains, with Plato's approval, sexual eros is "a raving and fierce master."

The sexual appetite is thus even hungrier than hunger for the greater part of one's life. Its power "persuades and drags the majority" to seek out and venerate sexual activity and its pleasures, just as geometrical proofs persuade the mind to inquire into and admire the beautiful truths about Number that they demonstrate. In fact, "erotic compulsions are probably fiercer than geometrical proofs" among the populace at large given the crazed intensity of fricative pleasure. The reproductive urge adds impetus to the sexual appetite, for this urge too is "autocratic, like an animal disobedient to reason," and its "raging lusts" force most people to give in to the reproductive imperative. Sexual desire thus never learns to cooperate with reason, given its double-barreled force. At most it can be controlled by a fear of punishment for going beyond reason's limits. This is why the sexual appetite in the *Phaedrus* bears the brunt of a cruelty to which Plato never subjects hunger and thirst. "The charioteer, as though recoiling from the starting gate, yanks back more intensely the bit from the mouth of the wanton horse, thoroughly bloodies its jaws and evil-speaking tongue, and, making the horse sprawl to the ground on its limbs and hips, gives it a painful lashing." The beatings do not stop until the sexual animal finally cowers in a corner, forced somewhat into compliance because it is hobbled by terror. Even in this condition, however, its swollen eyes retain a lascivious glimmer. The bad sexual horse still "has something to say to the charioteer and expects to enjoy some small treats for all its pains". Human sexual desire thus poses the greatest challenge Plato sees to reason's mastery over the rampant ways of appetitive pleasure. So relentless is it that it must be bludgeoned into following reason's command, and even then its rebellious spirit remains unbroken.

The continual struggle between the physical appetites and reason is central to Plato's conception of ethical human conduct. Human beings are virtuous when they regulate their appetites in a manner conducive to their own and the city's greater well-being. Conversely, they corrupt society and themselves when they give their appetites free rein. "Virtue is the outcome for those who conduct themselves well in relation to their threefold need and appetite, and the opposite is true for those who conduct themselves badly in relation to them". Persons behave with appetitive virtue if they act only on what Plato calls "necessary and salutary appetites". He considers appetition necessary and healthy to the extent that persons benefit from it physically, and they so benefit when the appetites cannot be avoided without inducing harm to bodily well-being. "The appetites that we cannot deflect and that are healthy for us when acted on are rightly called necessary." An ideal of nutritive simplicity also informs Plato's conception of appetitive virtue. He imagines that the dietary aspect of a good appetitive regimen would be met with the humble fare of the Greek countryside: wine in small amounts, bread, greens, and cheese for the main meal, chickpeas and figs afterwards, and roasted acorns for the occasional snack. The sexual appetite is likewise beneficial when its pleasures are kept to a salutary minimum. People become wicked, however, when their appetites are "unnecessary and lavish." In this condition they seek gratification in elaborate kinds as well as quantities. Broad culinary diversity, for example, is "bad for the body, bad for the soul, especially for its intelligence and capacity to be moderate." Persons who are wicked in their appetitive behavior are "stuffed on pleasures", be they gluttons, drunkards, sex maniacs, or some potent combination of the three. The appetites' voracity therefore drives an ongoing contest between virtue and vice in human affairs. The appetites seek vicious excess, and reason tries to restrain them within the limits of appetitive virtue. Showing proper restraint in dietary and sexual behavior is thus central to Plato's conception of what it means to be morally responsible.

Excessive pleasures are unhealthy partly because they upset the balance of pleasure inherent in appetitive human experience. Appetitive pleasures, as Plato sees them, are not simply pleasurable, but a mix of pleasure and pain. When they are immoderate, the pain overwhelms the pleasure, such as groaning from the feast. Pain indicates a body in unhealthy distress, which is something "neither to choose nor desire". Persons given to overindulging thus behave contrary to their bodily well-being. Sexual pleasure best exemplifies this health concern, for it is an especially intense mix of pleasure and pain. By Plato's diagnosis, then, excessive sexual pleasure is like the self-inflicting of wounds, because the pain far outstrips the pleasure. The disease is sexual madness and its symptoms are "a kind of panic" for sexual activity, burning with sexual desire, and becoming crazed during copulation and orgasm. Persons cannot be blamed for suffering this condition if they have not learned how to control their sexual desire, but they are blameworthy to knowingly resist Plato's treatment, as shown further below.

The contest posed by the sexual and other appetites goes far beyond the health concerns of the populace. In Plato's view, if one or another of them goes unchecked—and sexual eros especially they stimulate and commandeer numerous other desires of an acquisitive, extravagant, or violent sort. On this topic too, though, Plato is more eloquent than cogent. At best he sketches how and why unchecked appetition provokes this proliferation of desires by giving a quick guided tour of delinquent male character types who are afflicted and even criminal in their appetitively stimulated vices, such as the democratic man. The sexual appetite of Plato's tyrannical man, for instance, not only produces and rules over his desires for love affairs and for drinking parties, it also provokes him to steal from his own parents and neighbors and to loot temples in order to indulge these desires in a spendthrift way. Similarly, the man dominated by sexual passion is likely to commit any sort of murder as a crime of passion. Uncontrolled sexual desire, hunger, and thirst stimulate other desires as a means to attain these core appetitive ends, such as the tyrannical man's desire to have money for drinking parties so that he can seduce the drunken participants who stir his ardor. Plato's claim about proliferating desires, however, cannot adequately be explained as a means-end argument, for here he goes beyond such an argument without justifying why he does so. "Murder of any sort" is in many instances not explicable as a means to fulfill uncontrolled sexual desire, hunger, or thirst. Plato is contending that all vicious desires are propagated from the unregulated core appetites, and from sexual desire especially. The unrestrained appetites bring about "injustice, licentiousness, cowardice, ignorance, folly, and in general, every vice". A tree of vices to illustrate this idea would have a three-pronged taproot, with the longest root at the center being uncontrolled sexual desire.

Plato further contends that on a broader social scale the proliferation of desires goes beyond individual vices and leads to chronic wars of conquest and famine, with the greedy in power rapaciously consuming resources at the expense of the weaker in need. As he would have it, then, sexual eros and the other two core appetites, unless held in check by reason, are the origin of human-motivated social ills because they stimulate all vices from avarice to zealotry. If only we minded the necessary limits of sexual activity and ate and drank moderately, the society of peace and justice would be ours for the taking.

Plato sharply differentiates the sexual appetite from Platonic eros for bodily and transcendent beauty. The sexual appetite is inherently and dumbly drawn toward the fricative "pleasure of sexual activity," while Platonic eros is stimulated by a cognizant awareness of beauty in a beloved person and it recoils from the rub-a-dub-dub of sexual activity. Contrary to the straining of the sexual appetite toward pleasure, it strains with an opposing erotic intensity to perceive the nature of Beauty itself. Unlike the innate sexual appetite, Platonic eros is acquired, a learned taste for Beauty or the Good, which one gains through becoming enlightened by Platonic metaphysics. The sexual appetite cannot acquire or sublimate into developing this taste. Its satisfaction requires heated friction of the genitals. By contrast, Platonic eros finds its ecstasy in the "sweetest" pleasure of seeing visible and transcendent beauty. This pleasure is as sweet as sweet can be because it is free of the pain that accompanies genital pleasure. Sweet pleasure is experienced in its purest unmixed way through the study of geometry, when persons envision "the straight and the round, [which] are always beautiful in themselves and have their own pleasures. These are not at all like the pleasures of scratching". Sexual pleasure, by contrast, is a deep-seated scratching that involves "intensely sharp, piercing, and burning" sensations. Therefore, the sexual appetite is point for point the unregenerate opposite of Platonic eros.

Unlike the pleasure of studying geometry, however, the overall human experience of falling or being in love with another person combines the conflicting impulses of the sexual appetite and Platonic eros. This heady experience of being in love is a mixture of the two, not pure Platonic eros, and should never be confused with Platonic eros alone. Plato noticed such confusion brewing in his own day and attempted to clarify matters. As he explains in *Laws* 837b6–d2, Platonic eros remains unconditionally antisexual in its desire and end. It absolutely "forbids one from plucking the bloom" of sexual activity. Instead it thrills the soul with a desire to behold the form of Beauty itself, partly through the stimulus of seeing the bodily beauty of beloved persons. The experience of being in love is a "third sense" of eros, the "mix of [the two kinds of] eros." Platonic eros proper refers to the antisexual component, while the sexual appetite is the intensely sexual component. Even though Plato deploys erotic imagery rivaling that in Sappho' poetry to describe the desire of Platonic eros to view Beauty, eros in this sense has a pronounced aversion to sexual contact, contrary to sexually appetitive eros. The motive of Platonic eros is a longing to behold "the nature of beauty seated on a pure throne," not, as eros does for Sappho, to sexually worship Aphrodite seated on her "exquisite throne." To Plato, consequently, the sexual appetite as "wicked horse" is like an inflamed satyr 'groin in the soul' irrational faculty, while Platonic eros is an ecstatic rapture that makes the soul rational faculty flutter and throb with longing for the unadulterated pleasure of viewing Beauty in and of itself.

Human beings, insofar as they are embodied agents, do not experience Platonic eros on its own. Lovers are in a two-fold—and to Plato conflicting state of agitation. Through reason they seethe with Platonic eros for Beauty, but through the sexual appetite they whinny for sexual pleasure. Neither impulse comprehends or has any share in the other longing, at least as Plato construes them. Platonic eros, further, is no rarified substitute for sexual desire. On his view it is the more authentic eros, though it is not humanly possible to experience it in an unmixed form given the persistence of the sexual appetite. Plato accords little or no beauty to sexual pleasure, even though he accords considerable beauty to the human body. Such pleasure, far from having aesthetic merit, is at worst a violent outrage and at best a grotesque comedy with its contorted bodies, panting, and shouting. Not least among its unattractive qualities is sexual desire obliviousness to beauty and its capacity to transmit this insensibility to the person as a whole.

Plato extends the harmful repercussions of excessive desire beyond the body and society and into the afterlife of the immortal soul. This afterlife concern is no ancillary matter, for his thought is permeated with the Pythagorean dualism of body and soul and with a cosmic dualism between the realms of being and becoming. As his primary aim in ethics and politics, Plato strives to enlighten embodied souls through social and political change, and his sociopolitical reforms are a means to this end. "Not only once have we said that tending the soul comes first, of the three things that properly matter to human beings [namely, soul, body, and material goods]," for "the soul is truly the most honorable concern for all." The immortal soul, when embodied, is at great risk of being lured into myriad vicious and painful pleasures by the appetites. Appetite-driven concerns entice the soul and person as a whole into thinking that only the physical world of flux exists and that pure being is a Platonic fiction. The soul, once beguiled, loses its ability to recollect its immortal nature and becomes burdened with bodily and earthly qualities, buried alive with clods of proliferating vices. Souls that fail to recollect their nature cannot ascend to the Good or Beauty after they depart from the body at death. Instead they remain unenlightened, banished from their birthright in pure being, and from there descend into lower animal forms, encased in fur or fins, and never gazing upward again. Excessive sexual and other appetitive behavior thus must be curbed for pressing reasons of concern to the soul that go beyond bodily health and the good society, important though these are. Plato in the *Republic* and *Laws* is eager to do whatever it takes to restrict appetitive behavior individually, socially, and politically in order to facilitate the philosophical quest of immortal souls for the intelligible world. The clampdown begins with sexual desire.

Even though sexual desire is the most recalcitrant troublemaker of the core appetites. Plato argues that it is both harmful and unfeasible to starve or deny it altogether. The sexual horse should be given its requisite carrots now and then, for a strict regimen of moderation exemplifies Plato' notion of sexually appetitive virtue. Like hunger and thirst, sexual desire is unavoidable and beneficial to a degree. To this degree, persons ought to be sexually active for health reasons, because a "great compulsion" (Ünçgkh) drives human nature to fulfill the necessary appetites. Plato's more precise plans for reproductive reform are explored in the following section. Suffice it here to say that he allows moderate sexual hedonism for persons who have completed their procreative service for the good of the city. He does not try to restrict necessary and beneficial sexual activity throughout the human life span to the purpose of reproduction because he thinks sexual desire is far too compelling for so restrictive a limit. Complete sexual abstinence, further, would be unfeasible and inadvisably extreme even if some individuals were to prove able to emaciate their sexual desire. Moderation exemplifies Plato's conception of virtuous sexual conduct.

Plato underscores his position that sexual renunciation would be unhealthy by associating diseases with the total deprivation of sexual pleasure. If, for instance, women refuse to sate their urge for reproduction, their wombs precipitate respiratory ailments and other signs of ill health. Men too undergo a suffering on par with Io' if they leave their sexual appetite unfed. They become maddened from the stings and bites inflicted by their inner sexual horsefly. This physiological torture is especially unbearable if a man has more than the usual abundance of seed teeming in his spinal marrow. In order to avoid such diseases, persons should regard a law-abiding sexual moderation and "not complete sexual abstinence" as proper. To live by this standard would admittedly be about as exciting as a steady diet of chickpeas and acorns, brightened by the occasional fig. This is exactly how Plato thinks we should live, with the gift to be simple in the sexual and sibling appetites and the ensuing gift to be free from vicious desires, social inequity, and widespread indifference to the Good.

Plato's Procreative Ethics and Communal Social Ideal

Plato firmly believed that uncontrolled sexual desire had been allowed to run wild and plague the human condition. As far as he was concerned, its potential to run rampant was fully realized in Athens and elsewhere, with his fellow Greeks being afflicted with chronic sexual madness and yet denying that they were sick in the slightest. "Human sexual desires are the source of countless woes for people individually and for entire cities." As far as Plato's contemporaries were concerned, though, nothing made them happier than sexual pleasures and the more intense and frequent the experience, the better. What they called happiness Plato regarded as a widespread addiction to the leader of the hedonistic pack, sexual desire, and to its spawn of other violent desires waging gleeful despotism over reason and moderation. To his mind sexual desire held the lead because of its composite make-up, the ferocious sexual appetite with the equally wild reproductive urge riding on it bareback. Given this magnitude of the woes and their ostensible origin, Plato put reproductive and other sexual reforms first on his agenda to ameliorate the embodied conditions of the soul in society.

The reproductive regulations in the *Republic* and *Laws* are pragmatic in intent and motivated by Plato's aim to rationally patrol sexual desire for the duration of its power, from early youth through old age. To accomplish this project, "an audacious lone man," he declares, must fearlessly intervene in the appetitive status quo, "guided only by reason and having no backers to support him". Plato as maverick philosopher takes matters into his own hands through political philosophy, rather than directly on the political scene in Athens, for he fears that his ideas toward sexual and social reform would be unanimously voted down. Young adult males would protest the loudest, he thinks, for by his understanding young men are oversexed, "teeming with semen" in their spinal marrow. Rather than submit his proposals to a democratic vote, Plato started to teach young men philosophy, and as a recurrent theme in his ethics and political theory, he strove to reverse the conventional Greek measures of virility and happiness: Sexual restraint is the mark of a real man and genuine happiness, while sexual pleasure is for sissies. And in a more long-term investment beyond his immediate students, Plato wrote the *Republic* and *Laws,* not as bookish utopias, but as plans for real social change toward a future of appetitive restraint.

Plato presumes the ancient Greek norm that the persons to target for procreative regulations are the central enfranchised group in a city, the guardians in the *Republic* and the citizens at large in the *Laws*. The regulations serve partly to perpetuate the group and the distribution of labor within it. As in Greek society, Plato does not offer other possibilities, such as requiring a slave class to perform reproductive labor on a surrogate basis, or employing other social outsiders as procreative laborers to do the job. He has eugenic reasons for requiring the citizens and good guardians to reproduce their own social kind. In the *Republic,* city officials regulate the guardians in a preferential system that gives the best and most restrained guardians the greatest opportunity to procreate; the worst guardians, the least; and only the offspring of the best are to be raised once they pass inspection. The guardians have no choice but to comply. In the *Laws,* however, all the citizens must reproduce their fair share and regard it as unholy to do otherwise. They too, though, are to aspire toward moderation themselves and to reproduce restrained offspring. Male citizens face stiff penalties if they do not marry female citizens. Once married, the bridegrooms and brides must direct their attention toward procreation. Female overseers police the married couples to make sure that they obey. The obligation to procreate therefore applies to the guardians on a preferential scale in the *Republic,* and to the citizens without exceptions or preferential system in the *Laws.* In both plans, however, Plato's regulations aim to create a more purebred strain of human beings in control of their appetites.

Due to his assessment of the appetites, Plato regards society as a mixed blessing. On the one hand, human beings are not self-sufficient and require things to meet their basic needs or "necessary desires." People have rightly gathered into a city or polis to cooperate, share, and fulfill the needs of one another. Reproduction, for example, is one such civic need, for without a symbiotic populace, there are no persons to work and sustain the division of labor. Plato deems society good to the extent that it satisfies the necessary desires that lead to individual and collective well-being. The physical appetites, however, relentlessly push human beings as political animals to transgress the limit of necessary desires, and sexual desire is the strongest culprit. Civic mores should impede this corruption by encouraging the enlightened rule of reason in the person of the philosopher king.

According to Plato, the customs of private property and the free market inevitably breed appetitive excess and violence. Society becomes inflamed with vices when men have too much wealth in persons, goods, and resources at their disposal on which their own appetites and those of their families may feed and proliferate. Even if a city begins with material simplicity and restraint, it is only a matter of time until it ends up frenetically unrestrained when its inhabitants "buy and sell, [using] the marketplace and coinage as a means of exchange". As Plato sees it, in a free market there are no checks on what people may want to acquire, own, and consume for themselves and their kin. Excess is encouraged as though it were economic prosperity, and this unleashes the mob of appetites and related desires rather than keeping them subdued. As a result, an initially restrained city "will not satisfy." Its inhabitants will demand more luxury goods, and thereby make their once healthy community feverish. In such a diseased city, "men think they will be happy by owning land, big fine houses, fine furnishings, gold, silver, and all other such things and they spend money as they wish, such as giving it to mistresses". To rehabilitate the city from acquisitive license, Plato would prohibit private ownership, unrestricted consumption, and the free market. Given his diagnosis, a communal social order is the cure.

In the *Republic* Plato finds a Pythagorean-inspired communalism the most attractive option to implement for his envisioned city of Kallipolis. This social order works in the voluntary cooperative spirit that "friends should hold goods in common," though the social pattern is also mandated administratively by enlightened philosophical rule. Plato works from a Pythagorean model partly because he and the Pythagoreans alike sought to institute "as many impediments as possible on the exercise of human sexual activity" for the good of the city, as explored further in chapter four. Plato thus approaches his plans for communal sexual reform in a Pythagorean spirit, for he too aims to help friends help one another keep their sexual and other desires in beneficial check, with guidance from the wise king. He is utterly serious in this endeavor, given all that he sees at stake.

The first kinds of property that Plato would free from the ownership of men are women and their capacities for reproduction and nurture. Women gain first priority because the principles by which members of a society reproduce offspring are his fundamental law of social order. Procreative customs, he states, play a pivotal role in determining whether social customs in general are restrained or dissolute. "The beginning of [human] generation is the first law that the lawgiver would establish by regulating marriage customs, " because the patterns of "marriage, procreation, and raising children have a great and complete bearing on whether the social order proceeds rightly or wrongly. " If this primary law mandates, as Athenian society did in his day, that men own wives and daughters wives as household managers and mothers of their children, and daughters to be exchanged in marriage to other men then the society is bound to be disorderly and feverish. Plato thus long ago had the basic insight for which Engels is better known. He appreciates that the work of reproduction and childrearing sets the pattern of society itself and with it the quality of life that the people have, female and male members alike. Plato too advocates a kind of socialism, albeit on a city, rather than nation, basis. What brings him to this insight, however, sets him apart from Engels and makes his socialism puritanical. Because disorderly sexual desire and its progeny of vices are to blame for social and psychological corruption, he gives top priority to reining it in. In so doing Plato strives for a two-in-one efficiency. By regulating procreation as the first law of social order, he constrains the sexual appetite as well. The two-fold control mechanism that he devises works rather like a twisted leash that confines a dog by its neck and leg at the same time, though Plato's double leashing is deliberate. His communal rallying cry thus is not the Marxist-feminist "Workers of the world unite!" with a driving concern for female solidarity and freedom from male-mandated reproductive norms. Rather, he is the first voice of the Platonist Temperance Union. "Citizens, rein in your sexual desire! The reproductive urge first and the rest will stay in tow!" A Pythagorean communalism of the women best facilitates this aim because it severs sexual desire from possessiveness and consumerism, helps restrict sexual activity to the beneficial degree, and in other ways encourages an appetitively subdued society.

First, the communal pooling of women and reproductive labor removes kinship-based factionalism and the related competition for wealth in the city. Plato thinks "there is no greater evil than the fragmented city". A city must strive to be politically unified and psychologically holistic, so that it responds quickly to suffering in its parts, just as the human body responds to a sharp blow to a finger. Traditional procreation within marriage, however, hinders civic unity because it motivates families and clans to rival one another to acquire more for their own households at each other' expense. Families, preoccupied with their own material prosperity, tend to neglect and even contribute to suffering in the city outside of the kinship circle that claims their primary loyalty and identity. Alcmaeonid pain is likely to give pleasure to the rival Pisistratid clan. Both groups are ready to dishonor their rivals and put them at a disadvantage, even though they are all fellow Athenian citizens. Plato's communal reforms in reproduction and childrearing would dismantle the acquisitive bastions of kinship groups so as to produce a genuinely collective civic body committed to moderation.

Second, the communal pooling of women is of great benefit to women themselves. It frees them from the burden of running the domestic side of family-oriented acquisitiveness, such as purchasing goods for the household and maintaining it. Through this freedom they are much better positioned to help shape a holistic and unified city. When women are privately managed as wives, mothers, and daughters, the ensuing social order assumes that a married couple's desires to have their own children, house, and household goods are basic subsistence needs rather than acquisitive wants. A wife in this system belongs to a particular man and is the mother of his children. She is habituated to want her family's comforts foremost even if the cost, including her energy, would be better spent on a community project that matters to everyone. Her daily tasks inefficiently replicate the so-called women's work being done by neighboring wives and mothers in a house-by-house choreography that leaves them all with less time and initiative for more collective social pursuits. Their energy would not be drained in a society that shared the raising of children and other domestic work. Women find their opportunities to work for the collective good curtailed in societies where men and their families sharply distinguish among themselves between "my property and not my property". The problem becomes even more apparent the more consumer oriented the society becomes, which Plato thinks is inevitable in a society that extols the family, property, and mercantilism. The women have bigger houses, more furnishings, and so on, whose upkeep is a their responsibility regardless of whether they own female slaves, or, in the modern day, machines. Plato explains this argument by analogy with female guard dogs. If the dogs, like Athenian women, were restricted to feminine roles such as tending the pups and cleaning the den, then the pack as a whole would suffer. The female dogs would not go hunting as they do along with the male dogs to help meet the entire pack need for sustenance. This would be especially true if the den kept getting needlessly bigger and more elaborate due to covetous canine visions of the good life. Plato's communal reforms do away with the separate households that lead to unnecessary replication and proliferation of appetitive demands. Women are then freed along with the men to shape a holistic and unified city, rather than remaining pawns to the passions to have and to own.

Plato remains true to his conviction that the communal city ideally should supplant the society that privileges private ownership, favors the family, and encourages consumption. In the *Republic* he is optimistic that his proposals are feasible and practical. This reform would work successfully, so long as philosophers become kings and their subjects are collectively raised and educated according to the principle that friends should hold goods in common. Sexual communalism remains an elite practice in the *Republic,* however, restricted to the guardian class. In the *Laws* Plato reaffirms and broadens his conviction that communal reproduction and childrearing are the best way to ground a society. If he could, he would extend these reforms to all citizens, not only to an elite guardian class. "No one will ever posit a more correct or better definition [of the ideal city] in its pre-eminence toward human virtue than one in which the private ownership of women, children, and all other goods is everywhere and by every means eliminated from human life". Nonetheless, Plato by this time is resigned to thinking that such reform is not possible on a pragmatic level. Only "gods or children of gods dwell happily in the fully communal city", but mere mortals seem incapable of such enlightenment. Plato surrenders to the apparent inevitability of familial norms in the *Laws* because of the flood of reactionary responses that his communal sexual proposals elicited, an onrush that has only recently abated. The citizens of his envisioned city of Magnesia must make do with the given conditions of family and marriage, but still try to be moderate in all respects. For example, the rich and powerful should marry persons of modest means so that the ensuing generations of families are at most moderately affluent and roughly on par with one another. Here Plato is trying to deploy marriage to do what he knows a communal city would accomplish more effectively: to prevent social cliques of the wealthy from producing more of their own social kind, at the expense of shaping a more holistic and egalitarian city of moderation and justice for all. In the *Laws*, however, he shrinks from enforcing even this method of severing the reproductive urge from family wealth and power, unlike the forceful separation of the two that he sets out for the guardians in the *Republic*. "To mandate these things by law would be considered laughable and would stir up anger among many". Instead, the citizens must themselves learn to see the merit of marrying into appetitive temperance and voluntarily seek this middle class mean. In the *Laws*, Plato thus aims only to instill the norm of frugal economic parity within the more traditional Greek framework of marriage and the family. This alternative is second-rate in his view, because it leaves in place the appetitive breeding ground that should be supplanted for the moderate society to become a living reality the individual male ownership of women, their wombs, and children in the family.

Plato's Eugenic Aim in his Procreative Reforms

Plato in the *Republic* and *Laws* further restricts sexual desire through eugenic constraints on reproduction. Some of the measures derive from popular Greek culture, where they promoted generic well-being of the offspring and community at large. Plato, though, reshapes these measures to support his own conception of appetitive health. The guardians and citizens must obey population control measures, procreate only during their prime, abide by incest prohibitions, and conduct religious ceremonies in order to have the gods bless and ensure the production of healthy offspring. A few of Plato's other eugenic measures, though, go beyond retooling popular practices already in place. These measures aim even more pointedly to select for appetitive restraint so as to create a new order of lean human beings on the run like greyhounds toward virtue.

The guardians in the *Republic* and the citizens in the *Laws* must produce offspring in a limited number and of the best possible kind. In the *Republic* the ideal population should be large enough so that the city is self-sufficient and not so large as to preclude the city from being politically and psychologically holistic. "The guardians must guard in every way that the city will be neither big nor small but of adequate size and unified". The city officials monitor the frequency with which the guardians engage in procreative intercourse. The officials must, for example, take into account population losses due to natural deaths, wars, and diseases. In the *Laws* Plato is more specific about the preferred demographics of the polis. The adult male segment of the population and its concomitant number of households should amount to no more than the choiceworthy Pythagorean number 5,040. The wives should bear at least two offspring, one of each sex. Though Plato does not quantify the upper limit that each couple should produce, he does have such a limit in mind. Once married couples produce a "generous quantity of offspring," they must stop engaging in reproductive intercourse. The guardians and citizens thus must procreate strictly within the means of their community and respect its need for population control. This rule hems in sexual desire, for it is a civic duty to avoid sexual relations that lead to births exceeding demographic interests. Population control further curtails the appetites more generally by sparing the city from having too many mouths to feed.

The guardians and citizens also must reproduce only

during their prime of life so as to give birth to the healthiest possible offspring. For Plato, the prime is an age span during which human beings are "at their peak" of mind and body, ripe for producing the best offspring. For females it starts between 16 and 20 and extends to 40 years of age. For males it starts between 25 or 35 years of age, or "whenever a man reaches his peak as a runner," up to the age of 55. This rule is very strict. Since the guardians are committed to producing "the best possible men and women", transgressors who procreate outside of the age limits must either abort the fetus or expose the newborn infant. If they disobey, they commit a criminal act of impiety. In the *Laws* too, overage citizens who transgress this rule are to be penalized and dishonored with public humiliations and the occasional beating. Plato thus curbs human sexual desire further by imposing a rule of quality control in addition to population control. The guardians and citizens must refrain from procreating until they are at the right age and the city needs newborn members to add its populacc.

Incest prohibitions in the *Republic* and *Laws* serve partly to set another barrier to unregulated sexual desire. In the *Republic* he requires the guardians to obey a communal version of the traditional Greek rule to avoid parentchild incest. In the *Laws* he reverts to the traditional Greek rules. Sexual relationships between parents and children are "not in the least holy, but loathed by the gods and most shameful of shameful deeds". Though incest prohibitions prevent inbreeding, in Plato's cities they further tighten the reins of sexual desire, for the taboo in the *Republic* applies to guardians who are already retired from their reproductive duties and forbidden to produce more children, when the problem of inbreeding no longer applies. The guardians and citizens thus have to mind their place in the kinship structure as well as their age and demographic concerns before allowing themselves to engage in sexual activity.

In the *Republic* and *Laws* Plato insists that procreative relations elicit the benevolent involvement of the gods through the use of religious ceremonies. This requirement regulates sexual desire further by linking the reproductive urge with a piety that is both sexually explicit and solemn. The ceremonialism also reaffirms the presence and importance of the Greek gods, whom Plato has rehabilitated so that the gods are supremely good and impervious to corruption—models of divine virtue for the citizens to emulate. The worship of Plato's noble Olympians is required to ensure that the gods will recognize their mortal counterparts in virtue and favor the people production of appetitively sedate offspring. The rituals especially serve "the gods of reproduction (yeoð genüylioi)", such as Hera and Zeus, who were important deities presiding over the birth process in ancient Greece. The guardians and citizens must incorporate ample religious ritual into their mating through traditional feasts, hymns, and sacrifices. The gods receiving such worship gain in honor and strength, as is their due, and once gladdened in their hearts, the gods are then propitious toward the city and its reproductive efforts. The guardians and citizens thus are obliged to sustain the gods in order to bear appetitively well-bred children, and to raise children worthy of sustaining the rehabilitated gods, just as the Greeks had long been doing by Plato's day, though without his refurbished Olympian theology and express eugenic aims. The generations to come, Plato insists, are required to hand on this living torch of worshipping the good gods. He therefore supports the traditional polytheistic web connecting the Greek gods, city, adults, and children together in a symbiotic community, though his community and its Olympians are dedicated to appetitive virtue.

To Plato, as to the Greeks, the inaugural act of marital intercourse is itself a religious ceremony, such as the wedding night in the *Laws* or a communally reproductive event in the *Republic.* In the *Laws,* a personified deity of reproductive "Beginning" (Ürxá) presides over this initiation. She ensures reproductive continuity across generations and its ceremonial exchange between the citizens and their gods. This goddess "maintains all things provided that she receives due honor from those who make use of her". A male citizen thus would be outrageously impious if he refused to be a husband and father and abandoned this civic symbiosis with the gods. "It is never holy for a man to willingly and deliberately be deprived of a wife and children". The goddess of reproductive beginning helps prevent this impiety from occurring. As immortal overseer, she accompanies the newlyweds to the bedroom and sees to it that they carry out their procreative responsibility for the city and the gods.

Plato also proposes specialized methods of selecting for temperance that go beyond adapting popular Greek reproductive mores. In the *Republic* he proposes selective breeding, by analogy with purebred dogs, horses, and the like. Through a rigged system of lots of which the guardians are unaware, "the best" female and male guardians, that is, the ones most virtuous in their appetitive discipline, should have the most frequent opportunity to mate. The guardians who prove somewhat inferior and less restrained should have the least frequent opportunity and only with other inferior guardians. Their offspring are to be secretly taken away by officials and almost certainly left to die, along with the visibly defective offspring of the superior guardians. Appetitive moderation is thus its own limited hedonistic reward in the *Republic*. Since the best guardians are most capable of managing their sexual desire, they win most of the available occasions for experiencing sexual pleasure while they are passing on their traits. In the *Laws*, however, Plato abandons the breeding altogether and prefers to mate husbands and wives who complement each other psychologically as well as economically. The dispositions of the spouses should carefully counterbalance or offset whatever personality extremes the two partners may have. The intended result is to achieve the golden mean of temperance in the character formation of the offspring. For example, a rash man should marry and mate with a placid woman. This "will benefit the civic order" because their personalities will blend and form offspring who are more balanced and restrained. Plato thus ventures into innovative methods to implant the norm of appetitive virtue across generations. He is ready to be a political animal breeder or a marital chemist mixing character—whatever it takes to realize his reforms.

Plato offers a final eugenic plan in the *Laws,* and only in this dialogue, that is of great importance for the prominence it gains in Middle and Christian Platonism, albeit in a much transmuted form. The citizens of the hypothetical city of Magnesia must engage strictly in temperate and deliberately reproductive sexual relations when they first marry. This restriction pertains only to "the procreative union" and it is in force either until the couples have produced their requisite number of children or throughout their prime of life, if they do not meet the quota. The rule ceases to apply once they produce sufficient offspring or pass their prime. Plato imagines that the rule would be in effect for no more than ten years on average per couple. During this time their sexual interests and activity must be exclusively procreative. "The bridegroom must direct his mind to his bride and reproduction, and the bride must do the same,"especially when no children are born yet. Newlywed husbands in particular are prohibited from ejaculating in a willfully non-reproductive way. They must refrain from homoerotic sexual activity, masturbation, and sexual acts that are either actively contraceptive or performed with fingers crossed to prevent conception. They also must avoid intercourse that is carelessly indifferent to whether pregnancy will ensue. Through this conditioning, the citizens during their procreative duty should ideally come to find non-reproductive sexual activity as unthinkable as incest and avoid it voluntarily. In case the citizens still prove sexually unruly, however, Plato has backup forces ready. The female overseers, police, and city council must, if need be, stop them from shirking or transgressing their reproductive obligation. Transgressors must be stigmatized in public; their names posted in public view. They are prohibited from attending marriage and birth ceremonies, and other citizens may beat the reprobates with impunity if they dare to attend such ceremonies. The married couples thus must keep their sexual activity strictly procreative during their period of childbearing. The goddess Beginning is with them in the bedroom to reinforce compliance and a reproductive dragnet keeps them under surveillance.

The procreant male citizens in the *Laws* receive a list of sexual prohibitions against masturbating and so on because Plato finds them his main regulatory problem, oversexed as he thinks men are in their ideas about virile happiness, especially in youth. Keeping the young women in line seems less difficult to him because Athenian social mores already recognized no sexual venue for female citizens beyond marital sex, unlike the many venues that men were openly accorded—to the city detriment, as Plato saw it. As he puts it, through his anatomical displacement of the social imperative, the womb naturally commands women to become mothers, while men must undergo full-scale reprogramming.

Plato facilitates his goal to inculcate appetitive restraint by construing the temperate and reproductive regimen as a work of art for the procreant citizens to make. Reproductive activity, as he describes it in the *Laws* alone, is a skillful craft, and like other crafts, it requires a purposeful and controlled technique to do well. "All persons who are partners in any enterprise produce fine and good products when they direct their mind to themselves and the activity, and do the opposite when they are inattentive". If the prospective parents are not deliberate and sedate in their acts of reproduction, then they fail in their duty to be master artisans of offspring. Like careless woodworkers whose furniture wobbles, they produce badly wrought offspring who are bound to become dissolute. To drink and then copulate is particularly reprehensible, rather as "drinking and driving" is today. Intoxication interferes with the sexual craftsmanship required to shape embryos that are "well-built, steady, and tranquil". Plato further insists that the citizens can master this procreative skill only through life-long appetitive restraint in all respects. They cannot be undisciplined in other respects and then try to look restrained when they copulate to reproduce, such as by holding their breath or taking a sedative. Day after day they must avoid all the "diseased, violent, and unjust" activity that Plato associates with uncontrolled appetition. Thanks to this overall habituation to temperance, parents imprint their sober craftsmanship on the embryonic character of their offspring. They also bring the newborns into a society where rampant desires have in theory become unthinkable due to the vigilant monitoring of the appetites that concentrates primarily on sexual desire as the deepest root of all vice. This eugenic proposal is the consummate touch to the program of sexual restraint that Plato works out in the *Republic* and *Laws,* his key way to eliminate the profusion of human wrongdoing that uncontrolled sexual desire unleashes.

The sexual program in the *Laws* is far more restrictive than the one in the *Republic* due to its twist on reproduction as purposive craft. In the *Republic* Plato argues only that city officials must monitor the frequency and coupling patterns of the guardians' procreative activity. He does not demand that this activity be temperate and attentively purposeful. In the *Laws* Plato not only adds this major qualifier, he arms it with policing mechanisms for the procreant citizens. The *Republic,* moreover, never specifies that guardians in their prime must engage only in reproductive sexual relations it states only that their acts of procreation are to be strictly regulated. The *Republic* does not rule out autoeroticism, for instance, let alone stigmatize reproductive guardians for "killing the human race" if they occasionally masturbate to climax, whereas male citizens are so stigmatized in the *Laws.* Plato in the *Laws* creates a society that is more repressive due to this regimen of strict procreation that has no precedent in the *Republic.*

Plato's greater severity in the *Laws* is partly a compensatory measure for having to accommodate the family, clans, and the marketplace in Magnesia. Since these customs give sexual desire a ready way to breed myriad vices, he grants the reproductive urge and sexual appetite far less latitude. In the *Republic,* by contrast, the communal guardians are precluded from having sexual desire run wild through the conduits of the family and free market. Plato, if given a choice, would control sexual desire by eliminating these conduits rather than leaving them in place and having to clamp down on sexual desire. By the time he wrote the *Laws,* though, he found to his dismay that people refused to surrender familial clans and the market. Sexual desire thus pays the price and gets put under maximum security.

Despite the marital and procreative orientation of the *Laws,* in no dialogue does Plato require his citizens to engage in exclusively marital sexual relations. In the *Republic,* of course, he would prefer to do away with marriage altogether for the guardian class. In the *Laws,* where marriage is the norm, he takes it for granted that male citizens in their prime will occasionally impregnate female slaves as well as wives, though he requires this practice to remain discreet. "If a female slave mates with a free man, her offspring must belong to her master." Plato's position here is compatible with his eugenic rule that a procreant male citizen must not ejaculate into a woman unless he intends to make her pregnant. Because this rule is not as strong as requiring a male citizen to inseminate only his own wife, the men remain free to exercise a reproductive prerogative with female slaves so as to replenish the slave labor force on a locally grown basis. And though Plato does not say as much, if the men are temperate and purposive while copulating with female slaves, they in theory improve the slave breed too better workers who eat less. The *Laws* therefore does not mandate strictly marital sexual practices, while the *Republic* eliminates marriage outright for the main enfranchised group.

Plato in the *Laws* and *Republic* leaves the sexual behavior of the citizens and guardians unmonitored after they complete their reproductive service to the city. He is quite confident that they will heed the limits of necessary and beneficial sexual pleasure, for by this time they are disciplined to be moderate and their reproductive urge has quieted down. Plato also thinks that those who are finished procreating inevitably will be sexually active because of the sexual appetite driving force for much of the human life span. Assuming the *Laws* ten-year average period of reproduction, most of the women would be only in their later twenties and most of the men would be around forty, hardly too old for eros. In the *Laws,* likewise, post-reproductive sexual activity "should remain silently unregulated" so long as the citizens remain moderate, avoid incest, do not procreate, and refrain from copulating with citizens who are still serving reproductive duty. Even more permissively in the *Republic,* guardians past their prime need only obey incest rules and avoid reproducing. Otherwise the men are "free to have sexual activity with whomever they please, and likewise the women", whereas Plato offers no such carte blanche in the *Laws.* In the *Laws,* further, he keeps plans to enforce sexual moderation on standby, for the sexual appetite needs an extinguisher in case the citizens break away from their controlled burn. This outbreak is more likely to happen to them than to the communal guardians, for the family and private ownership fuel sexual desire.

Though Plato does not specify when postreproductive sexual behavior crosses the line from being necessary to unnecessary, what matters most is that necessary sexual activity takes place discreetly, not lewdly on display. Thus, even though he is stern in his restrictions, he is not so severe that he would require sexual abstinence from the guardians and citizens who have completed their reproductive service to the city. In fact, as he states in the *Laws,* citizens who have finished reproducing should regard moderation and "not complete sexual abstinence" as honorable, and they should act accordingly. In so doing they serve Aphrodite properly, which she naturally compels them to do until they become elderly. Plato therefore never seeks to limit all sexual activity to a strictly procreative function, even though this position has been attributed to him, both in Jewish and Christian Platonism and in the modern day. In the *Laws* the citizens adhere to a strictly temperate and deliberately reproductive function only for the time they must engage in their baby-making craft. In the *Republic* no such restriction applies. To Plato, then, temperate sexual hedonism is the mark of appetitive virtue, not sexual renunciation apart from the perfunctory performance of reproduction. This principle respects the force that Plato accords to the sexual appetite and is in keeping with the Apollonian tenor of his ethics, mhdän ìgan, "nothing in excess."

Summary

Sexual desire according to Plato is the most incorrigible of the inherently antirational physical appetites and gives rise to myriad ills individually and socially. It has plagued the human condition in its uncontrolled or poorly regulated form, and thus must be curtailed to the necessary degree. The sexual appetite, when successfully domineering, both deters the embodied soul from attaining enlightenment and places it at risk of reincarnating as a dumb animal, never to desire Beauty or even to think again. As a bodily health problem, further, excessive sexual desire and activity bring distress due to the gross imbalance of burning pain over pleasure. Finally, individual vices, crime in the streets, and warfare between cities and states are the seedy fruits of sexual desire, hunger, and thirst and sexual desire especially. The inhibition of sexual desire and the other appetites would consequently bring great benefits for individual health, the social good, and the enlightenment of the embodied soul, and the last benefit for Plato is the most important of all.

In the *Republic* and *Laws* Plato does not present one fixed plan to rein in sexual desire, but he aims to control it by managing the reproductive urge in a variety of ways. Despite the absence of systematic fixity, he supports several constant plans across both dialogues. First, he advocates communalism, and reproductive communalism especially, in order to eliminate divisive clan groups and the marketplace through which the appetites run riot. Crucial though this reform is, in the *Laws* Plato despairs of its feasibility and constructs a second-best plan, while still preferring his communal ideal. The compromise system retains the family along with trade in the marketplace. As a compensatory measure, he constrains sexual desire even more firmly as the primary origin of vices. Second, Plato advocates procreative age limits and strict measures of population control in the interest of appetitive restraint and the greater good. Third, he requires the guardians and citizens to honor the gods through Greek religious ceremonies in order to enhance the greater symbiotic community of noble gods and well-behaved mortals through the reproduction of children destined for appetitive virtue.

In addition to the constants, Plato promotes several eugenic options to inculcate sexual and other appetitive restraint. In the *Republic* he encourages breeding only the better-restrained guardians; in the *Laws* he has persons mate with spouses of counterbalancing personality traits and economic backgrounds. As his most ambitious and historically significant plan, Plato in the *Laws* maintains that reproduction is a skill that requires life-long controls on the appetites, especially during the delicate craftwork of procreative sexual intercourse. To prevent the slipshod production of children, he requires the ever-temperate citizens to be strictly and deliberately reproductive in their sexual activity, but only while serving their time of providing newborn human resources for the city. After the citizens have performed their service, Plato directs them to continue paying their virtuously moderate sexual dues to Aphrodite, which the sexual appetite presses them to do until its yearning for fricative pleasure fades away much later in life.

Despite Plato's repertoire of eugenic plans, their common goal is to regulate procreation so that uncontrolled sexual and reproductive activity become passÜ customs that a new breed of human beings have transcended the once sex-hungry men in particular. If Plato had his way, sexual practices and their progeny of vices would undergo major reduction and reform. So effective would the social reconditioning be that the citizens of the future would look back upon Plato's fellow Athenians as primitive sexual savages, much as we pride ourselves for our greater brain capacity over Australopithecus.

3

Socratic Methods in Philosophy

Introduction

In the Euthydemus Socrates mentions temperance, justice, and bravery as virtues; then he adds wisdom. Sometimes he mentions piety as a fifth virtue. These are the only virtues that Socrates discusses in the earliest dialogues, though they are not the only traits generally recognized as virtues by his contemporaries. The tendency to pick out some of the recognized virtues as primary does not begin with Socrates; but earlier sources do not show any clear agreement about which virtues are primary. We cannot assume that everyone would immediately agree with Socrates' list, but it would probably not be thought surprising.

While people agree fairly broadly in saying that the traits on Socrates' list are the virtues, or among the major virtues, they do not agree about what these virtues require. It is worth examining some widespread disagreements.

Redescriptions

Some literary sources contemporary with Plato present a

disagreement about the virtues that is expressed in (what I will call) redescription. This redescription is indicated by saying that certain innovators 'called F G', in order to praise F; 'F' is the name of some trait generally regarded as vicious, and 'G' is the name of some trait generally regarded as virtuous. The same sort of redescription operating in the reverse direction can be used to condemn F; in this case 'F' names a commonly recognized virtue, and 'G' a commonly recognized vice. This formula ('They called F G') is normally used by people (whom we may call, simply for convenience, 'conservatives') who disapprove of the views of the innovators; it is not clear that it is used by innovators to describe their own views.

Redescriptions are prominent in a familiar, but difficult, passage in Thucydides about changes and conflicts in common views about the virtues. Though Thucydides is talking initially about Corcyra, his remarks are supposed to apply to the Greek world in general. He describes how the dislocations resulting from war caused these changes:

> By their justification they changed around the accustomed valuation of names in relation to actions. For unreasoning daring was counted bravery in support of one's party; provident delay was counted fair-seeming cowardice; the temperate was counted a pretext for the unmanly, and the understanding in relation to everything was counted inactive in everything; the impulsively sharp was added to the attributes of a man, but to deliberate in safety [was counted] a specious excuse for deserting [the cause].

This passage raises some difficult questions of interpretation; these may be clarified by reference to some apparently parallel passages. In Republic VIII the adolescent son of the oligarchic man is persuaded by the arguments (logoi) that 'calling shame foolishness, push it out and calling temperance unmanliness and abusing it, expel it, and treating moderation and orderly expenditure as boorishness and illiberality, exile it'. Instead, they bring in ' insolence and anarchy and extravagance and shamelessness'. They celebrate these and put a good face on them, 'calling insolence good breeding, anarchy liberality, extravagance magnificence, and shamelessness bravery'. For our purposes the most important point is the fact that both writers present disagreement through redescription, whether or not they reach their descriptions independently.

The same pattern of redescription appears in some passages of Isocrates. He praises the age of Solon and Cleisthenes, when people were not encouraged 'to think licence democracy, lawlessness freedom, uncontrolled speech equal law, and freedom to stop at nothing happiness'. He argues that 'overreaching' (pleonexia) should be applied to gaining genuine goods, and therefore to the most just and pious people. In his day, it is different:

> Many things in the city are so turned upside down and confused that some people do not even use names according to nature any more, but transfer them from the finest things to the basest of practices. They call those who act the fool and are able to mock and mimic naturally gifted, whereas it is fitting for the people who are naturally most gifted in relation to virtue to receive this appellation.

Aristotle refers to redescription as a stock device of the orator. In contrast to the previous passages, which look at it from the point of view of the conservative, he takes the point of view of the innovator, and suggests ways to make redescription persuasive. We should treat qualities close to those that a person actually has as though they were the same qualities, so that we treat the cautious person as sluggish and contriving, or (in the opposite direction) the naïve person as honest. We should treat people with extreme degrees of some quality as though they had the relevant virtue, so that we treat the rashly confident person as brave and the extravagant person as liberal:

> For it will seem so to the many, and, moreover, it allows mistaken reasoning from the cause. For if someone is prone to face danger where it is not necessary, he would seem all the more [likely to do it] where it is fine to do so; and if he is openhanded to all and sundry, then [he would seem all the more likely to be so] to his friends; for it is an extreme degree of virtue to benefit everyone. Aristotle notices that, as the

previous passages also show, the technique of redescription can be used either to praise or to blame; and he uses the same term, 'putting a good face on' (*hupokorizesthai*) that Plato uses in Republic VIII.

The Significance of Redescriptions

In all these cases the innovators are presented as redescribing F as G, but we might still understand them in different ways. If we focus on the first of Thucydides' examples, 'They called mindless [lit. "unreasoning"] daring bravery', we have these options:

- People regarded 'Bravery is mindless daring' as the right answer to the question 'What does the word "bravery" mean?'.
- They regarded it as the right answer to the question 'What is bravery?'.
- They said or believed 'Mindless daring is bravery'.

They said or believed of actions (for instance, killing one's political opponent in broad daylight) that Thucydides regards as manifestations of mindless daring that they manifested bravery.

Only the first of these answers implies that the innovators disagreed with conservatives about the meaning of the relevant words. The third answer implies agreement about the meaning of the relevant words; innovators asserted, in so many words, 'Mindless daring is bravery', meaning just what the conservatives would have meant if they had used the same words. The fourth answer simply expresses the view of the innovators that actions condemned by the conservatives as mindless daring could be justified as bravery (according to the normal concept of bravery) in support of one's party. Similarly, they did not say 'Temperance is a pretext for cowardice', but they came to believe of temperate behaviour that it was a pretext for cowardice. According to the fourth answer, Thucydides is speaking of de re beliefs (believing of temperance that it is ...), not of *de dicto* beliefs (believing 'temperance is . . .').

The same options for interpreting the remarks about redescription are open in the other passages that I quoted above. In some of them, however, the fourth is the most plausible. Aristotle does not seem to be thinking of orators who actually want to say 'The rashly confident person is brave'. This claim would be controversial, and the orator has no interest in being drawn into such controversy. Aristotle is thinking of the orator who wants to apply the description 'brave' to a person whom other people might describe (even truly describe) as 'rashly confident'. The orator himself has good reason to avoid the description 'rashly confident' and to stick to 'brave'.

The same point applies to the innovators discussed by Isocrates, Plato, and Thucydides. If they want to apply favourable descriptions ('bravery', etc.), they are unlikely to want to apply unfavourable ones ('mindless daring', etc.) as well. The unfavourable descriptions seem to be the ones that (according to Thucydides) in fact apply to the relevant people, whereas the favourable ones are those that the innovators apply to them. This is the pattern that Thucydides seems to summarize:

> *Most people are readier to be called adroit while being [in fact] evil-doers than [to be called] stupid [while being in fact] good, and they are ashamed at the one [sc. the second description], but take pleasure in the other [sc. the first description].*

Several examples of this attitude have been displayed in the previous remarks, if we take the fourth answer to give the right account of the passage.

All the passages on redescription make good sense if they are taken (as in the fourth answer) to ascribe de re beliefs about virtues and vices to the innovators. In some cases they may also ascribe de dicto beliefs. Some people, on being told that innovators regard ordinary decency as mere stupidity, might want to deny that ordinary decent behaviour (avoidance of treachery or deceit, for instance) is stupidity. Others, however, might be ready to acknowledge that it is indeed stupidity, but reply that this is a point in favour of stupidity.

We can use these passages on redescription to identify some generally accepted assumptions about the virtues. In each case Thucydides (for instance) assumes that his readers will be surprised, even shocked, to be told that the innovators redescribed F as G, either because 'F' is properly applied to a good quality and 'G' to a bad quality incompatible with F, or for the reverse reason. He believes, for instance, that we will be surprised to be told that mindless daring could be counted as brave action, because we normally suppose that bravery excludes mindless daring.

While people agree on the assumptions that make the innovators' views surprising, they are also uncertain enough to give the innovators' views some plausibility. If A stabs his political rival B to death in broad daylight, Ns defenders may argue that A's action was not a piece of mindless daring; A took a risk for a worthwhile cause (the benefit of his party), and that is what brave people are expected to do. A just and temperate person refrains from aggression against people who have not offended him. His scruples make him afraid to seize the advantage that a less scrupulous person can seize by acting boldly; fear is the mark of a coward; hence (for reasons noticed by Hamlet) temperance makes us cowards.

A broader question raised by these arguments of the innovators concerns the connections between the virtues. Conservatives might point out that the allegedly brave actions advocated by the innovators are not the actions of a temperate and just person; but how good an objection to the innovators is this? Is it reasonable to expect that a genuinely brave action will always conform to the demands of the other virtues? Or, if different virtues sometimes support incompatible actions, which virtue takes precedence?

To formulate the questions in this way is to abstract and to generalize to a higher level than Thucydides does, and no doubt to a higher level than the people he describes ever did. Still, these questions are a useful startingpoint for considering Plato's early dialogues. Socrates, Plato, and Thucydides all lived through the last seven years of the Peloponnesian War, including the revolutions of the Four Hundred and the Thirty;

and perhaps Thucydides has these revolts especially in mind when he writes about the Corcyrean revolution. Like Plato, he writes about people of the period of the Peloponnesian War from a post-war perspective. If the Platonic Socrates considers the questions implicit in Thucydides' reflections, he cannot be accused of raising questions alien to the concerns of Plato's contemporaries. If, on the contrary, Socrates' inquiries make it reasonable for him to raise the Thucydidean questions, but he completely ignores them, then he seems to weaken his own position in the eyes of Plato's contemporaries.

Bravery

Thucydides' list of redescriptions begins with the redescription of mindless daring as bravery in support of one's party. We may reasonably compare this implicit view of bravery with Socrates' discussion of bravery in the Laches.

Lysimachus and Melesias wonder whether their sons should be given instruction in armed combat, but they are not trying to make their sons into professional soldiers. They want their sons to have the sort of training that will equip them to achieve 'many fine actions', as their grandfathers Aristeides and Thucydides did. Lysimachus and Melesias themselves are 'without renown', because (they think) their education was neglected. They want their sons to acquire bravery, because they take this to be the mark of 'fine and good men'.

We might infer that Lysimachus and Melesias believe that bravery, understood as the strictly military virtue for which they hope their sons are being trained, is enough to make someone a 'fine and good' man. Such a belief is not uncommon. Indeed, bravery (andreia) has a special place among the virtues, in so far as it is sometimes regarded as the pre-eminent virtue of a man (aner). Laches insists that he will listen to discussions about virtue only from people who are themselves virtuous and he welcomes the conspicuous proof of Socrates' virtue given by his brave actions at the battle of Delium. This close connection between being brave and being a good man is expressed in Pericles' remark that someone who has died bravely in battle has 'proved himself a good man'. Pericles does not mean that a noble death in battle suddenly endows someone with temperance and justice, but that a conspicuous display of bravery entitles someone to be called a good man, whatever else can be said against him.

Other common views, however, suggest that if bravery is understood as a purely military virtue, then bravery by itself is not enough to 'prove oneself a good man'. Indeed, the very quality of andragathia, 'being a good man', that is sometimes ascribed to those who display bravery in battle is sometimes ascribed only to those who display the sort of virtue that includes concern for justice.

Pericles (as presented by Thucydides) acknowledges and exploits both the narrow and the broad use of 'andragathia'. In telling the Athenians that they risk the loss of their empire, Pericles insists that if they want the honours, they will have to put up with the labour, and that the contest is not simply about freedom or slavery, but about the danger they will face from people whose hatred has been aroused by the empire. He warns against the views of people who are afraid of the risks of empire and want to mind their own business and be good men (andragathizesthai); this is not a reasonable option, since it is dangerous to abandon the empire, even though it seems unjust to have acquired it.

Pericles implies that the aspiration of people who want to display andragathia by opposing him is misguided. He acknowledges that some people will believe that andragathia requires them to be concerned about questions of justice; he answers them by asserting that such scruples amount to cowardice, and so do not reflect andragathia at all, in the present situation. This argument uses a narrow conception of andragathia, identified with bravery (itself narrowly conceived), to defeat the considerations that are derived from a broader conception of andragathia, including justice. Pericles suggests that if a proposed course of action is cowardly, there is nothing to be said for it from the point of view of andragathia. He takes his audience to assume both that (i) concern for justice is one aspect of being a good man and that (ii) bravery (conceived narrowly as fearlessness in the face of danger) is all it takes to be a good man.

These two assumptions exploited by Pericles are inconsistent. Lysimachus and Melesias in the Laches implicitly accept them both, without noticing the inconsistency. Though they begin by assuming that if their sons are brave, they will be 'fine and good men', they offer examples suggesting that bravery, as they understand it, is not enough to make someone a good man. For the fine actions of the elder Aristeides and Thucydides were achieved both in war and in peace, and especially in 'directing the affairs of the allies and of this city'. Aristeides and Thucydides gained their reputation partly in the military sphere, but they were also leading politicians with a reputation for wisdom and justice; Aristeides opposed the devious Themistocles, and Thucydides opposed the 'demagogic' policies of Pericles.

Nicias and Laches take up the discussion, by considering the value of military training, but they do not consider the relation between being brave and being 'fine and good' in general. Nicias argues that the knowledge and skill learnt in military training is useful in a military context, and that in fact it will encourage people to learn all that concerns a general (182b5-7). His assurance that armed combat will have these desirable results is rather hasty. Being a good general—in the Athenian context where the office of a general is both military and political—requires more than purely technical military skills; Nicias entirely overlooks this point, even though he is himself a general prominent in political life.

Laches' reply to Nicias is also rather narrowly focused. He argues that lessons in armed combat cannot be much use, since the teachers of them do not try to teach them in Sparta, where the Spartans' whole concern in life is to find the kinds of instruction and training that will allow them to dominate other people in war. He adds that he has seen one teacher of armed combat make himself ridiculous. He does not raise the wider question of whether this is really the way for young men to be spending their time if they want to acquire the qualities of the elder Thucydides and Aristeides.

Socrates' interlocutors, then, seem to be no clearer than Thucydides' speakers and audiences about how to choose between these three inconsistent claims that they accept: (1) Bravery is sufficient for being a good man (*andragathia*, being *kalos kagathos*). (2) Being a good man requires wisdom and justice. (3) Being brave is not sufficient for being wise and just. In the rest of the dialogue Socrates suggests that we resolve this conflict by rejecting the third claim. He suggests, against the innovators, that endurance (*karteria*) and daring (*tolma*) cannot be brave if they are harmful, mischievous, and senseless. Assuming that the *andreios* is *kalos kagathos,* Socrates infers that the brave person must meet the other conditions that a good person must meet.

Several questions can be raised about the cogency of Socrates' arguments, especially those that lead to the conclusion that the best account of bravery that they have found makes bravery identical to the other virtues. Here, however, I am simply focusing on the intuitive plausibility of his premisses and his conclusion. The conclusion is certainly meant to be surprising; but when we think about it, we see that it expresses (even if it exaggerates) a widely accepted assumption about bravery. It is the assumption that the conservatives rely on in expecting their audiences to be shocked at the thought that some people actually regard mindless daring as bravery.

Temperance

Temperance and bravery raise some sharply different questions. While common sense finds it fairly easy to describe the range of actions that count as brave, the standard uses of 'temperate' (*sôphrôn*) are far more various. Indeed, while 'temperance' is a fairly good rendering of 'sôphrosunç', as the term is used in Plato's *Republic* and Aristotle's *Ethics*, it is perhaps a misleading rendering of the term as it appears in earlier Greek and in the Socratic dialogues. In these contexts a uniform and fairly adequate translation of '*sôphrosunç*' would be 'sound mind' or 'good sense'; but this uniform rendering covers considerable variety in the actions recognized as temperate.

It is often supposed that the temperate person will 'know himself', his needs, and his limitations, and that as a result of this self-knowledge, he will not pursue excessive satisfaction of one desire at the expense of other interests and needs. Hence temperance is taken to imply the observance of the two Delphic maxims 'Know yourself' and 'Nothing too much'; indeed, the first of these maxims is taken to imply the second. On this view, the temperate person is moderate, self-controlled, and self-restrained.

Charmides' initial attempts to say what temperance is capture these aspects of the virtue. In suggesting that temperance is doing everything in an 'orderly and quiet' way, he alludes to the demand for young people to display self-restraint rather than self-assertiveness. When Charmides cannot explain what sort of quietness is to be identified with temperance, he tries a different account, and suggests that temperance is shame. Once again, this account suits many common beliefs about temperance; *aidôs*, rendered by 'shame', also covers modesty and bashfulness, both conventionally expected of a child or young person. It is also appropriate to suggest that temperate people will have the right sort of shame restraining them from acting wrongly. Someone who lacks temperance is prone to the wanton insolence (*hubris*) that displays itself in disregard for the rights and interests of others, and sometimes in a positively aggressive attitude to others for the sake of displaying one's own superiority.

The connection between temperance and order makes it appropriate to appeal to *sôphrosunç* in political contexts. While every form of government and constitution might be expected to claim that it promotes tranquillity and good order, these goals tend to be especially emphasized by oligarchs.

From the oligarchic point of view, an orderly and temperate constitution is one in which all the members of the society, and especially the lower classes, know their place and obey the laws. The demand for a more 'temperate' constitution was a characteristic oligarchic slogan.

These widely accepted views about temperance make Socrates' treatment of it in the *Charmides* easier to understand. He connects it with moderation, by focusing on the role of self-knowledge in temperance. He connects it with good order and good sense, by suggesting a line of argument that leads to the conclusion that temperance must be knowledge of good and evil as a whole. The steps of Socrates' argument are open to question, as they are in the *Laches*, but the conclusion is not as counterintuitive as it may appear at first sight. If we expect the *sôphron* person to display good sense on practical questions, and we expect this good sense to be embodied in a realistic estimate of oneself and in the proper sort of respect for others, someone will hardly meet these expectations without a general appreciation of what is morally important. This general appreciation is what Socrates demands in demanding knowledge of good and evil as a whole.

Piety

Many, though not all, of Socrates' contemporaries believed that piety simply consists in doing what the gods require in order to secure their favour, and that what the gods require need not conform to the requirements of the other virtues. Greeks were familiar with the view that the gods demand justice and punish injustice (in later generations or in an afterlife); but they still practised propitiatory sacrifice, seeking to placate the gods by material transactions independent of the moral character of the sacrificer. This traditional view is expressed by Cephalus in *Republic I*; he takes seriously the stories about the punishment of unjust people, but he does not make it clear whether sacrifices to win the gods' favour can be substituted for justice towards other human beings. Adiemantus suggests that this sort of substitution is quite reasonable, and he makes a good case for it from traditional authority.

While Socrates' own reputation for bravery and temperance was secure, his claim to be pious was disputed. In the *Apology* he answers the charge that he is guilty of impiety because he does not recognize the gods recognized by the City. While he defends himself against the charge of being an atheist, he does not argue that he believes what most people believe about the nature and activities of the Olympian gods. In particular, he does not claim to defend traditional views about the attitude of the gods to morality.

Euthyphro is the interlocutor whose views about piety are examined, and his views are by no means wholly traditional. In prosecuting his father for causing the death of a slave, Euthyphro violates a traditional bond of filial loyalty, but he does not acknowledge anything shocking in what he is doing. He simply argues that if an injustice has been committed, the gods demand punishment for it. He recognizes that his view is not the usual view; that is why he accuses most people of ignorance about the gods, because they do not realize that the gods require him to seek the punishment of injustice, no matter who has committed it (4b7-e3). Since this alleged rule of piety conflicts with the prohibition on harming one's father, Euthyphro can reasonably be asked for some justification for his claim that the rule requiring punishment of injustice takes precedence; and so Socrates asks him whether his knowledge of piety is so exact that he can defend his assumptions about the priority of one rule over the other.

Though Socrates challenges some of Euthyphro's arguments, he does not challenge the basic claim that piety requires justice. Indeed, that claim is stated and taken for granted in the last part of the dialogue (12C10-d4). Neither Socrates nor Euthyphro takes this claim to need argument; they can claim the support of a strong tendency in Greek thought about the connection of religious with moral obligation. In assuming this connection between piety and justice, Socrates displays the same tendency to harmonize the virtues that he displays in his treatment of bravery and of temperance. In each case, he implicitly resists any suggestion that one virtue could demand behaviour that is condemned from the standpoint of another virtue. In resisting any such suggestion, he takes the side of the conservatives against the innovators.

Justice

According to one isolated passage in Theognis, all virtue is summed up in justice; Aristotle finds this line worthy of quotation as a proverbial remark about justice. Justice is the characteristic virtue of the good citizen; the just person obeys the laws, and fulfils particular obligations to other people. It is not surprising that Cephalus mentions honest dealing and payment of one's debts as clear examples of just actions or that Polemarchus, on the authority of Simonides, tries to generalize this suggestion in the general formula that justice consists in giving what is due to each person.

Though Socrates recognizes that questions about justice are especially perplexing, he does not ask what justice is. In the earliest dialogues, he does not pursue the same sort of inquiry as the one he pursues into other virtues in the *Laches*, *Charmides*, and *Euthyphro*. He expresses his own unconventional views about justice, however, quite strongly and clearly.

Some of the issues that Socrates faces are raised by Neoptolemus in Sophocles' *Philoctetes*. Neoptolemus connects the requirements of justice with obligations to specific people, even when these conflict with the course of action that has the apparently best consequences for the public interest. He is easily persuaded by Odysseus to deceive Philoctetes, in order to steal the bow that the Greeks need to capture Troy. Neoptolemus changes his mind, however, regarding Odysseus's plan as immoral and dishonourable. Odysseus's plan can be represented as the only sensible course of action for the Greek expedition; and Neoptolemus does not dispute this view of it. If he thought that promotion of the general interest made an action just, then he should agree—given his belief about the public interest that it would be just to do what Odysseus tells him to do. But he is convinced that it is unjust, because it involves breaking obligations to Philoctetes.

Socrates seems to agree with some of Neoptolemus's doubts about appeals to the public interest. In the two cases where Socrates came into conflict with the dominant party in Athens, his opponents could make some case for the claim that their actions were in the public interest, even if they were illegal and unjust. The Thirty presumably claimed that the current emergency justified their summary proceedings against individuals; and the majority after the battle of Arginusae might have claimed that it was expedient to try the generals together, even though this action violated normal legal procedures. On the other side, many Athenians might well believe that, whatever might be true about the public interest, the actions were clearly unjust. Socrates does not suggest that he would have been justified in taking the stand he took against illegal action only if he could show that the illegal action was not in the public interest.

Nor, however, does Socrates identify justice with legality. He does not suggest that if the Thirty had taken the time to pass a law permitting their seizures and confiscations, it would thereby have been unjust to disobey them. Indeed, he threatens to disobey any order that would require him to act unjustly by giving up his philosophical activity as the price of remaining alive; he insists that he must follow his obligation to carry on with philosophy.

The Priority of Justice

Socrates not only holds strong views about what justice requires, but also maintains the supremacy of justice over other moral and prudential considerations. He imagines someone asking him whether he is not ashamed to be endangering his life by his present course of action. Socrates replies that the only question for him to consider is whether a proposed action is just or unjust, and whether it is the action of a good or a bad man. He claims that his action is just, and that it is shameful and bad to commit injustice by disobeying the order of one's superior. Similarly, he claims to be concerned about whether his actions are just, fine, and pious.

Socrates appeals to the example of Achilles, but adapts it to his present purposes. Two features need adaptation: (1) In killing Hector, Achilles was avenging the death of Patroclus, and eagerly returning evil for evil. (2) Achilles apparently chose the fine over the advantageous; 'he counted his own interest for little and did something fine'. For Achilles, 'such a death was finer, while being alive was expedient'.

Both of these features of Achilles are eliminated by Socrates. (1) A quotation from Homer is modified to suggest that Achilles' overriding concern was justice, not revenge. (2) Socrates agrees that Achilles chose the finest course of action, but strongly denies that he sacrificed advantage in order to choose it.

In claiming that the virtuous action is the fine course of action, Socrates simply assumes what he assumes elsewhere in the earliest dialogues. In the Crito, he also claims that living finely is beneficial to the agent, since living well and happily is the same as living justly and finely. In his view, acceptance of the priority of justice requires acceptance of his view that justice promotes the agent's advantage.

Virtue and Happiness

Socrates' defence of justice by appeal to advantage is not a special claim about justice, but a general claim about the connection of virtue with happiness. He does not allow the possibility that justice might conflict with any of the other virtues. It cannot properly be condemned as cowardice (as Thucydides' innovators suppose). Nor can it conflict with temperance, if this is understood as good sense in considering one's own interest. Socrates' belief in the close connection of virtue with happiness is simply a consequence of his refusal to allow conflicts between the virtues.

This attitude to virtue and happiness is not simply the product of Socrates' theoretical assumptions. The outlook of two Sophoclean characters suggests why many people would find Socrates' position intelligible. Both Antigone and Electra make choices that other people regard as unreasonable and imprudent. They are often accused of lacking 'good deliberation' (euboulia), since they choose a course of action that seems to involve them in some severe loss. But this is not their view. Antigone and Electra do not claim that they are following duty or obligation or honour or pride against self-interest and prudence. They claim that prudence and good deliberation really justify the course of action they choose.

Other people defend justice on a more theoretical level. One writer denies any opposition between justice and the demands of nature. Everyone benefits, he argues, from law and justice because they meet the natural need for security. Moreover, the legitimate desire for worldly success need not lead us to violate conventional morality; we can secure admiration and honour by being law-abiding, without needing to dissemble and without going to the effort of struggling against the interests of the many. Once we see this, we will no longer be tempted to regard a law-abiding outlook as mere cowardice.

Democritus defends justice differently. He believes it is not enough to argue that justice results in honour and reputation; for these can be gained by astute dissembling (B264). He argues for a much closer connection between justice and success. In his view, happiness requires undisturbed harmony in the soul (which Democritus interprets in atomic terms, B191); this harmony requires the wisdom that prevents disharmony (B31); and the appropriate wisdom requires us to avoid the distress resulting from greedy and intemperate action.

We cannot say whether these theoretical defences of justice influenced Socrates or reflect his influence. But it is worth mentioning them together with Antigone and Electra, to show that Socrates' position is not wholly eccentric or unprecedented. Once we see the widespread support for the conservative view that refuses to allow the virtues to impose conflicting requirements, we can see why someone who finds this conservative view plausible might also take Socrates' conclusions seriously.

Socrates' Assumptions

Socrates' assumptions about the virtues may be summarized in two main assumptions: (1) Socrates takes for granted the unity of each virtue, taking it to be a single trait of character rather than a collection of loosely connected traits. (2) He assumes the harmony of the virtues with one another and with happiness, so that he does not allow the possibility of conflict between the requirements of two virtues or between virtue and happiness. The unity of each virtue is most clearly assumed in the Charmides; the harmony of the virtues with one another is most clearly assumed in the *Laches*; and the harmony of virtue and happiness is most clearly assumed in the arguments about justice. In each case Socrates shows how we can reject the suggestion of the innovators that, for instance, justice and temperance might encourage cowardice, or bravery might move us to act unjustly.

These arguments recognizably defend the position taken by the conservatives, who resist the redescriptions offered by the innovators. His defence leads him to claims that his contemporaries no doubt found surprising, but even his most surprising claims turn out to reflect lines of thought that would be widely accepted as plausible.

Socrates' assumptions about unity (in each virtue) and harmony (between the virtues and between virtue and happiness) do not appear bizarre or indefensible when we take the trouble to compare them with common beliefs. However counter-intuitive they may have initially sounded to his contemporaries, they correspond to recognizable strands in common beliefs. One way to reconcile different strands in ordinary views about the 'fine and good' person supports the assumption of the harmony of the virtues. Even Socrates' most counter-intuitive assumption, about the harmony of virtue and happiness, can claim the support of the Sophoclean Antigone and Electra.

This is a one-sided picture, however, of Socrates' treatment of contemporary views. To form a more accurate picture, we must consider some conflicting elements in contemporary views—elements that conflict with Socrates' attitude to the virtues and that are not recognized in the earliest dialogues.

Conflicting Elements in Bravery

We saw that in Thucydides andragathia sometimes requires nothing more than firmness on the battlefield in the face of life-threatening danger. If this is all it takes to be brave, it is easy to identify bravery with mere boldness; Laches at one point finds it obvious that bold and fearless animals are also brave.

If we conceive bravery in these terms, we may doubt whether it really makes someone a good man. Indeed, it seems to conflict with other virtues. To be brave, we need to pursue our own aims vigorously and fearlessly; but to be temperate, we need to moderate our own aims and desires to fit our plans for our own welfare or to fit other people's demands. The training that develops bravery may seem to make it more difficult to acquire the other virtues.

This conception of bravery raises further questions about how we should conceive a 'fine and good' man. One of the young men in the Laches is Aristeides, the grandson of Aristeides 'the Just'; and this famous Aristeides is a paradigm of a 'fine and good' man. His justice did not always seem to benefit him. According to stories found in later sources, he was regarded as someone who wanted to be just, not merely to seem just; one citizen even voted for Aristeides' ostracism because he was tired of hearing him called 'the Just'. It was at any rate not obvious that his justice was always an advantage to him in the political struggle with Themistocles.

We might say that Aristeides' justice was a particular proof of his virtue, or we might say that his justice interfered with his virtue, and that he would have done better for himself if he had been less scrupulous and more like his devious and daring rival Themistocles.

If, then, we pursue the implications of some ordinary views about bravery, they reveal the conflict between self-assertive and other-regarding virtues. This conflict raises an awkward question for Lysimachus and Melesias: do they want their sons to be as just as Aristeides, or would they be willing to sacrifice some justice for the sake of greater worldly success? Socrates does not draw attention to this question. The deepest sources of conflict between bravery and the other virtues are not explored in the *Laches*. Some of Laches' initial replies suggest how the conflict might arise, but these replies are soon rejected, and do not receive the discussion they deserve. Socrates' questions lead his interlocutors to agree that a genuinely brave person must also have the other virtues, so that they can no longer allow conflict between bravery and other virtues.

Socrates cannot fairly be accused of simply imposing his own views about bravery and the other virtues on interlocutors who have no tendency to accept them. For we have seen that ordinary views about the connection between bravery and *andragathia* and between *andragathia* and justice support Socrates' moves. It is not so clear, however, that Socrates' treatment is the only plausible treatment of bravery and the other virtues. Why would it not be better to affirm clearly that bravery is only one virtue, and that it is separable from the others? This would also be an intelligible response to common views about virtue. The *Laches* seems to fail us when we ask why this response is inferior to Socrates' response.

Conflicting Elements in Temperance

The different kinds of outlook and behaviour attributed to the temperate person make it difficult to say how temperance is related to the other virtues. A temperate person with self-control and moderation is likely to be undemanding and law-abiding; but this sort of moderation may not always be a good thing. The attitude of the 'non-interfering' (*apragmôn*) citizen who sticks to his own business might be regarded as a rather passive acquiescence in the face of superior power. Pericles argues that such a person is simply useless in a community that demands active citizenship and bold decisions. He insinuates that such 'non-interference' is part of the andragathia that is really a cowardly avoidance of danger.

More generally, we may doubt whether it is always a good idea to restrain one's own desires because of other people, or even in one's own long-term interest. While traditional Greek moral thought is full of the praises of temperance, the attitudes characteristic of temperance seem rather antagonistic to some conspicuous aspects of the traditional heroic outlook. The most famous actions of Achilles and Ajax are not exactly striking examples of temperance and moderation. The temperate, well-balanced outlook is more characteristic of Odysseus, as Sophocles' *Ajax* makes clear from the beginning. Odysseus's caution and sagacity leave him open to suspicion. Self-assertion rather than self-restraint might well seem to be the most admired characteristic of a firstclass hero; caution and self-control might seem to be a second-best, commendable only in a second-class person who needs moderation because he cannot achieve the extreme of greatness. While many Greek moralists advocate temperance and reject aggressiveness, self-assertive aggression is a persistent ideal. Suspicion of temperance supports the view that bravery and temperance are not only distinct, but actually in conflict.

Sometimes moderation may be rejected because it involves a cowardly deference to the demands and interests of others. But even if we confine ourselves to one's attitude to oneself, there might still be reasons for suspicion of *sôphrosunç* as cowardly calculation. Achilles and Ajax lack temperance not only in their attitudes towards others, but also in their attitudes towards themselves; both of them are moved by their immediate reactions, even though these reactions tend to frustrate their longer-term aims.

These doubts about temperance raise a question about the attitude of the innovators. Do they actually mean to claim that temperance is not a virtue? As we have seen, Thucydides' presentation of them as believing that mindless daring is bravery and that the temperate is a pretext for the cowardly might be taken to attribute de dicto or de re beliefs. The de re interpretation is far more plausible in the case of bravery. In the case of temperance, the *de dicto* interpretation deserves consideration. If it is right, then the innovators express explicit opposition to temperance.

The *de dicto* interpretation is not required, however. When Callicles and the Unjust Argument reject temperance, they connect it with moderation and self-restraint. Their reasons for rejecting moderation do not require rejection of *sôphrosunç* altogether; for since *sôphrosunç* also includes good sense, someone who pursues his own interests sensibly might claim to be *sôphrôn*. In the appropriate circumstances the self-seeking pursuit of one's own power and advantage at the expense of others might be attacked as an obvious lapse from temperance; but it might also appear to be the proper thing for a *sôphrôn* person to do. This aspect of *sôphrosunç* is exploited by Polyphemus in Euripides' *Cyclops*, who says he will reject the traditional gods and conventional morality, sacrificing to no god but himself and his belly, because eating and drinking daily and freedom from pain are Zeus for a *sôphrôn* human being. Polyphemus uses '*sophrôn*' equivalently with 'wise'. From this point of view, both Thucydides' innovators and Polyphemus might claim to be defenders of temperance.

For these reasons, Socrates' interlocutors might reasonably be puzzled about whether temperance is really a virtue at all, whether it conflicts with the other virtues, and whether it is really just one virtue, rather than different virtues or traits of character that happen to have acquired the same name. The Charmides, however, does not explore these puzzles for us. Socrates assumes throughout, and reaffirms at the end, that temperance is just one trait, that it is a virtue, and that it is clearly good for the agent. A reflective student of contemporary views would find good reasons for challenging all these assumptions, and might reasonably expect Socrates to examine them, rather than take them for granted.

Conflicting Elements in Piety

If Euthyphro had failed to prosecute his father, he might well have been taken to show indifference to the pollution that was widely believed to result from homicide. This pollution rested on the killer himself, but could be communicated to anyone who associated with him in the normal way. This traditional fear of pollution, however, is not Euthyphro's motive; he relies simply on his conviction that the gods require the punishment of injustice—a quite different requirement from the traditional appeal to pollution. Since this traditional issue about pollution is not considered in the *Euthyphro*, the dialogue does not make it clear how Euthyphro's views about piety and justice may conflict with traditional views.

The demands of justice may conflict not only with traditional views about the inevitable connection, irrespective of motives or justifications, between homicide and pollution, but with a quite different strand in traditional religion that emphasizes the freedom of the gods to act as they please. If the gods can demand whatever they please, and can reward whomever they please for the right sorts of services, why should we assume that what the gods demand will also be what justice demands? If sacrifices and other services will conciliate the gods even if we commit injustice, piety does not require justice. One view of the gods suggests that they are indifferent to the social virtues of temperance and justice, and do not expect such virtues in their favourites. At the end of the *Medea*, for instance, *Medea* escapes to Athens, despite what she has done. The gods, no less than human beings, are jealous of their power and status; and their ways of demonstrating their power against human beings who displease them do not always seem to have much to do with justice.

We might argue, indeed, that in some circumstances piety conflicts with justice. This is one way to describe the conflict between Antigone and Creon; Antigone claims (according to this view) that specific religious obligations to one's family are absolutely binding, whether or not they can be reconciled with the demands of justice. We might draw the same conclusion from the cycle of hereditary guilt and punishment in the house of Atreus. Orestes and Electra are required to avenge the death of Agamemnon no matter what further destruction they cause to the society they live in, and the demands of family piety seem to be indifferent to any other considerations of justice or humanity.

This view about piety and justice may not be the predominant view expressed or suggested in Sophocles' *Antigone* and *Electra*, and we may be confident that it is not Sophocles' own view. Still, it is one possible view that is clearly suggested by these plays of Sophocles; it is suggested even more sharply by plays of Euripides on similar topics (in particular by his *Electra*). Socrates, however, does not confront this issue about piety. By examining Euthyphro, rather than a defender of a less moralized view of piety, Socrates leaves some controversial assumptions (accepted by him and Euthyphro) about piety unexamined.

Conflicting Elements in Justice

Justice is a source of disputes partly because it is difficult to decide what is due to different people, and what should be done when what is due to one person or group of people seems to conflict with what is due to another. The *Crito* allows us to compare Socrates' convictions about justice with the convictions of Crito, who, while sympathetic to Socrates, is sufficiently influenced by common sense to be doubtful about Socrates' proposed action. Sometimes Crito challenges Socrates' view about what the just course of action would be. He suggests that Socrates is really acting unjustly (45c5-8) in allowing his enemies to defeat him, and in betraying his children and his friends. His friends are ready to help him; and if he refuses their help, he will make it seem as though they were unwilling to help; hence refusal will be unjust to them, and shameful both for them and for him.

Crito's doubts show that common sense distinguishes justice from simply obeying the laws or acting in the public interest. We owe obligations of justice to particular people, especially to our families and friends, and it does not seem clear why the benefit of the community should take precedence over these. The suggestion made by Polemarchus in *Republic I*, that justice should simply be identified with helping friends and harming enemies, seems to go beyond any explicit claim made in a non-philosophical source; helping friends and harming enemies is associated with justice in so far as it is thought to be required by a general principle of repayment of benefits and harms, and that general principle is characteristic of justice. Crito's doubts show how that general principle might result in doubts and conflicts about what justice really requires.

These doubts do not affect Socrates. In the *Apology* he recalls his willingness to reject any appeal to the public interest as an excuse for illegal action against the generals or against Leon. In the *Crito* he argues that it would be unjust to harm the city in return for all that the city has done for him. Might his obligation not to harm the city conflict with his obligation to particular individuals? Socrates does not discuss this question directly.

Neoptolemus sees the possibility of a conflict between justice and the common good. He is willing to concede Odysseus's claim that the scheme is the most effective one for the benefit of the Greeks, and hence the 'wise' (*sophon*) course of action; but he prefers acting justly over acting wisely and for the common good (1244-6). Cleon in Thucydides exploits the same thought that calculation of gains and losses is the sort of wisdom that interferes with simple justice. If Neoptolemus and Cleon are right, justice and wisdom may conflict in ways that Socrates does not consider.

Conflicts about Virtue and Happiness

Socrates' willingness to assume without argument that justice promotes his happiness is especially surprising in the light of the fact that many of his contemporaries rejected his assumption. Crito objects that it is shameful and humiliating for Socrates to accept a sentence of death, and Socrates admits that some people will agree with this objection. The objection suggests that in some cases justice and bravery conflict. The brave person will be ready to defend his own life and interests, and will not be deterred by the short-term threat of punishment. Crito suggests that Socrates will show shameful cowardice, if he fails to look out for himself in the present circumstances. Excessive attention to scruples about injustice may present itself—as it does to Callicles in the *Gorgias*—as mere cowardice.

In these cases the obligations of justice seem to conflict with the demands of self-interest; and in those cases it is not clear why justice should always win. Alcibiades suggests that love of one's city does not imply the sort of loyalty that excludes conspiracy against it, but actually justifies him in trying to return to Athens by intriguing with its enemies. He implies that when the other-regarding virtues get in the way of his success, he has no reason to follow them. This is Euripides' complaint about Alcibiades in Aristophanes' Frogs, and Aeschylus in his reply does not disagree. While these self-assertive views focus especially on justice, they extend to the other-regarding virtues generally.

This criticism of justice is not adequately answered by Anonymus Iamblichi, who defends justice by appeal to the benefits of law for everyone, and to the benefits of good reputation for an individual. As Antiphon points out, the argument about reputation proves at most that a sensible person will avoid getting a reputation for injustice. Admittedly, one way to get a reputation for being just is to be just and to avoid the trouble of dissembling; and this point would give us a good reason to be just if there were little to be gained by dissembling. In fact, however, there is often a great deal to be gained by committing injustice; if this is so, it is more sensible to dissemble than to be just. The argument from the general benefit of law and justice is indecisive; for not every unjust action destroys the whole system, and an astute person can gain from his injustice without having to destroy the whole system.

These disputes make it clear that Socrates' contemporaries have not made up their minds about the relation between the virtues and happiness. Many people agree that the other-regarding virtues are genuine virtues; and even if some people, agreeing with Neoptolemus, are sometimes willing to say that virtue should be followed even if it conflicts with the agent's own happiness, no one explains why we should follow virtue against happiness. On the other hand, ordinary views about happiness might well lead us to doubt whether the other-regarding virtues promote happiness; such doubts may well lead us to deny that they are genuine virtues.

All this gives us a further reason for expecting Socrates to focus on questions about justice and happiness. But he does not focus on them. In the earliest group of dialogues, he does not say what conception of happiness he relies on, or what conception of justice makes it reasonable to accept his strong claim that justice is sufficient for happiness. He does not even distinctly recognize that there is any controversy about his claim that the just person is happy.

Since many people would regard Socrates' commitment to justice as evidence of his lack of wisdom, questions about justice also raise questions about the virtue of wisdom. Answers to these questions might support Socrates' own controversial moral positions. In fact, however, none of the earliest dialogues explores these questions. They do not inquire into the just, the fine, and the good, which he identifies as the main sources of controversy. Socrates does not seek an account of the virtues and other moral properties that raise especially difficult practical questions for him.

Function of Allusions

In so far as Socrates develops the conservative position, he allows the reflective reader to trace an intelligible route from common sense to the Socratic conclusion. He cannot reasonably be expected to endorse every aspect of common sense, since he is looking for a consistent position, and common sense contains conflicting elements and tendencies. Some elements of common sense have to be rejected, and Socrates makes it clear that he appeals to powerful tendencies in common sense that support his decisions about which elements should be accepted and which rejected.

Still, his argument is open to objection. It is not the only way of selecting from common sense to reach a consistent position. Nor is the possibility of other consistent positions merely a logical possibility. The views of the innovators show that many people tend to prefer a consistent development of, and selection from, common sense that is sharply opposed to Socrates' position. Socrates does not explain why we ought to discard the other aspects that are prominent in some people's views some of the time. While we might sometimes be attracted to Socrates' particular emphasis, we might sometimes be impressed by the aspects of common sense that imply the disunity of a virtue, or conflicts between the virtues, or conflicts between virtue and happiness. Socrates does not tell us why his emphasis is to be preferred over the contrary emphasis, because he does not even explicitly acknowledge the aspects of common sense that conflict with his emphasis.

How are we to explain Socrates' silence on these aspects of common sense? We cannot reasonably suppose that the historical Socrates or Plato was unaware of the disputes that are ignored by the Platonic Socrates, or that Plato thought his readers would be unaware of them. We might suggest that Plato makes Socrates pass over certain disputes because Plato does not think it important to call his readers' attention to them. We must reject this suggestion, however, if we discover that in fact Plato calls his readers' attention to the disputes. We can discover this, despite what we have found about the topics actually discussed in the dialogues, if we consider the extent of allusion in the dialogues.

Allusions in the Laches

The dramatic date of the *Laches* is later than the battle of Delium in 424 and earlier than the death of Laches in the battle of Mantineia in 418. It is therefore placed during (or close to) the so-called Peace of Nicias, in which Nicias's reputation as a general and politician probably reached its height. The dialogue happens before the Sicilian expedition, in which Nicias's judgement was found to be unreliable. Plato's readers could hardly avoid thinking of this, and Plato perhaps helps them to think of the unfortunate end of Nicias's life.

The relevance of Nicias's career is suggested more directly by part of the discussion with Nicias. Socrates suggests that the diviner must be subordinate to the general. First Laches agrees, and then Nicias seconds the agreement between Laches and Socrates. The emphasis given to this point about diviners might easily remind readers of Nicias's notoriously superstitious behaviour. According to one story, he kept a diviner in his house, ostensibly to advise him about public affairs, but actually to advise him about how to run his silver mines. Above all, the reference to diviners is highly relevant to the occasion at Syracuse when Nicias listened to the diviners and failed to move the Athenian forces when he should have.

This allusion to Nicias counts against the suggestion that Plato intends his readers to ignore the possibility of separating bravery from the other virtues, and specifically from practical wisdom. His implicit judgement on Nicias may be compared with Thucydides' remark that Nicias did not deserve the misfortunes he suffered, since he had practised all of conventional virtue. Plato does not necessarily reject Thucydides' judgement entirely Nicias is not one of the innovators who take bravery to conflict with justice and temperance. Nonetheless, he makes the mistake that the innovators also make, of separating the virtues. He is an apparently brave man who conspicuously lacks practical wisdom; his hesitation about retreating did not betray unwillingness to face danger (indeed, he remained facing danger for too long), but did betray failure to appreciate the most important considerations relevant to his situation. Nicias's sort of bravery showed itself incapable of coping intelligently even with the dangers of war, which were supposed to be the proprietary concern of bravery. A reader of the *Laches* might reasonably be expected to notice this point.

We might speculate, though less confidently, that Plato intends a similar point about Laches. At the beginning of the dialogue Laches expresses his admiration for Socrates' bravery in the retreat from Delium. It is a little surprising, then, that his first account of bravery mentions only standing firm and facing the enemy; Socrates has to remind him that bravery can be displayed in retreating. Neither of them mentions any example parallel to the retreat from Delium, even though Laches himself acknowledged this example earlier. This silence about Delium perhaps becomes more significant in the light of Alcibiades' remark in the *Symposium* that Socrates was far more self-possessed than Laches in the retreat. A similar fact about Laches would be salient to anyone who recalled his later death in the battle of Mantineia, where he was among the Athenians who failed to stand firm at the crucial moment and ran away before they were even engaged. In both battles the Athenians panicked before fighting, in circumstances where a more realistic estimate of the dangers and of their resources might well have avoided a defeat.

We cannot be sure that Plato intends these allusions. But since Laches himself suggests that we look at a person's record to assess his virtue, it would not be too difficult for a reader to consider the record of people as well-known as Laches and Nicias. In both cases a reader might reasonably notice that these people who think of bravery in separation from the other virtues did not do so well even in the military emergencies that most obviously called for bravery.

Allusions in the Charmides

We noticed that the discussion in the *Charmides* ignores common views about temperance that might raise difficulties for Socrates' belief in the unity of the virtue. Some different aspects of temperance, however, are alluded to in the characters and action of the dialogue. It begins with examples of Socrates' moderation, suggesting that he behaves in the ways normally regarded as temperate. He has just come from a fierce battle at Poteidaea, where (as at Delium) his brave actions were recognized. He now displays temperance—a virtue that was often supposed to be entirely separate from bravery. When he sees Charmides, he loses his former 'boldness' about speaking to him (155c5-7), and when he sees Charmides' cloak, for a moment he feels 'no longer in control of myself' (155d4); but eventually he recovers his composure and speaks to Charmides (155e2-3). This episode alludes clearly to an accepted conception of temperance as self-control and moderation. In this case (concerned especially with appetites, and specifically with sexual appetites), moderation in one's own desires might reasonably be expected to make one less aggressive in one's attitude to others.

In contrast to Socrates, Critias lacks self-control. When he believes he could defend his position better than Charmides defends it, he 'had difficulty in containing himself before, but now could contain himself no longer' (162c3-4); he intervenes in the discussion out of anger at Charmides (162d2). Critias's disorderly and self-assertive interruption displays his lack of temperance.

The dialogue alludes more obliquely, but still quite clearly, to the political use of appeals to *sôphrosunç*. Plato positively harps on the family and background of Charmides and Critias, who are his own relatives. Socrates and Critias comment on Charmides' physical attractiveness; Socrates remarks that Charmides will be unbeatable if his psychic qualities are equally outstanding, and suggests that it is 'fitting' for a member of Critias's house to have these qualities.

Critias assures Socrates rather complacently that Charmides is well equipped in this area too (154e3-4), since he is 'philosophical', and composes poems, which seem to be rated more highly by Charmides himself and by others than by Critias (154e8-155a1). Critias says that Charmides has poetic gifts 'as it seems to other people and to himself' (155a1); Critias does not himself endorse this general view. Socrates suggests that this poetic gift is hereditary, coming from Charmides' ancestor Solon. Before beginning the discussion with Charmides, Socrates emphasizes the antiquity of Charmides' family and the poets' encomia on how his ancestors excelled in 'fineness, virtue, and the rest of what is said to be happiness'; as a result of this, it is reasonable to expect (*eikos*) that Charmides will come first in everything.

In considering these remarks about Charmides' background and his apparent prospects, are we expected to remember that Charmides and Critias later became prominent members of the deservedly hated regime of the Thirty? It is difficult to see how Plato could expect us not to bear this in mind, since he takes some pains to identify these two characters with the well-known historical figures. And if we are to keep the historical Critias and Charmides in mind, what are we to think about them as exemplars of temperance?

From one point of view, temperance is the hallmark of the political programme of the Thirty. Athenian oligarchs thought that by concentrating the government in fewer hands they would make the constitution more temperate; so concentration of power in the hands of the Thirty seemed a move in a temperate direction. The Thirty discouraged political initiative, and even any form of criticism or dissent, among the citizens, who were certainly required to 'mind their own business'. One story in Xenophon suggests that Critias actually tried to make Socrates mind his own business by refraining from comments with any apparent political significance. From another point of view, however, the Thirty and their supporters were conspicuously intemperate, proceeding against their opponents with lawless violence and showing no respect for the rights or interests of most of their fellow citizens. This aspect of the Thirty is mentioned directly in the *Apology*, in the story of Leon.

Some of Socrates' remarks in the *Charmides* suggest that Plato intends us to keep this in mind. Socrates mentions Charmides' illustrious ancestry as a reason for expecting him to be temperate; but he does not say that it is a good reason. (In the case of Charmides' poetic compositions, even Critias does not seem to think that Solon's talent has been inherited.) In contrast to the beginning of the *Laches*, Plato does not raise any explicit doubts about whether the virtues are passed down in families; but he clearly invites us to ask whether the hereditary conception is at all plausible.

In the light of Charmides' later life, his inability to identify the sort of quietness and shame that are proper to temperance may be significant.

Charmides and Critias pursued the self-assertive ideal that clashes sharply with the self-restraint characteristic of temperance. The behaviour of the Thirty in asserting themselves without regard to law or justice is a clear example of aggressiveness (*hubris*); they took quietness to be appropriate for other people, but not for themselves.

Critias's contribution to the discussion reflects the same political point of view. He supports the view that temperance is 'doing one's own'; in political terms, 'one's own' is often construed as 'one's own business', as contrasted with interfering in other people's business. 'Interfering' (*polupragmonein*) was a common oligarchic accusation against a democracy; and 'doing one's own' and 'not interfering' were taken to be characteristic of a well-ordered (*kosmios*) and quiet (*hçsuchos*) lower class that allowed its betters to govern. This attitude might plausibly be attributed to Socrates also, by anyone who had heard him draw an analogy between political knowledge and the knowledge characteristic of the different crafts. Surely Socrates must think that there are political experts; and if so, does he not favour an oligarchy?

Plato has a good reason for wanting Socrates to distinguish his view on temperance from the view of those who regard it as a useful virtue for subjects that is not required of rulers, and who want to enlist this limited version of the virtue in their political programme. While the *Charmides* does not mention these questions, the reader who is aware of them, as Plato's original readers must have been, can see that Plato is also aware of them.

Socrates suggests that knowledge of what I do or do not know about (170d1-3) might be morally and politically useful (171d1-172a5); it would allow us to know the limits of our own knowledge, and to find the people who have the appropriate knowledge so that they can rule over us (171d8-e7). These remarks are relevant to the political aspects of temperance. Socrates describes a community in which everyone does what he knows how to do, and every activity is regulated by the relevant kind of specialized knowledge (173a7-d5). On Critias's interpretation of temperance, this is a community that is thoroughly regulated by temperance; but Socrates denies that it achieves happiness. To achieve happiness, we must add the science of good and evil.

The effect of Socrates' remarks is to challenge an assumption made by those who advocate oligarchy as a temperate form of government. He argues that it is not enough to pick out some people as rulers; the temperate person will also want to be assured that these people have the right sort of knowledge to qualify them as rulers. Plato's comment on the political treatment of temperance is indirect, but not obscure.

These allusions make it difficult to maintain that Plato thinks it unimportant to remind his readers of the commonly recognized aspects of temperance that are not explicitly discussed in the dialogue. In particular, he reminds them of the view of temperance that denies its harmony with the other virtues. Denial of such harmony is characteristic of the self-assertive outlook of a Charmides or a Critias; we may well suppose that they are not a good advertisement for the outlook that we are committed to if we dispute Socrates' assumptions.

Disputes and Agreements

These allusions must be given their proper weight in a discussion of the questions that are raised and ignored in the earliest dialogues. If we attend to them, we cannot claim that every question about the virtues that is not discussed is taken by Plato to be irrelevant to the dialogue; nor can we claim that Plato wants us to overlook the fact that Socrates does not discuss certain questions. On the contrary: Plato's allusions draw our attention to the fact that Socrates does not discuss certain questions. We ought, therefore, to seek an explanation of Socrates' silence on the assumption that it reflects both Plato's deliberate decision and his expectation that his readers will notice his decision.

We have one clue to Plato's reasons for his decision if we notice that Socrates begins from agreements rather than from disputes. At the beginning of the *Laches* and *Charmides*, no one suggests that there is serious controversy about the sorts of actions that are required of a brave or a temperate person. Laches acknowledges that Socrates showed bravery in the retreat from Delium. At the beginning of the *Charmides* Charmides himself is generally acknowledged to do what is expected of a temperate person. Moreover, Socrates does not suggest that he himself rejects common views. In the *Euthyphro* a dispute about whether Euthyphro's action was pious is the starting-point for the discussion. Though Socrates' own actions raised questions about his piety, it is Euthyphro's action, not Socrates' action, that provokes the discussion in this dialogue.

The *Laches*, *Charmides*, and *Euthyphro* ask for accounts that answer the 'What is it?' question about three of the cardinal virtues. Why is no dialogue of inquiry devoted to seeking an account of wisdom or justice? We surely cannot suppose that Socrates and his interlocutors face especially difficult and pressing questions about bravery, temperance, and piety, but less difficult and less pressing questions about wisdom and justice. Indeed, the virtues that Socrates discusses are considerably less open to controversy than are the virtues that he does not discuss. Perhaps Socrates picks out bravery, temperance, and piety because they raise fewer obvious disputes than he would raise if he set out directly to discuss justice and wisdom.

This suggestion becomes still more plausible if we notice that when Socrates considers the less controversial virtues, he even sets aside the controversies that arise about these virtues. He begins with an initial consensus on intuitive views about the virtues. He seeks to show that some aspects of this initial consensus are difficult to defend, and indeed must be abandoned. We are expected to see on reflection that the most plausible elements in our intuitive views really lead us to take the counter-intuitive Socratic views more seriously than we ever expected we would.

Laches, Nicias, Charmides, and Critias embody non-Socratic conceptions of particular virtues; but if we consider what we know about these people, we will not find this non-Socratic conception very attractive. We might concede, on Socrates' behalf, that the Socratic assumptions about unity and harmony do not provide the only possible way to understand the virtues; but we might reasonably add that other ways of understanding the virtues raise obvious objections.

We can now suggest a general conclusion about Socrates' strategy in the earliest dialogues. He takes some aspects of his views to need argument, and regards other aspects as sufficiently obvious to need no argument. Argument is offered to show that the Socratic position is a reasonable development of common beliefs; Socrates shows that his claims about unity and harmony offer a solution to some puzzles and difficulties in ordinary beliefs. Argument is not offered to show why Socrates' reconstruction and revision of common beliefs are preferable to other possible reconstructions and revisions. Plato suggests to us that no argument is needed, because these other possibilities can soon be rejected on moral grounds; the allusions in the dialogues help us to see why.

This strategy is open to objections – (1) We might not be convinced that alternatives to the Socratic reconstruction of ordinary beliefs will turn out to be morally unattractive. Plato suggests or hints that if we disagree with Socrates, we will find ourselves advocating the outlook of a Nicias or a Critias; but we may reasonably ask for some more precise argument to show that this is the only alternative to agreeing with Socrates. (2) We might not be convinced that it would be wrong to prefer Nicias or Critias over Socrates. Perhaps we should simply face the fact that bravery is separable from the other virtues, and that it cannot be relied on to find the best action in all dangerous situations. More radically, perhaps we should acknowledge that the restrained, non-aggressive behaviour characteristic of temperance and justice involves a sacrifice of one's prospects for one's own happiness.

The earliest dialogues do not answer these objections. We can see this if we return to Thucydides' comments on conflicts about the virtues, and compare them with Socrates' discussions. Socrates presents a clear line of argument for an account of the virtues that disagrees with the outlook of the innovators who regard mindless daring as bravery and regard temperance as cowardice. He does not show, however, that this account is superior to the account that would support the outlook of the innovators.

Plato's Development

I have assumed that the *Protagoras* and the *Gorgias* are later than the shorter Socratic dialogues I have discussed. These two dialogues take up many of the disputable features of Socratic ethics that I have identified; the *Gorgias* shows a particular concern to face and to answer certain criticisms of Socrates. Indeed, I would go further, and claim that the *Protagoras, Gorgias, Meno,* and *Republic* show increasing attention to the disputes that I have described. While the earliest dialogues neglect certain questions and disputes, later dialogues do not neglect them at all, but actually focus our attention on them.

We ought not to take any particular view about the order of the dialogues as an assured starting-point. Suppose that we abandon the assumption I have made so far, and that we regard the *Gorgias* as one of Plato's earlier Socratic dialogues. In that case, we cannot accept my previous suggestion that Socrates largely ignores challenges to his position that arise from contemporary disputes. The puzzles that I have been trying to explain simply disappear; we need not attribute any indirect defence to Socrates, since his reply to radical critics is clear and direct.

An early date for the *Gorgias*, however, raises other puzzles. If Plato had formulated answers to radical critics of Socratic method and ethics, why should he have gone on to write the shorter Socratic dialogues, which are completely silent about these answers? Admittedly, Plato need not say everything he believes in every dialogue; but it would often be easy and relevant to indicate his views by summary or allusion. He offers neither summary nor allusion, even though they would dispel the appearance of unsupported dogmatic assertion.

This consideration helps to persuade me that the *Protagoras* and *Gorgias* are in fact probably later than the dialogues that I have placed in the earliest group. In fact, I believe that if we attend to the questions I have discussed in this paper, we find further reasons to accept the order that I have assumed. If I am right, the earliest dialogues display an indirect approach to critics, while the *Gorgias* displays a more direct approach; moreover, the *Protagoras* fits well between the earliest dialogues and the *Gorgias* in its attitude to these questions. For these reasons I believe we have discovered an important aspect of Plato's development in the early dialogues.

My appeal to development may appear to be a mechanical and unimaginative answer to a question that I could answer more plausibly if I took a less rigid view of the point of the Socratic dialogues. In speaking of what Socrates assumes and what Socrates argues, I have accepted a rather narrowly doctrinal conception of the dialogues, supposing that Socrates uses the conversations with different interlocutors to advance or to defend views that he accepts. But I have also pointed out that if we accept this conception, then Socrates' arguments are open to serious objections because they omit views that seem to deserve consideration. Would it not be more sensible to abandon a doctrinal conception of the dialogues? Ought we not to suppose instead that Socrates simply examines the beliefs of his interlocutors, in order to expose their inability to defend their own positions against his objections?

I certainly admit that I have assumed a doctrinal conception of the dialogues. Even if we reject such a conception, however, the questions I have raised are difficult to avoid. Even if Socrates is simply examining the beliefs of his interlocutors, why does Plato present these interlocutors holding these beliefs? Why should Socrates not have examined interlocutors with the sorts of beliefs that would have raised the controversies I have mentioned?

Laches, Nicias, Charmides, Critias, Euthyphro, and Crito would be very suitable interlocutors for the discussion of controversies about the virtues; indeed, as I have suggested, we might even expect them to have some of these controversies on their minds. As far as we can tell, considerations of verisimilitude do not explain why these interlocutors are not represented as raising such questions. We still have to ask why Plato restricts the range of questions that Socrates considers. I am inclined to answer that a doctrinal conception of the dialogues actually gives a better answer than other conceptions give to the questions I have raised.

If the account I have given is right, then Plato might fairly be expected to discover the weaknesses in Socratic argument that we have noticed, and to recognize that Socrates' reasons for avoiding the most acute controversies about the virtues are inadequate. If he recognizes these things, then we would expect other Platonic dialogues to face the controversies more squarely, and to use different kinds of argument to deal with them. I believe that this is what we find, in the *Gorgias* and in later dialogues.

4

Assumptions about Knowledge and Scepticism

Introduction

In modern epistemology, or theory of knowledge, certain assumptions are common. Among them is the view that the existence of knowledge must be justified against the sceptic, that is, the person who thinks that we can never know anything, because he holds that we can never meet the conditions for knowledge. Knowledge is taken to be, at least in part, a matter of being in the right relation to facts or information. (What is this right relation? Here we find very different views, which can barely be indicated here. Some philosophers stress justification, others the right causal connection, and there are sophisticated variants and combinations of these positions.) It is hard to imagine a modern epistemologist being impressed by the thought that your mechanic *knows* how to fix cars. It is equally hard to think of her finding it important that someone who knows lots of facts in science, say, may lack understanding of them. And what modern epistemologist would greet an authoritative pronouncement that she in fact possessed knowledge by trying to refute it?

We can start to understand what is distinctive about ancient attitudes to knowledge by beginning with Socrates. His friend Chaerephon, we are told, asked the oracle of the god Apollo at Delphi whether anyone was wiser than Socrates, and Apollo replied that nobody was. On being told this, Socrates was surprised, and wondered what the oracle could possibly mean, since he was aware that he possessed no wisdom or expertise of his own. So he went round people considered experts, questioning them about their alleged expertise, but always finding either that they could produce no remotely adequate account of what they were supposed to be experts in, or that the expertise they did have was less important than they thought it. He concluded that Apollo's meaning must be that the wisest person is the person most aware of their own ignorance.

Of all ancient philosophers, Socrates is the most recognizable. There is good reason for this; for ancient culture in general Socrates serves as the symbolic figure of the Philosopher. However, it is also remarkable, given that his Life is elusive, he wrote nothing, and Left a series of wildly differing philosophical Legacies.

Socrates lived from about 468-399 BC. His father was a stonemason called Sophroniscus, his mother a midwife called Phainarete. His circumstances were initially prosperous, but by the end of his Life he was poor, as a result of neglecting his practical affairs in his devotion to philosophy. His wife, Xanthippe, has an aristocratic name; she passed into Legend as the shrewish wife of the undomestic philosopher, but we do not know what Lies behind this. They had three sons, one young at the time of Socrates' death. Later, unreliable tradition ascribes to him a second wife, Myrto.

In 399 Socrates was tried and executed. The charges are strikingly vague and prejudicial, and it has always been suspected that the real agenda was political. We shall never know the facts. Clearly Socrates was widely regarded as an annoying and subversive presence in Athens.

Socrates identified the practice of philosophy with personal discussion and questioning, refusing to write anything. His followers elevated him to the founding figure of their mutually conflicting approaches to philosophy. Through his austere disciple Antisthenes, Socrates was regarded as the inspiration for the convention-rejecting Cynics; through his disciple Aristippus, he was claimed as the first hedonist. Through the tradition of Plato's Academy he was hailed as the first sceptic; through the Stoics he was regarded as the first ethical philosopher. In the writings of his younger follower Xenophon he appears as a conventional moralizer. In the writings of Plato, Socrates appears in a variety of guises. Sometimes he is the questioner who undermines the pretensions of others to understanding; sometimes he puts forward positive claims about ethics and metaphysics; sometimes he merely introduces other philosophers who have things of their own to say. Socrates continued to be influential as the figure of the philosopher par excellence, and his refusal to commit himself to authoritative teaching made him a usefully plastic figure whose influence could be claimed for widely different views and approaches.

This minimal construal of what a god means by calling a human 'wise' is in keeping with a Greek tradition of emphasizing the gulf between human and divine capacities. It also brings out some assumptions about ancient epistemology. Socrates goes round denying that he has knowledge, but this is never understood to mean that he does not know ordinary, everyday facts; he is aware of knowing large numbers of these. Further, he sometimes claims to know quite substantial pieces of moral knowledge, such as that he should never do wrong, or abandon what he regards as his divine mission. What he denies having is knowledge in the sense of wisdom or understanding, which goes beyond mere knowledge of isolated facts and is assumed to be found, if at all, in people who are experts in something. When Apollo says that he is the wisest person, then, Socrates is troubled by it, since if a person is an expert in something, he would normally be expected at least to be aware of what he is an expert in. He responds to the oracle by trying to find someone wiser than he is, then, not out of a rude desire to show Apollo wrong, but because he does not understand the oracle, and the only way to find out how he is the wisest person is to find out what the expertise is which he is supposed to have. And, since this is obviously not self-declaring, the only way to find it out is to see how well he compares with other people in understanding what they are supposed to be wise about or experts in; and this can only be achieved by questioning them about what they are supposed to understand.

The Trial of Socrates

'The following sworn indictment has been brought by Meletus, son of Meletus, of Pitthos, against Socrates, son of Sophroniscus, of Alopeke. Socrates does wrong in not recognizing the gods which the city recognizes, and in introducing other, new divinities. Further, he is a wrongdoer in corrupting the young.'

This indictment against Socrates was preserved in the archives of Athens and reported by Later scholars. Socrates was found guilty by about 280 votes to 220. (Juries consisted of 501 citizens.) The prosecutor proposed death as a penalty. Socrates at first refused to allow that he had done anything deserving of a penalty, but eventually suggested a fine. The jury voted for death by a Larger margin, about 360 to 140.

A number of points emerge in Socrates' response to the oracle. Philosophically interesting questions about knowledge are taken not to concern our relation to particular facts how I can *know*, for example, that the cat is on the mat. Philosophical attention is focused on a more complex matter: the possession of wisdom (*sophia* - the wisdom loved by the *philosophos*). It is assumed, taken to be a matter beyond argument, that wisdom is not just knowing individual facts, but being able to relate them to one another in a unified and structured way, one that involves understanding of a field or area of knowledge. (A useful parallel is that of knowing a language, which obviously involves more than knowing individual pieces of information about vocabulary and syntax, and requires the understanding of how these fit together in a unified way. The language example also brings out the way that this unified understanding is not a theoretical grasp cut off from practice, but may itself involve a practical ability to apply the understanding in question.) The philosophically interesting kind of knowledge involves a complex of items grasped together in a way that enables the knower to relate them to one another and to the structure as a whole. In all but the simplest cases this grasp will require an articulate ability to do this relating, one which will explain why the different items play the roles they do in the system. Such a grasp will typically be found in someone who has expertise (*techne*) in a subject.

Socrates never raises the question whether there is such a thing as wisdom or expertise. This would be silly, since there obviously are experts in some fields, such as crafts. Presumably, though, Apollo meant more than that Socrates had the kind of expertise to be found in weavers and potters, so Socrates' search is for expertise in matters of importance in human life. Hence he is particularly keen to question self-styled experts in virtue, or what is worthwhile in life, such as the sophists claimed to be. He questions them on the topics that they claim to be experts in, and always succeeds in showing that they lack understanding of these topics, since they fail to explain satisfactorily why they say what they do, and indeed often make inconsistent claims. Socrates' questions do not start from a position of his own, since this would only weaken the point that it is the other person who is supposed to display understanding of what he claims to know. When Socrates deflates the self-styled experts by showing them, just from premisses that they accept, that they don't understand the subject they have been pontificating about, they cannot defend themselves by faulting his views, since these have not come into it.

Differing Views of Socrates

'Mankind can hardly be too often reminded, that there was once a man named Socrates, between whom and the legal authorities and public opinion of his time there took place a memorable collision. This acknowledged master of all the eminent thinkers who have since lived whose fame, still growing after more than two thousand years, all but outweighs the whole remainder of the names which make his native city illustrious was put to death by his countrymen. Socrates was put to death, but the Socratic philosophy rose like the sun in heaven, and spread its illumination over the whole intellectual firmament.'

John Stuart Mill, *On Liberty*

'Socrates — that clown from Athens!'

Zeno of Sidon, Epicurean philosopher, second century BC

'We shall ignore Chaerephon's story about the oracle, since it is an utterly sophistical and cheap trick.'

'Socrates, the arguments you worked out are bogus. The conversations you had with the people you met are one thing, and what you did was another.'

Colotes, early Epicurean philosopher, third century BC

Understanding and what it involves

What would show that a person has wisdom and understanding comes to be referred to as 'giving an account', *logon didonai. Logos* is the ordinary Greek word for reason; what you say about the topic you are supposed to understand must give reasons in a way that explains the matter. Socrates' victims can produce plenty of words, but they fail to give a reasoned account of their subjects, and so are shown not to understand what they are talking about.

What are the standards for 'giving an account'? This is obviously crucial for the question of whether you really know, that is, understand something. Minimally, of course, you have to be able to keep your end up in an argument and show that your position is consistent. But something more positive than this seems required too. One major strand of ancient epistemology consists of exploring the requirements for 'giving an account', providing the reasoned basis necessary if you are to have understanding of a field of knowledge.

In many of Plato's dialogues Socrates suggests that you have to be able to provide a satisfactory answer to the questioner who wants to know what virtue is, or courage, or friendship, or the like. This is obviously not provided by trivially appealing to the meaning of words; it has to express the nature of virtue, or courage, in such a way that the person to whom it is successfully conveyed will be able not only to recognize examples of virtue, or courage, but to explain why they are examples of the virtue in question, relating them to its nature. This exploration is sometimes called a search for 'Socratic definitions', although 'definition' is an unhappy term here.

One standing puzzle about these dialogues is the following. Socrates is ambitiously searching for understanding of difficult concepts like virtue and courage. But his approach is always to question others, starting only from shared premisses. This kind of *ad hominem* arguing relies only on what the opponent accepts and what it produces, time after time, are conclusions as to what virtue, courage, friendship and so on are not. Some self-styled expert makes a claim as to what virtue, etc. are, and Socrates shows that this cannot be the right answer. This does not, however, seem to move us towards understanding what virtue, courage and so on are. Socrates shows that others lack understanding, but not in a way that seems to be cumulative towards obtaining understanding of his own. There appears to be a mismatch between the goal and the methods. There are many ways of resolving this puzzle, and philosophers are divided over it.

Plato has a variety of concerns with knowledge, to some of which we shall return. Some of his most famous passages, however, show the dominance of what we can call the expertise model for knowledge. What is taken to matter for knowledge is whether you can, as an expert can, grasp the relevant items in a way that relates them to one another and to the field as a whole, and can give a reasoned account of this, one which explains the particular judgements you make and relates them to your unified grasp of the whole. And in some places Plato rethinks the crucial idea of giving a reasoned account, taking mathematics as his model.

In the *Republic*, Plato develops possibly the most ambitious model for knowledge that any philosopher has put forward. Now the aspiring knower has to complete an apprenticeship of many years' mathematical studies. Mathematics — by which he is primarily thinking of the kind of systematized geometry of which we have a later example in Euclid is remarkable for its rigour, system and clarity. It struck Plato as a perfect example of the kind of structured body of knowledge that had been presupposed all along by the expertise model. Moreover, all the features of the expertise model seem to fit mathematics in a clear and impressive way. Mathematics is not a heap of isolated results; particular theorems can clearly be seen to depend on other results which are proved in turn. The whole system begins from a clear and limited set of concepts and postulates. The way in which we get from these first principles to particular results is also lucid and rigorous. It is easy to see why Plato might see in an earlier version of Euclid a splendid model of knowledge as a structured and unified system, one where it is absolutely clear what the knower knows and how she knows it, how the system holds together and what it is to give a reasoned account of what you know — namely, a proof.

Mathematics as a model for knowledge also introduces two new notes. One is that mathematical results are peculiarly unassailable; we do not waste time arguing that Pythagoras' theorem is wrong. We have seen that certainty and justification of what is known are not prominent in the cluster of issues that are the focus of the expertise model, where what matters is understanding that can be applied in practice. But Plato is clearly at some points attracted by the idea of a body of knowledge that is not open to serious questioning.

The other point flows from the fact that mathematics provides us with a body of firm knowledge which does not seem in any plausible way to have as its object the world that we experience, in an everyday way, through the senses. Pythagoras' theorem was not discovered by measuring actual drawn triangles and their angles, and irregularities in these are obviously irrelevant to it. Plato is attracted to the view that a body of knowledge can exist to which our access is solely by using our minds and reasoning. He is not the last philosopher to be tempted by the view that the powers of philosophical reason are more developed versions of our ability to reason mathematically.

In the *Republic*'s central books, we find that to have knowledge requires mastery of a systematic field whose contents are structured as rigorously as the axioms and theorems in Euclid, and linked by chains of proof. Moreover, Plato goes one better than the mathematicians in claiming that philosophy actually proves its own first principles something which mathematicians fail to do and so does not begin from assumptions, but shows how everything flows from a first principle which is proved and not assumed. (Here matters get obscure, particularly since Plato makes everything depend on what he calls the Form of the Good.) As with mathematics, what is known is a formal system — what Plato famously regards as the world of Forms and not the world of experience revealed to us by the senses; indeed, Plato goes out of his way to stress the extent to which the person thinking in abstract mathematical terms will come to conclusions at odds with experience.

This is, of course, an *ideal*, something emphasized by the way that the only people who, Plato thinks, have a chance of attaining it are those who are exceptionally talented by nature and have been brought up in ideal cultural circumstances. This warns us against thinking that we can find any actual example of knowledge. The expertise model on its own seemed to hold out the chance at least that knowledge was attainable. But when the requirements are made as formal and demanding as they become when mathematics is the model, the conditions for knowledge get set so high as to be unattainable by us.

Understanding and the Sciences

Aristotle, in this as in many matters Plato's greatest pupil, takes over the *Republic* model, but with important modifications which make it philosophically far more fruitful. He develops the idea in his work on the structure of a completed body of knowledge, the unfortunately titled *Posterior Analytics*.

For Aristotle, Plato goes wrong in thinking that all knowledge hangs together in a unified structure. This makes the mistake of thinking that all the objects of knowledge together make up a single system, and can be known as such. But, Aristotle thinks, there is no such single system; different branches of knowledge employ fundamentally different methods, and do so because their subject-matters are fundamentally different. Aristotle does not disagree that something like Euclid's geometry is a reasonable model for knowledge; like Plato, he is willing to appeal to mathematics to beef up the idea of expertise. But there is no such thing as knowledge as a whole, only the different kinds or branches of knowledge or, as we are tempted to say, sciences. (The Greek word for knowledge, *episteme*, forms a plural, but we cannot say 'knowledge', and have to make do either with 'branches of knowledge' or 'sciences'. This can obscure the way that, for example, Aristotle's notion of a science is a restriction of Plato's conception of knowledge.)

As well as this radical 'departmentalizing' of knowledge, Aristotle imports a further difference. Whereas Plato focuses relentlessly on the individual knower, Aristotle widens his epistemological view to take in many aspects of the *social* production of knowledge. It is not for nothing that 'science' is more appropriate to Aristotle's discussions of knowledge than to Plato's. Aristotle is aware of the way that the development of a science, such as biology, requires research and observation from many people, and also that the single investigator does not reinvent the wheel every time, but relies on others' results and data and, more importantly, on their questions and setting of the problems. He himself begins his enquiries in a number of fields by first canvassing views on it that are reputable and widely held, or put forward by philosophers or other investigators. It is by entering into this tradition of previous enquiry and exploring the problems that it has thrown up that the investigator can make progress.

Hence Aristotle can distinguish (though it would have been nice if he had done so more clearly) between different aspects of the development of a body of knowledge. The data and observations a science relies on, built up by the co-operative activities of many people, are material for a science, not science itself. Pieces of information do not constitute knowledge until they are fitted into and form part of a structured system. Hence before they amount to knowledge, the results of research and observation must be given a place within the appropriate structure. In the *Posterior Analytics* this structure is laid out very rigidly, and the influence of the mathematical model is very obvious. The first principles of a science must be true, primary and immediate, hold necessarily and be explanatory of the results that they are the first principles of. Much effort has gone into exploring ways in which a science like, say, biology could fit such a model, and it is generally agreed that the model is unsuitably rigid for many Aristotelian sciences. The overall point is not lost, however: empirical research is needed to gather any information worth knowing, but knowledge comes only when we see how it fits into a formal explanatory structure.

Both Plato and Aristotle have an extremely ideal model of understanding. Neither doubt that knowledge is possible in principle, though for Plato particularly the conditions become very idealized and removed from everyday life. Of course, given that they are working with the expertise model, the idea that knowledge is possible is not very radical. But what they are claiming is that we can have knowledge not merely of humdrum matters but of philosophically challenging and worthwhile subjects. Some version of this claim is common in most ancient philosophical schools.

Scepticism and Belief

This is not the only approach to knowledge, however; we find very different ones. The most radical of these is traced in part to Socrates and in part to Pyrrho, a later philosopher who also wrote nothing. This is ancient scepticism (making Socrates one founder of scepticism). Unlike modern scepticism, the ancient movement does not limit itself to denying that knowledge is possible, leaving us with true belief. Ancient scepticism is as concerned with holding beliefs as with knowledge, and is best thought of as an intellectual position concerning the powers of reason, one far more radical than modern scepticisms.

The sceptic begins like everyone else, by searching for truth and for knowledge. This he does by investigating, querying others' reasons for what they claim, and looking for supporting reasons for positions of his own. So far there is no disagreement with the basic idea that knowledge requires the giving of a reasoned account. Knowledge of any kind worth Pyrrho of Elis (*c.* 360 - *c.* 270 BC) is, like Socrates, an influential philosopher who inspired others but wrote nothing himself. His life is even more elusive than that of Socrates, and unlike him he left no visual image.

Originally a painter, Pyrrho at some point was influenced by various philosophical schools. He accompanied Alexander the Great on his conquest of northern India, where he encountered Indian 'gymnosophists' or naked wise men. It has been claimed that this encounter was decisive for his own philosophical stance, and similarities have been claimed between reports of his arguments and early northern Indian Buddhist texts. The Greeks, however, found no problem in interpreting Pyrrhonism in Greek terms, especially as Pyrrhonists always argue against the views of others, and so developed a repertory of attacks on existing philosophical theories.

Pyrrho himself impressed others by the example of tranquillity and impeturbability he gave in refusing to commit himself to any dogmatic belief. Stories about him abound, but are mostly hostile jokes to the effect that he suspended judgement in everyday matters, thereby making himself ridiculous. Other stories say that he Lived a respectable life and that Elis exempted philosophers from taxation in his honour. His pupil Timon wrote satires against dogmatic philosophers, and also prose accounts of Pyrrho's arguments which, though problematic, show them as forerunners to the Later versions of these arguments, especially those found in our main sceptical text, Sextus Empiricus' *Outlines of Pyrrhonism* (of uncertain date but probably second century AD).

having (that is, not knowledge of everyday bits of information) requires that you be able to give satisfactory reasons for what you claim. What distinguishes the sceptic from other philosophers is just that he never regards himself as having got to that point. The Greek term *skeptikos* means, not a negative doubter, but an investigator, someone going in for *skeptesthai* or enquiry. As the late sceptic author Sextus Empiricus puts it, there are dogmatic philosophers, who think that they have found the truth; negative dogmatists, who feel entitled to the position that the truth cannot be found; and the sceptics, who are unlike both the other groups in that they are not committed either way. They are still investigating things.

Why the problem? Surely if you investigate you will turn up *some* results that can count as knowledge or at least as belief. Sceptics think that, while we want to think this, it will always turn out to be rash (or 'precipitate') assent: we committed ourselves too soon. Real inquiry, thorough investigation, will reveal that the situation was more complex and problematic; we turn out never to have reason to commit ourselves one way or the other, and so end up suspending judgement that is, having a detached and uncommitted attitude to whatever the issue was.

At first this sounds ridiculous, indeed unserious. Does the sceptic really hold that we can never establish what time it is, that the sun is shining, that this is bread and not grass? This is an ancient reaction, but a mistaken one.

Pyrrho, the founding figure of one branch of scepticism, is someone about whom we know little, and our accounts of his intellectual attitudes are frustratingly meagre. His uncompromising attitude about our never having reason to commit ourselves to anything led to unfriendly jokes, such as that he had to be looked after by unsceptical friends to stop him walking off cliffs, and the like. But there is an alternative tradition to the effect that he lived a normal life, so it is most probable that, like later sceptics, he took it that even when we cannot commit ourselves to beliefs we can live by the way things appear to us.

Later sceptics who took their inspiration from Pyrrho developed the idea that we 'live by appearances'. That is, all we need to live is for things to appear to us in one way rather than another. If we go beyond this (which we get inclined to do when we move on from everyday matters to issues where there is dispute and complexity) and try to commit ourselves to beliefs, we will always in fact find, if we investigate rigorously, that we cannot commit ourselves; there turns out to be equally good reason on both sides of the question, so that we find ourselves equally inclined both ways, and so end up uncommitted, suspending judgement on the issue. This does not leave us paralyzed, however, since we still have the appearances to live by. The fact that I cannot commit myself does not stop things appearing to me one way rather than another. Being rationally uncommitted does not do away with all the other sources of motivation that get us by — habit, desire, fear of the law and so on. The view that if reason does not commit us we cannot go on living comes from an over estimation of the powers of reason, which we do not always need and which tempts the dogmatist into committing herself prematurely to the truth of some theory.

Moreover, the sceptics go on the offensive here. What we want out of rational commitment to our beliefs, they hold, is happiness, which is to be found in peace of mind; we want to feel confident about the way things are and not worried by our uncertainty about them. But commitment to positive or negative theories on the topic can never do this; all it can do is displace or redirect the original anxiety. Only the sceptic, who realizes the futility of commitment to belief, is tranquil; rigorous investigation brings suspension of belief, and this brings the peace of mind that had been sought in the wished-for answers. Hence only the sceptic gets what everyone else is looking for, peace of mind. But she gets it only by not looking for it, merely being there when it arrives; and it arrives as a result of the rigorous investigation that makes it impossible to commit yourself for or against any position.

There is much in the sceptical story that is implausible, or seems forced. Moreover, problems lurk which can be barely mentioned here. What is the scope of the sceptic's suspension of belief? Does it extend only to matters on which she investigates? If so, does she have some beliefs, namely the unproblematic ones? Anyway, what is the sceptic doing telling us all this about how to achieve peace of mind, how others fail, and the sceptic succeeds? How can she do this without holding beliefs?

Ancient scepticism is one of the most interesting and subtle philosophical positions. Like its dogmatic cousins, it embodies strong assumptions about reason, though subversive rather than positive ones, and is both deeper and broader than modern forms of scepticism which limit themselves to complaints about knowledge, and may reject some subject-matters on the basis of uncritically accepting others. Ancient sceptics, unlike moderns, are uninterested in carving out a position within philosophy; they think that philosophical reason, when exercised, will always undermine itself.

Socrates provided an alternative inspiration for the other branch of ancient scepticism, which took over Plato's Academy from the middle of the third century BC until its end in the first century BC. The Academics held that philosophizing in the spirit of Plato should take the form of doing what Socrates did, namely undermining the claims of others while putting forward none of your own. Hence the sceptical Academics spent their time arguing *ad hominem* (that is, not from any position of their own but only from premisses the opponent accepts) against dogmatic philosophers whose claims they thought inadequately grounded, mostly the Stoics. Unlike the Pyrrhonists, the Academics made no claims about happiness or peace of mind. Their assumption about reason is simply that dogmatic philosophers have always been too hasty; their claims can be overturned from within and not by relying on the establishment of other positions.

Varieties of Knowledge

So far we have seen bold and radical positions, both positive and negative, about knowledge and belief. It would be misleading, however, to give the impression that ancient concerns with knowledge always focus on wisdom and understanding; we can also find concerns which overlap with modern ones. Plato, for example, produces interesting arguments against relativist theories of knowledge which do not rely on any of the special features of his own ambitious account. A relativist, such as Protagoras, against whom Plato argues in the dialogue *Theaetetus*, claims that for someone to have a true belief is no more than for something to appear true to him, and hence that truth is relative to the believer. This can seem at first like a liberating discovery, especially since it defuses all disagreement. The wind appears hot to me, cold to you; we are both right, and there is nothing to argue about. Protagoras, however, puts his relativist theory forward as a *theory*, something we should accept and take seriously (if only in order to be liberated from our disagreements). But if Protagoras is right, the truth of his own theory is relative to him that is, it is just the way things appear to him. And why ever should we accept, or be interested in, what happens to appear a certain way to Protagoras? If we are to take relativism seriously as a theory, then relativism cannot hold of it.

Plato is also interested in the question of what is going on when we are said to know particular facts, and this is developed by the Stoics, who retain the expertise model for what they call knowledge proper, but also develop an account of what they call apprehension, which amounts to one way of thinking of knowledge, especially in some modern epistemological theories. Apprehension is what you have when you are so related to an empirical fact that you cannot be wrong about it. The Stoics put some effort into working out what the conditions have to be for this to hold. Roughly, the thing in question has to make an impact on you, an impression; and this impression must come from the thing in the right way the causal story must be the right one; and the impression must be one that you could not have had from any *other* thing, however similar. These conditions were seen as a challenge to produce counter-examples, where the conditions are all met, but we have to agree that we do not have knowledge. The Academic Sceptics in particular carried on a long debate with the Stoics on this topic, as a result of which the Stoics seem to have introduced further conditions and modifications.

Finally, we do find, in the range of ancient epistemological theories, one which seems to meet the desiderata for a modern theory, namely that of Epicurus. For Epicurus does worry about scepticism in the modern sense that is, the person who rejects the idea that our beliefs might ever meet the criteria for knowledge and he thinks that he has to establish the possibility of knowledge against this challenge. He thinks of knowledge not in terms of the expertise model, but in terms of the knower's relation to particular matters of fact. What I know, then, are for Epicurus primarily particular pieces of information to which I am related in such a way that my relation to them constitutes knowledge; these are the primary items that are known. Anything more ambitious than this has to be shown to be built out from these primary items in the most economical and careful way that is feasible.

Epicurus' theory is, untypically for ancient theories, rigorously empiricist – that is, it begins from and relies on our sense-experience. What I know comes to me through the senses, since only sensations relate information to me in a way which is unmediated by a process which could involve error. My ordinary beliefs, arrived at in ways which involve inferences going beyond experience, contain truths, but also falsehoods that have crept in through the human propensity to get things wrong. But if I concentrate only on what the senses tell me, I cannot go wrong. For Epicurus, belief and reasoning are sources of error, not, as for most other schools, the source of our ability to correct error. Error, then, comes in only when I start adding beliefs to what the senses tell me. Hence it turns out that what the senses tell me is not even as extensive as claims about tables and towers — since obviously these can be mistaken, as when we judge from a distance that a square tower is round. Rather, the reports of the senses are limited to how the tower appears to us from a particular perspective at a particular place, and so on. Hence we have knowledge, since we cannot be wrong about this. We could, however, be wrong about the tower, since we might make a claim that did not make due allowance for perspective, distance etc. Our knowledge turns out to be far more limited than our everyday observations about the world around us.

Epicurus' theory of knowledge was not regarded as particularly impressive; indeed it was widely regarded as hideously crude. Later Epicureans, however, did develop interesting analogues of what we think of as issues of induction how, from a number of particular observations, we can come to make justifiable generalizations about *all* occurrences of this kind of thing. Are we justified, for example ('we' being Epicurean philosophers living in Italy) in inferring that because all the humans we have observed are mortal, so are humans in hitherto undiscovered countries, such as Britain? (If there are any humans there, adds Philodemus, the philosopher whose example this is.)

Empiricist theories of knowledge, like an emphasis on the knower's relation to particular facts, are the minority stream in ancient epistemology. What emerges from even a cursory survey of ancient concerns with knowledge, however, is the width and diversity of approaches. A student of epistemology in the ancient world would find a number of challenging theories and an extensive tradition of debate. She would find several ways of understanding *knowledge*: theories about wisdom and theories about apprehension of particular facts, theories privileging abstract reasoning and theories privileging the basic reports of the senses. She would also find extensive engagement not just with knowledge, but more generally with problems of belief and the powers of reasoning, both positive and negative.

5

Invention of Logic by Aristotle

Introduction

Aristotle was rightly proud of his discovery, and so it is not surprising that he greatly over estimated its power, apparently thinking that syllogistic would be sufficient to represent the deductive structure of demonstrative sciences, including geometry or mathematics in general. It is only natural that the modern logicians who vindicated Aristotle's position in the history of their subject should have gone on to find Aristotle also pursuing other interests of his modern successors, such as proof theory and other parts of logical theory. For example, Jonathan Lear in his *Aristotle and Logical Theory* sets out to show that Aristotle was 'not only the father of logic, but also the (grand)father of metalogic'; and an article by Robin Smith describes "Aristotle as Proof Theorist". I do not wish to deny that these subjects can be found in the *Analytics*, but it seems to me that some of his more recent commentators have been inclined to ascribe to Aristotle an interest in the formal theory of deduction independent of the wider purposes of the *Analytics*, thus painting him as more of a logician in the modern sense than he probably was.

Just as there was a dispute in late antiquity over whether logic was a part or merely an instrument of philosophy, So there is some uneasiness today about whether logic properly belongs to philosophy or not. Logic has developed into a formidable technical discipline that may perhaps better be seen as a branch of mathematics certainly one needs to be a trained mathematician to do any significant work in the field. But most philosophy departments still require their students to take at least a course in elementary logic. Even if the connection between informal argument and formal logic has become harder to see, it is still the case that we need a clear understanding of such notions as consistency, inference, and validity; and though philosophical arguments usually are not deductive proofs, they had better not be logical fallacies. Furthermore, formalization can often help us to clarify distinctions that are hard to detect in ordinary language, even if we do not believe that formalized languages are in some way better or more scientific than natural ones. So a part of logic, at least, continues to be an instrument of philosophy or rather, of any discipline that makes use of reasoning and argument.

Aristotle was interested both in logic as a theory and in its more humdrum uses in philosophical, or indeed everyday, argument, and more than half of the text of the *Prior Analytics* is concerned with the uses of logic in argument, rather than with either the exposition of a formal system or what we would call logical theory. This is what one should expect, since Aristotle invented formal logic for the purposes of his general theory of argument, not just as a formal theory of deductive proof or an 'underlying logic' for demonstrative science. In order to show how the perspective of a general theory of argument differs from that of logical theory, I will argue that although syllogistic can be shown to be complete in the modern logician's sense, it was not considered by its author to be complete in the sense relevant to his project. A deduction system is complete in the modern sense if it allows one to deduce all (and only) the valid formulae. What Aristotle had in mind when he set out to show that 'every deductive argument (*sullogismos*) is in one of the (syllogistic) figures' was the claim that every valid deductive argument can be formulated as one or more syllogisms in the narrow sense. This, as Aristotle recognized, is not the case. However, I will also argue that he thought syllogistic captured at least a necessary component of every valid deductive argument, and perhaps that it was indeed sufficient as an account of the logical form of scientific demonstration.

The system of syllogisms is introduced in *Prior Analytics* A4 as part of a general theory of valid deductive argument, more general than the theory of scientific proof, which is set out in the *Posterior Analytics*. Formal logic is only a part of such a general theory, and that is why, after presenting the system of syllogisms as an account of the valid forms of deductive argument, Aristotle goes on to discuss heuristics how to find premisses for theses that one wants to prove and what he calls analysis that is, how to discover the syllogistic structure of premisses and terms in arguments formulated in ordinary language. The title of the whole work, "'*Analutika*'", refers to this part of the treatise, not the formal theory set out in its opening chapters. Much of book B can be seen as concerned with argumentative strategies and the detection of fallacies, and its last five chapters contain the sketch of a theory of rhetorical argument. So although the introductory lines of the *Prior Analytics* describe the treatise as a preliminary to the treatment of demonstrative science, the general theory developed here should serve the practitioner of dialectic and rhetoric as well as the scientist or philosopher.

In the context of such a general theory, the system developed in A1-22 is only a beginning, not the complete account of valid deductive argument that Aristotle in his more optimistic moments claims to have found, and that too many of his later followers have taken it to be. We do not have to think that Aristotle would have agreed with the arguments which Alexander of Aphrodisias presents for not pursuing the subject of valid inference for its own sake. But it may be that Aristotle developed his formal theory only to the extent that he thought he needed it for his account of demonstration, leaving many loose ends that seem to have been picked up by his students Theophrastus and Eudemus. That may be the reason why, for example, he did work out a system of modal syllogistic, but did not try to offer a formal account of the second type of valid deductive argument he recognizes in A23 what he calls 'argument (syllogism) based on a hypothesis' although he saw that it was not covered by the system of the syllogistic figures.

The point that Aristotle himself considered his formal logic as incomplete may have been obscured by the fact that he actually purports to offer a completeness proof, and that the first half of this proof can be read as a completeness proof in the modern technical sense. In order to show in what sense formal syllogistic was not complete, then, I have to draw attention to some differences between the system of syllogisms as described and developed by Aristotle in *Prior Analytics* A1-7 and its best modern models.

I take it to be generally agreed by now that formal syllogistic is best represented as a system of natural deduction, rather than an axiomatized theory. Aristotle explicitly introduces all the elements of such a system, and several scholars have shown that within its limits it is complete—that is, allows one to deduce all and only the valid formulae. Nonetheless, I think it is misleading to assume that Aristotle regarded formal syllogistic as a system of deductive inference. Although it would be correct to say that he uses such a system, it is not what he is talking about when he sets out to prove completeness, or when he shows, in A7, that all syllogistic moods can be reduced to the two universal moods of the first figure, rather than the four he had introduced as perfect in A4.

This is so because Aristotle is focusing on the notion of valid argument, not logical consequence or valid inference in general. His definition of 'syllogism' stipulates that a syllogism must have at least two premisses, and that the conclusion must not only follow, but also be different from the premisses. This shows, I think, that he thought of syllogisms as arguments or argument forms, not just valid deductions or inferences. The notion of a valid deductive argument may be hard to define precisely, but it is clear that it is narrower than the notion of a valid deduction. For example, any proposition can be validly deduced from itself, but no one would wish to present an inference of p from p as an argument. When Aristotle says, as he does several times, that nothing follows of necessity from a single proposition, he should not be taken to deny that any proposition implies itself, or to maintain that nothing can be inferred from a single premiss. After all, in A2 he actually proves the validity of four types of single-premiss inference: the conversion rules he is going to use in his proofs in A5 and 6. But he apparently thought that such inferences could not be used as arguments, because their conclusions would not state anything different from their premisses and hence they would be question-begging. The syllogistic moods *Barbara* and *Celarent* have a different status, and when it comes to showing that the two particular moods of the first figure can be reduced to them, Aristotle does not mention any of the other rules of his system, but speaks as though all syllogistic moods could be derived from *Barbara* and *Celarent* alone. So he is not trying to establish the minimal number of primitive rules of inference for the system he uses, but the number of primitive forms of argument presupposed by it. What he thought about the deduction rules conversion, *reductio, ecthesis*—we do not know, since he never discusses their status.

Again, the first half of the completeness proof in A23 takes the form of showing that any direct deductive argument with two or more syllogistic premisses can be transformed into a chain of two-premiss syllogisms which will therefore consist entirely of arguments in one of the syllogistic figures. This can be read as a completeness proof in the modern sense, but it is actually only one half of Aristotle's own purported proof. The second half sets out to show that all arguments 'based on a hypothesis' and most importantly, all *reductio* arguments will also fall into the figures; and this part is a failure. Aristotle first offers an analysis of hypothetical arguments according to which such arguments consist of a syllogistic deduction plus one more step, which he describes as 'based on a hypothesis'. This is the step that distinguishes hypothetical arguments from normal direct syllogisms. In the *reductio* arguments discussed almost exclusively in A23, the step would appear to be the move from '*p* implies a falsehood' to '*p* is false', and hence to the assertion of not-p. In the direct hypothetical arguments analysed in A44, the step seems to be, in modern parlance, an application of the rule of *modus ponens*. In any case, the hypothetical arguments are clearly not complete without the last step which leads to the conclusion, and so it is astonishing to see Aristotle assert, at the end of A23, that these arguments too will be in one of the figures. The most he can say at this point—and he has not proved that either is that such arguments must contain a syllogism in one of the figures. And at the end of A44 he does acknowledge that this type of argument cannot be analysed as a syllogism in the narrow sense.

With regard to the modern formal models of syllogistic, this should show that although the natural deduction system Aristotle uses can indeed be shown to be complete, Aristotle's syllogistic as a formal theory of valid deductive argument is not complete, and Aristotle did not think it was. The divergence between Aristotle and his modern commentators was, I think, because they treat *reductio* as a deduction rule, the validity of which need not be proved within the system. Aristotle so uses it himself in A2, 5, and 6, but in A23 he considers reductio as a distinct type of argument, and he is right in pointing out that it is not covered by the syllogistic moods. This is not a minor omission in Aristotle's projected theory. For it appears from A44 that the class of hypothetical arguments is supposed to contain most, if not all, of the argument forms treated in the *Topics*, and Aristotle emphasizes that these need to be investigated and clearly distinguished (50a39-40). But it seems that he left this task to his students.

Now the explicit recognition that hypothetical argument is not syllogistic comes much later than the completeness proof in A23, and so one might be tempted to fall back on a developmental explanation, saying that Aristotle believed what he claims in A23, and came to realize only later that hypothetical argument will not fit into the figures. But speculation about chronology should obviously be a last resort, and it would seem particularly implausible in this case. The *Analytics* are among the works that Aristotle himself cites by their traditional title, and though they obviously do not constitute a polished treatise, and do seem to contain sections (such as modal syllogistic) that were inserted into already existing drafts, there is good reason to think that it was Aristotle himself who put together the materials collected in the four books. Moreover, the argument of A23 actually shows that hypothetical arguments are not strictly speaking in the figures. Hence it seems more plausible to suppose that Aristotle was content with the weaker claim that every proof or every valid deductive argument must at least contain a syllogistic deduction. If this were true, then anyone who tried to produce a formally valid argument would need to rely on the syllogistic moods, even if the argument consisted of a hypothetical step in addition to the syllogism.

But why did Aristotle think that hypothetical arguments had to contain a syllogism in the narrow sense? This assumption appears unargued in both A23 and A44, and that in spite of the fact that the example Aristotle gives in A44 might actually be taken to show just the opposite. I think that the reason why Aristotle still thought he did not have to argue for his claim has to do with his conception of syllogistic necessity: he thought that the necessity that forces one to accept the conclusion of a hypothetical argument depends upon the necessity of the preceding syllogism.

Aristotle did not have the notion of a propositionally complex sentence or proposition. He thought that one should in principle be able to reformulate any given valid argument as a series of categorical propositions in which 'one thing is said of one thing'. Simple sentences are not contrasted with complex ones formed by logical connectives, such as conjunctions, conditionals, and so forth, but with sentences that express more than one categorical predication. For Aristotle, what we would call a 'conjunction' appears to be a set of two propositions, and similarly for the other complex sentence forms. An Aristotelian syllogism in one of the figures consists of at least two categorical premisses and a categorical conclusion which is said to result of necessity, because what is asserted in the premisses is (supposed to be) the case. But the premisses assert that some one thing holds or does not hold of all or some of some other things, and so the conclusion will follow necessarily only if the term relations asserted to hold in the premisses necessitate the term relation asserted in the conclusion.

In a hypothetical argument, on the other hand, it will indeed be necessary to accept the conclusion, but not because one has asserted some premisses such that the term relations asserted necessitate the term relation in the conclusion. The conclusion is accepted because its contradictory has been shown to be false, or because some other proposition has been proved and one has agreed beforehand to accept a proof for that proposition in lieu of a proof for the conclusion. Aristotle contrasts the two sorts of necessity in A44, saying that 'it is necessary to agree [sc. to the conclusion]; not on the basis of (ek) a syllogism, however, but on the basis of a hypothesis' (50a25-6). An anachronistic way of describing the difference would be to say that in the strictly syllogistic case, the inference is justified by the term relations asserted in the premisses, while in the case of hypothetical argument it is justified only by the (assumed) relations between the truth-values of the propositions involved. Aristotle did not realize that truth-value relations could in fact be asserted in complex propositions such as conditionals, and so he thought that the conclusion of a hypothetical argument, though validly established, had not been reached in the same way as the conclusion of a proper syllogism.

This does not yet show, of course, why a hypothetical argument would have to contain a syllogism; but one can see why Aristotle would have thought so from looking at his description of the two types of hypothetical argument he recognizes. One type is described as follows. One begins with an agreement to the effect that a proof for a proposition q will be accepted in lieu of a proof for another proposition *p*, the original demonstrandum. One then produces a proof for *q*, and because of the initial agreement, the interlocutor will have to agree that *p* has been proved as well. An example of this type of argument—no doubt the paradigm case that accounts for the label 'hypothetical'—would be Socrates' argument 'from a hypothesis' in the *Meno*. Socrates and Meno agree that if they can show that virtue is knowledge, they will have shown that virtue can be taught. Socrates then sets out to find a proof for the thesis that virtue is knowledge, and it is clear that if he had found such a proof, he and Meno would have been satisfied that virtue is indeed teachable. Aristotle calls the proposition for which a proof is to be offered the 'substitute' (*metalambanomenon*) the thesis that virtue is knowledge is substituted, as it were, for the original demonstrandum and he claims that it must be proved by a direct syllogism. Now unfortunately his example in A44 does not bear him out, for he clearly envisages an indirect proof for the substituted thesis, as the ancient commentators already point out. But this will not invalidate his general claim that every valid deductive argument must contain a syllogism if it can be shown that every *reductio* argument contains a syllogism; so we must look at the other type of hypothetical argument.

A *reductio* is an argument in which one derives a falsehood or absurdity from the contradictory of the demonstrandum, and then concludes that the demonstrandum must be true because its contradictory has been shown to be false. In order to derive the absurdity, one cannot use another indirect argument, since presumably nothing absurd can be derived from the thesis to be proved. Given that all premisses are assumed to be categorical, it would seem that the absurdity can only be deduced by a categorical syllogism, as Aristotle maintains. For since Aristotle does not recognize the possibility of a direct *modus ponens* argument, he cannot consider the option of deriving either the so-called substitute proposition or the falsehood in a *reductio* from a conditional together with the proposition that forms the antecedent. The necessity involved in hypothetical argument thus seems to be parasitic upon syllogistic necessity in the narrow sense, because the final step can only be reached if a proof has been given, either for the falsity of the contradictory or for the substitute thesis, and that proof cannot itself be hypothetical, on pain of a regress.

So much for Aristotle's claim that every valid deductive argument must contain at least one syllogism. It would assure him that he had established the indispensable core of a general theory of argument, and although he could not in fact prove the ambitious thesis of A23, the first half of his argument there the completeness proof for direct syllogistic deductions retained its importance as a proof that the core theory was indeed complete.

Furthermore, he may have thought that this part would provide all that was needed for scientific demonstration, even if it did not adequately cover the wider field of dialectical argument, or indeed scientific reasoning in general, because demonstration in the strict sense would not have to rely upon hypothetical argument. Though both forms of hypothetical argument recognized by Aristotle may have been taken over by the philosophers from Greek mathematics, Aristotle may have thought that they belonged to a heuristic or preliminary stage of scientific investigations. Plato's Socrates claims to have learned the hypothetical method of reasoning from the mathematicians, although the geometrical example he uses to explain the method is notoriously much harder to understand than the dialectical procedure it allegedly serves to illustrate. It seems clear, however, that the example does not illustrate a method of proof, but a heuristic strategy. The *Meno*'s argument about virtue and knowledge appears, together with another geometrical example (not Plato's), in *Prior Analytics* B25, the chapter dealing with 'leading away' (*apogôge*). This procedure clearly serves a heuristic purpose: namely, to 'lead away' from a given problem that appears for the moment intractable to another one that can be more easily solved. Aristotle describes the *Meno* example as follows: 'let A be teachable, B stand for science, and C justice. That science is teachable, then, is obvious, but it is unclear whether virtue is a science. If, therefore, BC is equally convincing as AC, or more so, it is a leading away' (69a24-27, trans. R. Smith). It seems that this will bring us 'closer to scientific understanding' because it shows us that if we can find a proof for the minor premiss (BaC), then we will have a (syllogistic) proof for the desired conclusion, 'virtue is teachable' (AaC). It is interesting to note that the argument considered here is not 'hypothetical' in the sense of A23 or A44; the additional assumption is simply the minor premiss in a regular syllogism. What was earlier described as a hypothesis or agreement 'If (we can prove that) virtue is knowledge, then (we have shown that) virtue is teachable' turns out to link the minor premiss and conclusion of a proper syllogism. The hypothesis, then, was by no means arbitrarily chosen, and the example invites the consideration that in the direct case, at least, one might try to eliminate the need for an agreement by finding an additional premiss that will turn the hypothesis into a syllogism. Thus direct hypothetical argument might be thought to figure in scientific reasoning only as a preliminary to the discovery of syllogistic proof.

That still leaves indirect argument, and Aristotle obviously knew that this was in fact quite common in Greek mathematics; his own example of a *reductio* argument is the proof for the incommensurability of the diagonal with the side of a square. Nevertheless, he maintains in several places that any indirect argument can be replaced by a direct one, so that *reductio* could in principle be dispensed with. The argument for this claim, as far as I can see, comes from his treatment of syllogism 'through an impossibility' (*dia tou adunatou sullogismos*) in B11-14. There he describes indirect argument as an argumentative strategy, to be employed if an opponent is not willing to accept a premiss one needs to derive the conclusion one is aiming at. An indirect argument, Aristotle explains in B14, is one in which one assumes what one wants to refute, and leads on from there to an agreed falsehood. So if the opponent will not agree top, you ask him to accept its contradictory he can hardly refuse to do that if he has rejected the original proposition and then try to derive an obvious falsehood from this assumption together with some other, already accepted premiss. This will serve to show that the contradictory of the premiss you tried to introduce must be false, and hence allow you to use the desired premiss after all.

In the simple cases Aristotle considers in B11-14, it is also true that the desired proposition could have been derived from the contradictory of the 'obvious falsehood' together with the other accepted premiss, and so Aristotle concludes that the same terms can (always) be used to construct either a direct or an indirect argument. When one tries to discover a scientific proof, as opposed to refuting an opponent in a dialectical debate, one will presumably not have to resort to such stratagems, and hence indirect proof will be dispensable. Since the difference between direct and indirect argument thus seems to be merely strategic, and the same terms will be used in both cases, Aristotle thinks that the heuristic devices used for constructing direct syllogistic deductions will be sufficient to cover indirect argument as well. The hitch is, of course, that not every indirect argument will be as simple as the ones Aristotle analyses in B11-14. The examples he has in mind there probably do not come from mathematics, but from the indirect proofs he himself had offered in A5 and 6, where the 'impossibility' arises in each case because the contradictory of one of the assumed premisses has been derived from the 'hypothesis' (i.e. the contradictory of the conclusion that follows from the premisses). It is probably significant that Aristotle does not seem to distinguish between deriving an 'obvious falsehood'—that is, a patently absurd but not logically false proposition—and deriving a contradiction. Only belatedly, in B15, does he acknowledge that one might need more than one syllogism to derive a contradiction namely, in those cases where one has not assumed the contradictory of the derived proposition in advance. But it is not clear that this would have led him to revise his view about the dispensability of indirect proof. He knew that such proofs were common in mathematics, and hence he found it important to show that his theory could deal with them; but he probably did not try to derive, for example, the incommensurability theorem from the premiss 'no number is both odd and even' together with other mathematical truths.

Aristotle may also have thought that in a truly scientific system of demonstrations, indirect proofs *should* be replaced by direct ones. He thought that direct arguments were preferable to indirect ones for epistemological reasons: as he points out in *Posterior Analytics* A26, when one derives a falsehood in an indirect argument, the premisses of the syllogistic deduction one uses will not state the facts on which one's eventual conclusion is based, and hence will not be 'prior to the conclusion' in the way required for demonstration. Only when the argument has been transformed into a direct syllogism which uses the contradictory of the 'obvious falsehood' as a premiss will the correct order of epistemological priority be restored. I suspect that what Aristotle disliked about indirect proofs was that they do not do what an Aristotelian demonstration is supposed to do: namely, explain why the conclusion must be true. The incommensurability proof does show that the diagonal in a square cannot be commensurable with the side; but one can hardly say that it explains or states a reason why the diagonal must be incommensurable, least of all by providing an appropriate middle term. So perhaps Aristotle hoped that in principle, at least, demonstration could proceed without indirect proof.

However that may be, even if formal syllogistic did not provide the comprehensive theory Aristotle had promised at the beginning of A4, the system of the figures would be the foundation of all valid deductive arguments, whether scientific or not, and its applications in heuristics and analysis would be as important for dialectic or rhetoric as for science or philosophy. In the rest of the *Prior Analytics* after A26 and before he turns to his official treatment of demonstration, Aristotle is concerned to show how formal syllogistic should be used to construct or to criticize arguments, and his main focus appears to be on dialectic. I will now briefly illustrate these uses of logic by a few examples.

In *Prior Analytics* A27-31, Aristotle describes an ingenious method for finding premisses for any given categorical conclusion. Once one has the complete list of valid syllogistic moods provided in A4-6, one will no longer have to collect and memorize long lists of propositions about various fields, as Aristotle had recommended in the *Topics*. Instead, one can construct lists of terms that either follow or are followed by a given term. The thesis under discussion—the *problçma*, as Aristotle calls it here, using the terminology of the *Topics* will have to contain two terms; hence by looking for terms that occur in the lists for both of the requisite terms, one will be able to find an appropriate middle term to construct one's syllogism. Alexander of Aphrodisias illustrates the procedure by a delightful example: lists of terms one can use to argue that pleasure is or is not a good, as the occasion demands. Aristotle's system is more efficient and economical than Platonic division, which is therefore demoted to 'a small part' of heuristics in A31; and Aristotle insists that his method is the only one guaranteed to locate all the premisses that can be used to construct valid syllogisms. At the same time, it may also show, depending on the exhaustiveness of the lists, where a syllogism can not be found.

Another advantage, not emphasized by Aristotle himself, is that it is arguably more general in its scope, and certainly much easier to use, than the system of the predicables that Aristotle had used to organize his materials in the *Topics*. It is hard to imagine an orator holding forth about questions of genus, species, and definition, while it is clear that she would be interested in the quantity or quality of her premises whether some predicate is or is not true of some or all members of a given class. Syllogistic shows that the formal validity of an argument can be established or checked regardless of the specific type of predication that occurs in its premisses and conclusion. Hence special conditions regarding the different types of predication can be treated separately from a general account of deductive validity. This certainly simplifies the task of the orator, who can now just study the system of the syllogistic moods (she might, indeed, memorize them with the help of mnemonic verses, as the medievals did), instead of delving into the arcane metaphysical questions that fill so many pages of the *Topics*.

It is not surprising that Aristotle seems to replace references to dialectic as a general theory of syllogisms by references to the *Analytics* in the chapters that deal with argument in the *Rhetoric*: for syllogistic provides all that the orator needs in order to construct valid arguments; she does not have to study up on the predicables. This does not mean that the orator will have to learn about scientific proof instead of dialectical argument, of course. The syllogistic figures will have to be part of the equipment of the dialectician as well; and given that the *Analytics* do not offer a detailed account of hypothetical argument, the *Topics* may still be needed as a handbook for the orator. What is missing from the *Analytics* is an account of the so-called general, or subject-neutral, *topoi*. In the framework of the classification of argument forms Aristotle uses in *Prior Analytics* A23, these should probably be described as general types of 'hypothesis' that one might expect one's interlocutor or one's audience to agree to. The sketch of a formal treatment of arguments concerning things preferable to their opposites in *Prior Analytics* B22 may show that Aristotle at some point planned to work out a formal theory of such arguments, but he evidently did not get around to this project. However, it invites the suggestion that a revised handbook for dialecticians might have paid less attention to the predicables than the *Topics* does.

The *Topics* as we have it is largely a handbook for *Academic* dialecticians; a manual based on the syllogistic moods, by contrast, could equally well have been used by people who had no special interest in genus, definition, or proprium. Hence the method of heuristics introduced in *Prior Analytics* A27-31 is at least as important for dialectic and rhetoric as for the theory of scientific proof. In fact, although Aristotle does briefly discuss the use of his method in the context of science in A30, it seems rather obvious to me that lists of terms are more likely to be used by a dialectician than by a scientist. A science, as Aristotle says, will have to begin by assembling, as completely as possible, the observed facts about its subject-matter. These will have to form most of the premisses and conclusions of its demonstrations, and at this stage it may be helpful to look for common terms in order to find out what can or cannot be derived from what. But as the *Posterior Analytics* shows, this will hardly be enough to establish, for example, the correctness of a proposed definition, or the claim that a thing's being F is to be explained by its being G rather than the other way around. Alexander was right, I think, to illustrate the use of heuristics by an example from the dialectician's repertoire.

The next section of Prior Analytics A32-46, deals with 'analysis'—that is, the question of how to reduce given arguments to syllogistic form. Aristotle declares at the beginning (47a5-8) that his previous claims about the universal scope of the syllogistic figures will be confirmed if it can be shown that it is indeed possible so to analyse any given argument. This is no doubt correct, but unfortunately the following chapters do not in fact confirm Aristotle's optimism. Since it is already clear how one has to deal with explicitly categorical propositions, this section concentrates on difficult or recalcitrant cases examples of obviously valid arguments that are not syllogistic in form, or fallacies that appear to be formally valid syllogisms but are not really so because, as Aristotle wants to maintain, their premisses have not been correctly analysed. Aristotle never shows any serious doubt about the adequacy of the syllogistic moods to capture the form of all valid arguments, but he often emphasizes the difficulty of uncovering the proper structure, and the need for more detailed investigations.

From a modern point of view, several of these chapters could almost be read as collections of counter examples to demonstrate the inadequacy of syllogistic. But Aristotle evidently did not see things this way. A36 may show most clearly why he was so confident: there he declares that the technical term '*huparchein*' (belonging) covers much more than straightforward cases of predication. It appears that his method of analysis allows him to treat just about any sort of proposition as a categorical premiss. In other words, he thinks that he knows what the 'logical form' of an argument has to be, and does not consider formalization, as modern logicians might, as a way of exploring or discovering different logical structures. The shortcomings of syllogistic as a way of representing complicated arguments are too well known to need spelling out in detail. With respect to the possible usefulness of syllogistic, however, it seems more important to emphasize that in spite of the difficulties so candidly discussed by Aristotle himself, analysis or reduction to syllogistic form can be very useful in cases where the form of the premisses presents no problem.

This comes out most clearly, perhaps, in the discussion of rhetorical arguments from 'signs' (B27) and the *Rhetoric*'s brief treatment of *lusis*-dissecting an opponent's arguments (*Rhet.* B25) which refers back to the *Analytics*. Aristotle shows that all but one of the customary types of sign argument are formally invalid, so an orator who has studied the *Analytics* will know exactly how to show that the argument, even if it has some merit, will not be sufficient to establish its alleged conclusion. Also, given some acquaintance with modal premisses, one may be able to show that an apparently cogent objection is not in fact conclusive. For example, if an orator has used what appears to be a universal premiss, say, 'Those who walk around late in the night are thieves', and the objection is raised that the generalization does not hold without exception, one can retort that what one was actually claiming was only that all those who walk around late at night are likely to be thieves—a proposition much harder to disprove, since one might have to show that the alleged suspects are in fact more likely not to be thieves than to be thieves. Despite its limitations, then, syllogistic can be used quite successfully at times to identify types of invalid argument, and in this respect it can serve an important function that modern logic also fulfils: namely, to spot faulty inferences or gaps in arguments. I should admit, however, that Aristotle's attempts to trace fallacies to faulty ways of rendering the supposedly categorical structure of premisses do not look like an improvement on the treatment of fallacy in the *Sophistici Elenchi.*

Now the use of syllogistic as a diagnostic instrument to discover weaknesses or faults in arguments seems, as in the case of heuristics, more important for those who engage in debate or in courtroom pleading than for those who try to construct scientific proofs. Presumably a serious scientific researcher will carefully try to avoid fallacious inferences, and therefore use only forms of argument that she knows to be valid. Given Aristotle's preconceived notion that proofs just *have* to be syllogistic in form, it is not likely that the chapters on analysis were meant to persuade the reader that mathematical proofs, for example, could be presented in syllogistic form. Aristotle's examples tend to be of the sort known from the Topics, and what is being confirmed, to the extent that anything can be said to be confirmed here, would seem to be the claim that the syllogistic figures are adequate to deal with all sorts of arguments *beyond* the field of scientific demonstration.

The sections on heuristics and analysis in Prior Analytics A complete a project to which Aristotle briefly adverts in the opening paragraph of A32. The three parts he mentions there are probably the system of the syllogistic moods, heuristics, and analysis. The contents of book B are more difficult to classify, partly no doubt because the book contains some notes or sketches that do not cohere very well with their context. For example, the book begins with a chapter that seems to offer some corollaries to formal syllogistic, and in effect bring in the syllogistic moods that were later classified as belonging to the fourth figure. At the beginning of B23 Aristotle makes a remark that indicates that he has so far been dealing with dialectical and demonstrative syllogisms, and is going to extend his investigation by applying the doctrine of the syllogistic moods to rhetorical argument. They either try to establish metatheorems regarding deductive argument in general, or deal with questions of argumentative strategy.

One theorem of which Aristotle was understandably proud is proved in B2-4; namely, that a true conclusion can be validly derived from false premisses. One may find it pedantic and tedious that Aristotle goes through all the syllogistic moods to show how this is possible in each case, with one or both premisses false, when two examples would have sufficed to establish the general claim. But this should not divert our attention from the fact that Aristotle's proof is a considerable achievement. It is one thing merely to assert that the truth of the conclusion tells us nothing about the truth of the premisses, another to offer a rigorous proof to show that this is so. Aristotle also shows that if a false conclusion is derived from apparently true premisses, then either one or more of the premisses is false, or the conclusion does not follow. These are points that may appear trivial to readers trained in modern logic, but they still need to be made in any introductory class on reasoning and argument, and Aristotle was the first not just to state, but to prove, them.

The chapters on the so-called conversion of syllogisms may look like a debater's exercise: showing how a given set of propositions and their negations can be combined in different ways to deduce different conclusions. But once again it is important to note that formal syllogistic enables Aristotle to prove his claims, not just to tell his students that they should try out various combinations to see if anything follows. Although Aristotle did not go on to develop a theory of evidence, he obviously recognized that not every thesis can or should be justified in the same way, and even that formally inconclusive evidence may be just as convincing as an elaborate deductive proof.

Despite its obvious limitations as a general theory of deduction, formal syllogistic allowed Aristotle to establish a number of fundamental points in the theory of argument. The crucial step, of course, was his discovery that the validity of an argument depends on the form of its premisses and conclusion, not their content or the peculiarities of the subject-matter under discussion. For a general theory of argument, the distinction between formal validity and truth may well be more important than the notion of a deductive system or an axiomatized theory. I hope to have shown that Aristotle's formal logic need not be seen exclusively as an attempt either to provide the underlying logic for axiomatized theory or to develop a system of deductive inference. It is at least as much a contribution to a theory of valid argument in general, and in this role it was correctly described by the ancient commentators as a tool of philosophy.

6

Dialectic and Philosophy in Aristotle

Introduction

A problem (*problçma*) is posed: is pleasure choiceworthy, or not? The answerer claims that it is or, alternatively, that it is not. The questioner must refute him by asking questions, by offering him premisses (*protaseis*) to accept or reject. He succeeds if he forces the answerer to accept a proposition contrary to the one he undertook to defend. He fails if the answerer always accepts or rejects premisses in a way consistent with the proposition he undertook to defend. To a first approximation, dialectic is the craft (*technç*) that enables someone to play the role of questioner or answerer as successfully as possible.

At the heart of dialectic so characterized is the dialectical deduction (*dialektikos sullogismos*). This is the argument that lies behind the questioner's questions, partly dictating their order and content, partly determining the strategy of the questioner's attack. Understanding dialectic more precisely is very largely a matter of grasping the nature of dialectical deductions and the type of premisses they employ.

In *Topics* I. 1 these deductions are contrasted with three other types of arguments: scientific, eristic, and paralogistic. In *Sophistical Refutations* 1. 2 they are distinguished from didactic, peirastic, and eristic arguments.

Scientific, Eristic and Fallacious Arguments

Dialectical deductions differ from scientific ones only in their premisses: the latter are deductions from first principles, and hence are demonstrations (*apodeixeis*). With eristic arguments the differences are potentially twofold. Eristic arguments are either genuine deductions from apparent *endoxa* or apparent deductions from genuine or apparent *endoxa*. Paralogistic arguments differ from all these: unlike dialectical and eristic arguments, their premisses are not endoxa, but 'premisses proper to a specialized science'; unlike scientific demonstrations, their premisses are false.

The sharpness of the divide between apparent deductions or apparent endoxa and the genuine articles suggests that the divide between dialectic and eristic is also sharp. But how can this be when dialectic is the single craft involved in constructing both genuine and apparent deductions from both genuine and apparent endoxa?

In the Rhetoric, we are told that rhetoric and dialectic differ in an important respect:

> *In the case of rhetoric, one person will be called a rhetorician on the basis of his scientific knowledge and another on the basis of his decision (proairesis), while in dialectic a sophist is so called on the basis of his decision, and a dialectician is so called not on the basis of his decision but on the basis of his ability.*

If dialectic is understood thus, a sophist is a dialectician who decides to employ eristic arguments. This alone is not enough to make him a sophist, however, since a contender (*eristikos*) also employs such arguments. What makes him a sophist is that he employs eristic for a particular purpose:

Sophistry is a way of making money out of apparent wisdom. Contenders and sophists use the same arguments, but not to achieve the same goal. If the goal is apparent victory, the argument is eristic or contentious; if it is apparent wisdom, sophistic.

Who is it, then, that makes the opposite decision and avoids eristic argument in dialectical debate? If the *Topics* and the *Sophistical Refutations* are to be our guide, he is the dialectician himself, since in both treatises dialectic differs from eristic precisely in employing genuine endoxa and genuine deductions, rather than merely apparent ones.

Pretty clearly, then, the *Topics* and the *Sophistical Refutations* do not observe the distinction which the *Rhetoric* draws between rhetoric and dialectic. Nevertheless, that distinction solves the problem we uncovered in the relationship between dialectic and eristic. Dialectic considered simply as a craft includes eristic. But if dialectic is what is practised by someone who decides to employ genuine *endoxa* and genuine deductions, it does not include eristic. To mark this distinction, let us call the latter *honest* dialectic and the former, which includes eristic, *plain* dialectic. Notice, however, that plain dialectic is a single craft, which contenders, sophists, and honest dialecticians use for different purposes. Thus there is just one kind of dialectic and three different styles of employing it styles that impose different restrictions on which of its various resources are to be employed.

Peirastic Deductions and Sophistical Refutations

Peirastic is 'a type of dialectic which has in view not the person who knows (*ton eidota*) but the one who pretends to know but does not'. In other words, it is the type of dialectic particularly useful in arguments with sophists—the archetypal pretenders to knowledge and wisdom.

Is peirastic, like plain dialectic, a neutral skill, or is it the honest employment of certain particular dialectical resources? The best answer, as we shall see at the end of the present section, is that peirastic is like dialectic: plain peirastic is a neutral skill; honest peirastic is the honest employment of that skill. In point of fact, however, Aristotle usually uses the term *peirastikç* to refer to honest peirastic. Thus, for example, he says that peirastic deductions employ premisses that must be known to anyone who claims to know the relevant science. If that is the case, they cannot be merely the kind of apparent *endoxa* that a sophist, but not an honest dialectician, is content to use, since, as known, they must be true.

The problem now is to distinguish honest peirastic from honest dialectic pure and simple. The best way to tackle it is by exploring sophistical refutations, which are the dishonest twins of honest peirastic arguments. The latter expose the genuine ignorance of a sophist answerer, who has only apparent knowledge and wisdom; the former give the appearance of exposing the ignorance of someone who really does have scientific knowledge.

Sophistical refutations come in two varieties. An A-type sophistical refutation is 'an apparent deduction or refutation rather than a real one'; a B-type sophistical refutation is 'a real deduction that is only apparently proper (*phainomenon oikeion*) to the subject in question'. Thus A-type sophistical refutations are eristic arguments, whereas B-type ones are closely akin to paralogisms.

Paralogisms proper to a craft or science are those based on the first principles and conclusions that belong to it. For example, Hippocrates' argument for squaring the circle by means of lunes is a geometrical paralogism, because it 'proceeds from principles that are proper to geometry' and 'cannot be adapted to any subject except geometry'. But someone who uses Bryson's method of squaring the circle, or who uses Zeno's argument that motion is impossible in order to refute a doctor's claim that it is better to take a walk after dinner, has produced a B-type sophistical refutation, because Bryson's and Zeno's arguments are not proper to geometry or medicine but 'common (*koinos*)'. Moreover, this sort of argument is paralogistic, even if it is sound: ' Bryson's method of squaring the circle, even if the circle is thereby squared, is still sophistical because it is not in accord with the relevant subject matter'. Hence the only difference between paralogisms and B-type sophistical refutations is this: the former have premisses that are proper to the answerer's science but false; the latter have premisses that are not proper to it but true.

Because paralogisms depend on premisses proper to a science, it is the business of the practitioner of that science to refute and diagnose them. But it is not his business to deal with B-type sophistical refutations, since these depend on common things, on *koina*. They are the business of dialecticians: 'it is dialecticians who study a refutation that depends on things that are common, that is to say, that do not belong to any [specialized] craft'.

I note in passing that it is also the business of dialecticians to deal with Antiphon's argument for squaring the circle, which is an A-type sophistical refutation. This is so for the following reason. Antiphon's argument assumes that a circle is a polygon with a very large (but finite) number of sides. Hence it 'does away with the first principles of geometry' specifically, with the principle that magnitudes are divisible without limit. Consequently, it cannot be discussed in a way that presupposes those first principles, but must be discussed on the basis of *koina*.

A natural thought about *koina* is that they are what Aristotle elsewhere calls axioms (*axiômata*), which are principles common to all or many sciences. These include such laws of logic as the Principle of Non-contradiction, which hold at least analogically of all beings, as well as other somewhat less general laws, such as the axioms of equality, which are not universally applicable, but are also not proper to a single science or a single genus. The trouble with this thought is that it is impossible to construct a B-type sophistical refutation using axioms alone. Axioms are common to all or many sciences, and so cannot by themselves entail a proposition contrary to a conclusion proper to a specific science. Yet that is precisely what B-type sophistical refutations must do. It is not an axiom that walking is a type of motion. But without such a premiss, no conclusion contrary to the doctor's principle that it is good to take a walk after dinner can be soundly derived from Zeno's arguments. It follows that the *koina* employed as premisses in this type of sophistical refutation cannot just be axioms.

But if *koina* are not axioms, what are they? We know that only *endoxa* or apparent *endoxa* can figure as premisses in plain dialectical arguments. We know, too, that *koina* are the dialectician's business:

> *It is plain that it is the dialectician's business to be able to grasp the various ways in which a real or apparent refutation—that is to say, one that is an example of dialectic or apparent dialectic or peirastic—can be achieved on the basis of common things.*

This suggests that *koina* are *endoxa* or apparent *endoxa*. The following passage from the *Rhetoric*, taken together with the passage from the *Topics* to which it refers, settles the identification:

> *Even if one had the most exact sort of scientific knowledge, it would not be easy to persuade some people by arguments based on it . . . rather, it is necessary to construct our persuasions and arguments on the basis of common things, as we said in the* Topics *about ordinary discussions* (enteuxeis) *with the many.*

[Plain] dialectic is useful in ordinary discussions (enteuxeis) because once we have catalogued the beliefs of the many, our approach to them will begin from their own views, not from other people's, and we will redirect them whenever they appear to be to be wrong.

Since the opinions of the many are real or apparent *endoxa*, *koina* too must be real or apparent *endoxa*.

This does not mean, however, that axioms cannot be *koina* in precisely this sense. They will be *koina* if they are *endoxa* of some sort. And many of them are sure to have this status if for no other reason than that the non-paradoxical views of philosophers have it.

The premisses of B-type sophistical refutations, whether axioms or not, are either *endoxa* or apparent *endoxa*, then. But since these arguments must be sound, the endoxa they employ must be true. What makes the arguments sophistical, as we saw, is simply and solely the fact that they employ these *endoxa* as if they were proper to the answerer's science, rather than merely being *koina*. We should expect, therefore, that honest peirastic arguments differ from B-type sophistical refutations in just this way: they have *endoxa* as premisses, but *endoxa* that are in fact proper to the answerer's science.

Armed with the evidence that has led us to form this expectation, we are now in a position to see that it is in fact met by Aristotle's somewhat opaque characterization of honest peirastic deductions. These, he tells us, 'deduce from premises that are accepted by the answerer, and that must be known (*eidenai*) by anyone who claims to have the [relevant] scientific knowledge. In a later passage, he explains that premisses of this sort are taken not from the things from which one knows (*ouk ex hôn oiden*) or even from those proper to the subject in question, but from the consequences (*tôn hepomenôn*) that a man can know (*eidota*) without knowing (eidenai) the craft in question, but which if he does not know (*mç eidota*), he is necessarily ignorant of the craft.

In other words, they are not the first principles of the answerer's science–not 'things from which one knows' or other principles proper to it, but 'consequences' of them. It follows, of course, that peirastic premisses, unlike those of B-type sophistical refutations, must be proper to the answerer's science, since they are syllogistic consequences of its principles.

Later in the same passage these consequences are identified as *koina*, that is to say, *endoxa*:

> *everybody, including those that do not possess a craft, makes use of dialectic as peirastic; for everyone tries to use peirastic to some extent in order to test those who claim to know things. And this is where the common things come in; for the testers know* (isasin) *these things for themselves just as well as those who do possess the craft even if they seem to say quite inaccurate things.*

Hence, as we were led to expect by our investigation of B-type sophistical refutations, the premisses of honest peirastic deductions must indeed be genuine *endoxa* that are proper to the answerer's science the one that the sophist undergoing honest peirastic examination is pretending to know.

Aristotle says that honest peirastic premisses are known (*eidenai, isasin*), that they can be known without having scientific knowledge (*epistçmç*) of the science the answerer pretends to have, and that they are consequences of the principles of that science. It follows that they are true, and potentially objects of scientific knowledge a potential that would be realized if they were in fact demonstrated from first principles. Since such premisses are *endoxa*, it follows that some *endoxa* also have these features.

But why do *endoxa* have to have them in order to serve as honest peirastic premisses? A person who really has scientific knowledge may yet be the victim of a sophistical refutation he may find himself caught in a contradiction when he is interrogated by a clever sophist. Hence the mere fact that someone can be bested in a dialectical argument is not enough to show that he lacks scientific knowledge. What is further required is, first, that this argument not be a sophistical refutation, that its premisses be true and proper to the science in question. But even that is not enough. They must also be premisses that anyone who knows that science would have to know. Otherwise, an answerer could reject them and still know the science. Finally, they must be premisses that it is possible to know without knowing the science. Otherwise, they could not figure in arguments available to non-scientists. Thus the various features that the premisses of an honest peirastic argument must have are entailed by the purpose which such arguments are intended to serve of enabling non-scientists to unmask the ignorant pretender to scientific knowledge.

In *Topics* VIII. 5 Aristotle discusses 'dialectical explorations (*sunoidois*) that are not competitive but are conducted for the sake of examination (*peiras*) and inquiry'. It is clear from the account he provides of how such explorations should be conducted that they do not fit the characterization of honest peirastic that we have been exploring. For example, the questioner is not restricted to using true premisses; he can, and sometimes must, use false ones:

> *Since arguments of this kind are conducted for the sake of practice and examination (*peiras*), it is clear that the questioner must deduce not only true conclusions but also false ones, and not always from true premises but sometimes from false ones as well. For often, when a true proposition is put forward [by an answerer], the dialectician is compelled to demolish it, and so he has to offer [the answerer] false premises.*

When Aristotle tells us in *Sophistical Refutations I.* 2 that he has already discussed peirastic arguments, therefore, there is good reason to take him to be referring to the discussion of dialectical explorations that examine and investigate, which occupies *Topics* VIII. 5-11. But to secure that reference, in the face of the manifest differences between what the two treatises say about peirastic, we must recognize that *Sophistical Refutations* mostly deals with honest peirastic, whereas the *Topics* deals with plain peirastic.

Didactic Deductions

According to *Sophistical Refutations*, didactic deductions (*didaskalikoi*) are 'those that deduce from the principles proper to each subject matter and not from the opinions held by the answerer, since learners have to take things on trust' (165b1-3). This pegs these deductions as scientific demonstrations of some sort. And, indeed, the *Rhetoric* characterizes them as "arguments based on scientific knowledge" (1355a26). But if didactic deductions are scientific demonstrations, why are they included with honest dialectic, peirastic, and eristic arguments as one of the four types of argument used 'in question and answer discussions'.

That is one problem. But there are two others that will turn out to be related to it. In the *Sophistical Refutations* Aristotle says that didactic deductions are not deductions 'from the opinions held by the answerer' (165b2). Yet, in the Topics, he says that 'the student should always grant [only] what seems to him to be the case' (159a28-9), suggesting that didactic arguments are indeed deductions from the student's opinions. That is the second problem. A third problem is also one of apparent inconsistency or discontinuity of doctrine. In *Topics* VIII teaching sometimes takes the form of a question-and-answer discussion. 10 teaching is contrasted with asking questions: 'the teacher should not ask questions but make things clear himself, whereas the dialectician should ask questions'.

To solve these three problems, and grasp the coherence of Aristotle's thought about didactic, we need to appreciate the relevance to them of the distinction between an argument 'taken by itself (*kat' auton*)' and 'presented in the form of questions'.

Suppose that a student has acquired the first principles of a science through perception or habituation and that his teacher wants to test him on his knowledge of that science. The natural thing for him to do is to examine the student by offering him propositions to accept or reject. And, of course, 'the student should always grant [only] what seems to him to be the case', since otherwise the teacher will not be able to discover what the student really knows. Here the teacher's didactic argument is 'presented in the form of questions'. But the admissions made by the student are not premisses in the didactic argument the scientific demonstration taken by itself that underlies these questions and partly dictates their order and content. *It* is not a deduction 'from the opinions held by the answerer' .On the other hand, suppose that a phrase that occurs in a scientific proposition has a double meaning, but that the student 'neither has considered nor knows nor conceives that a second meaning is possible'. Then 'the teacher should not ask questions but make things clear himself'. Here, unlike in the previous case, the teacher is not trying to find out what the student knows by asking him questions. He already knows that the student is ignorant, and is providing him with information. Here he may use a didactic argument 'taken by itself' to make things clear to the student.Once we see that teaching can involve question-and-answer discussion, as well as straight forward demonstration; once we see that didactic arguments can be understood in two different ways, we can see that these arguments do have a place in question-and-answer discussions, and that Aristotle's account of them is consistent.

The Classification of Deductions

In *Topics* I. 1 deductions are divided into four classes:

(T1) scientific

(T2) paralogistic

(T3) honest dialectic

(T4) eristic.

In *Sophistical Refutations* I. 2 they are also initially divided into four classes:

(S1) didactic

(S2) peirastic

(S3) honest dialectic

(S4) eristic.

Then two more are added:

(S5) A-type sophistical refutations

(S6) B-type sophistical refutations.

We are in a position to see that these classifications fit together to constitute a single systematic classification of dialectical deductions.Deductions come in two broad varieties:

(D1) genuine (valid)

(D2) apparent (invalid).

Their premisses are of six kinds:

(P1) true and proper principles of a science

(P2) untrue but proper principles of a science

(P3) *endoxa* that are true and proper to a science (because consequences of its principles)

(P4) *endoxa* that are true but only apparently proper to a science

(P5) *endoxa*

(P6) apparent *endoxa.*

(D1)-(D2) and (P1)-(P6) together determine the various kinds of dialectical deductions:

(D1)-(P1) deductions are scientific demonstrations (T1), and the type presupposed in didactic arguments (S1).

(D1)-(P2) deductions are paralogisms (T2).

(D1)-(P3) deductions are peirastic deductions (S2).

(D1)-(P4) deductions are B-type sophistical refutations (S6).

(D1)-(P5) deductions are honest dialectic arguments (T3), (S3).

(D1)-(P6) deductions are eristic arguments or A-type sophistical refutations (T4), (S4), (S5).

(D2)-(P5) deductions are eristic arguments of A-type sophistical refutations (T4), (S4), (S5).

A striking feature of this classification manifest once it is set out in tabular form is that it includes only one type of invalid deduction: namely, (D2)-(P5). This is so for a reason. The various kinds of formally valid and invalid deductions have already been studied in the *Prior Analytics*. The *Topics* and *Sophistical Refutations* are primarily concerned not with them, but with sound or unsound ones with the choice of premisses rather than with the logical form of arguments. Once that is noted, however, we see how complete and systematic the classification is. This is a further reason to think that our account of its various constituents is correct.

Indirect Endoxa and Protaseis

The first of three dealing with *endoxa* explores the notion of a dialectical premiss (*protasis*), to see what light it throws on *endoxa*.

Dialectical premisses, obviously enough, are premisses in a dialectical argument. Aristotle's initial account of them is as follows:

> *A dialectical premise consists in [A] making a question out of something that is* endoxos *to everyone or to the majority or to the wise—either to all of them, or to most, or to the most notable of them, provided it is not paradoxical; for a person would accept the opinion of the wise, provided it is not contrary to general opinion. Dialectical premises also include*

> *[B] things that are like* endoxa, *and [C] propositions that contradict the contraries of what seem to be* endoxa, *and also [D] all opinions that accord with [the principles of] the recognized crafts since a person would accept the opinions of those who have investigated the subjects in question for example, on a question of medicine they will agree with the doctor, and on a question of geometry with the geometer.*

Later, in a reprise of this passage, he adds what appear to be two new clauses to his account:

> *[E] Furthermore, statements that seem to hold in all or in most cases, should be taken as a starting-point, that is to say (kai), as an accepted thesis; for such statements are accepted by those who do not notice that there is a case in which they do not hold. [F] We ought also to select [premisses] from written accounts and draw up lists of them on each type of subject, putting them under separate headings for example, 'Dealing with good', 'Dealing with life'. And the one dealing with good, should deal with every kind of good, beginning with the essence.*

How are we to understand (A)-(F)?

(A) corresponds closely to the definition of genuine *endoxa* given in *Topics* I. 1: '*Endoxa* are things that are held by everyone, by the majority, or by the wise—either by all of them, or by most, or by the most notable and most *endoxos*'. It follows, as was in any case to be expected on general grounds, that genuine *endoxa* are, or can serve as, dialectical premisses. But (A) also tells us something new: namely, that views held by all, most, or the most reputable wise people have to meet a negative condition if they are to count as *endoxa*—they cannot be 'paradoxical'. What does this mean? According to (A) a proposition is paradoxical if it is 'contrary to general opinion' (104a11-12). But a later text shows that this is only a special case. A proposition is paradoxical if 'the many disagree with the wise' about it or if 'one or the other of these two classes disagree among themselves'.

The fact that (B) speaks of propositions that are 'like *endoxa*' and (C) speaks of the contraries of what 'seem to be *endoxa*' suggest that these clauses refer to apparent *endoxa*. Likelihood becomes certainty when we turn to Aristotle's illustrative examples: (1) 'If it is an *endoxon* that the science of contraries is the same, it might appear to be an *endoxon* that the perception of contraries is also the same' (104a15-17). (2) 'Propositions contradicting the contraries of *endoxa* will appear to be *endoxa*' (104a20-3). (3) 'If it is an *endoxon* that there is a single craft of grammar, it might also seem to be an *endoxon* that there is a single craft of fluteplaying' (104a17-20). (1) and (2) explicitly refer to apparent *endoxa*. (3) makes sense only if it too has apparent *endoxa* in view, since if a proposition is an *endoxon*, its contrary cannot be (Top. 159b4-6). Hence it cannot be an *endoxon* that there is a single craft of grammar, and also an *endoxon* that there is more than one such craft.

It is clear, then, that both *endoxa* and apparent *endoxa* are (plain) dialectical premisses. Consequently, we cannot identify genuine *endoxa* with such premisses, or infer that everything said about them applies willynilly to genuine *endoxa*.

This brings us to (D). Since the propositions referred to in (D) are accepted by most people, they must be *endoxa* of some sort. Since they are in accord with the principles of the recognized crafts, they cannot be merely apparent, and so must be genuine. Thus (D), like (A), concerns genuine *endoxa*. Moreover—and this is another respect in which it resembles (A)—(D) also tells us that a proposition can be an *endoxon* if all or most people would accept it. They do not already have to accept it for it to count as an *endoxon*.

(E) includes as *endoxa* statements that merely seem to be true to those 'who do not notice that there is a case in which they do not hold'. Hence it is plain that (E), like (B) and (C), refers to apparent *endoxa*.

(F) is almost certainly a new source of something already listed, rather than a wholly new addition to the list, since written accounts are likely to have wise people or practitioners of the recognized crafts as authors. Aristotle himself suggests as much when he says that we should note in the margins of the lists we distil from these writings the identity of the thinkers, such as Empedocles, who hold them, 'since anyone might assent to the saying of some reputable thinker'.

(D) refers to practitioners of the recognized crafts; (A) to wise people. What exactly is the difference? What is the difference between *endoxa* included under (A) and those included under (D)? The most intelligible answer is no doubt the right one. The opinions of a doctor who is known to have studied medicine carry weight with all or most people, whether or not the doctor himself has already acquired a reputation as a doctor. This is because medicine is itself an acknowledged craft, a recognized area of expertise. Hence, if a person can show that he has been trained as a doctor, that is enough (everything else being equal) to guarantee that all or most answerers would accept his opinion on medical matters.

Of course, someone can be wise without being a practitioner of a recognized craft. But his epistemic authority cannot then flow from that of his craft and his training in it. Nor is it enough that he actually be wise. If his opinions are to have any cachet with all or most answerers, they must recognize him as a wise person. In other words, like Solon or Thales, he must be *notable* for his wisdom, he must have a *reputation* as a wise man-hence the reference to notability and reputation in the relevant clause of the definition of *endoxa*. Of course, if a proposition is held by all or most of the wise, it will very likely be held by someone whom all or most admirers recognize as someone notable for his wisdom.

The difference between the *endoxa* characterized in (A) and those characterized in (D) is, therefore, this: some of the *endoxa* characterized in (A) are accepted by all or most answerers, because they are accepted by someone whose epistemic authority flows from his reputation for wisdom. Those characterized in (D) are accepted because they are accepted by someone whose epistemic authority stems, not from his reputation, but from his having been trained in an acknowledge area of expertise.

Some of the *endoxa* characterized in (A) and all of those characterized in (D) are therefore indirect *endoxa*: they are (or would be) accepted by all or most answerers, because they are accepted by someone whose authority such people recognize. But the other *endoxa* characterized in (A) are direct: they are accepted on other grounds. The epistemic credentials of indirect *endoxa* are as unproblematic as those of the crafts and sciences themselves.

7

Aristotle and Moral Education in Philosophy

Introduction

Ethical activity is not a mere means to other goods; so there is no convincing defence of it that can be given to those who see no intrinsic value in it. Aristotle therefore comes to the conclusion that it is fruitless to address his lectures to everyone capable of following an argument. Recognizing the limitations of his theory, he restricts his audience to those who have already decided to lead a life of virtue.

But now consider another passage—this time, one that is not so well-known or strategically positioned. At *Politics VII.*13 Aristotle says that people 'do many things contrary to their habits and their nature, because of reason, if they are persuaded that it is better to do otherwise'. The statement is a conditional: *if* they are persuaded, they will contravene their nature and their habits. But Aristotle would not have bothered to formulate this conditional if he had thought that its antecedent were never true. So he seems to be saying that in some cases those who have received an inadequate moral training listen to argument, become convinced that they have deficiencies, and change their ways, resisting the force of habit. Note that he is not limiting himself to a statement about what reason *can* do; he says that people *do* suppress their habits, because they are persuaded to change. But if this is what he means, then why does he not admit morally defective people to his classroom and address his lectures to them? Perhaps they can never become perfect, because even if he persuades them that the virtuous life is best, the effects of their early habits can never be entirely eliminated, and they will always suffer from the tension between the rational part of their soul and the emotions produced by their early training. Even so, it is hard to deny that there would be at least some improvement in their condition if they could be persuaded of the correct theory of the good, and were to put this theory into practice. If Aristotle is optimistic about the power of reason to reverse the force of habit, it is curious that he has no interest in trying to achieve these gains.

Our first passage suggests that Aristotle has modest expectations of what can be rationally established by moral philosophy. The second suggests the opposite, and it leads us to wonder why he is so restrictive in the first. Clearly, one of the interpretations proposed must be modified or rejected. In fact, I will argue that we should reject both. It is a mistake to infer from the second passage that, according to Aristotle, even those who have been badly brought up are capable of being persuaded by his ethical arguments. As I will try to show, he thinks that such people have a deficiency that makes them incapable of properly assessing ethical arguments. This is precisely what he is alluding to in the first passage. Those who are badly educated have failed to perceive a sufficient number of moral facts, and their narrow experience will lead them to reject the conclusions he comes to. At the same time, we should not take him to be conceding in the first passage that there are limitations in the arguments he uses. The reason why he excludes the badly trained from his lectures is not that he will be using premisses they have no reason to accept. On the contrary, his methodology leaves him free to search for premisses that *ought* to be accepted by everyone, not merely by those who have been well brought up. He restricts his audience to the well-trained because of the inadequacies of the poorly trained, not because he concedes that there are limitations in the arguments he uses.

To understand Aristotle's reason for addressing a restricted audience, we must consider a distinction he observes between arguments (*logoi*) and facts (*erga*). This contrast occurs in *NE* X. 1, where he mentions two groups of thinkers who say that pleasure is bad. Some sincerely hold this position, having been persuaded that it is true; but others say that pleasure is bad without believing it, because they think it will benefit most people to hear pleasure attacked. Aristotle then states his opposition to this strategy:

For arguments (*logoi*) about what has to do with feelings and actions are less persuasive (*pistoi*) than facts (*erga*). So when they clash with what accords with perception (*aisthçsis*), they are regarded with contempt, and furthermore they destroy the truth.

He then predicts that the strategy will backfire: when someone attacks pleasure and is then seen to pursue it, people will infer not simply that he takes *this* pleasure to be good, but that he takes *all* pleasure to be good. And Aristotle then commends 'true arguments' for their usefulness: since 'they harmonize with the facts (*erga*), they are believed, and for that reason they incline those who understand them to live in accordance with them'.

Here he is making two points. First, when we ask ourselves what we should accept in the field of ethics, we should not confine ourselves to examining arguments. We must also pay attention to facts, which are obtained by means of perception. Second, it is possible for arguments to conflict with facts, and when they do so, we should continue to believe the facts and infer that the arguments are bad. It is this second point that is especially noteworthy, for it will prove helpful in understanding why Aristotle limits his lectures to the well-educated. Here in X. 1, he unequivocally assigns arguments a subordinate role in the conduct of ethical life. He does not say (although we may wish he had) that when arguments conflict with the facts of perception, we must go back and forth between them, making adjustments or determining, case by case, which is more credible. Rather, he proposes a one-sided solution to such conflicts: the arguments must go, and the facts must remain.

This is not the only passage in which he proposes this methodology; the same point is made in *NE* X. 8. After noting that his arguments regarding happiness are in accord with certain statements made by the wise, he adds that although such things are persuasive (*pistin*), 'the truth in practical matters is judged from the facts (*erga*) and from life (*bios*); for these are authoritative (*kurion*)'. And then he spells out the meaning of such authority: whatever conflicts with the facts must be rejected.

Part of what Aristotle is saying here has long been familiar to students of his thought, because he calls attention to it in the methodological remarks cited at the beginning of this essay: in moral philosophy, we do not start from scratch, but from what we know (1095b3-6). Although it is the job of moral theory to seek arguments, there are certain truths we are already aware of before we begin our study of the subject, because we are familiar with the material it discusses. What seems to have escaped the attention of scholars is his thesis that part of what we start with propositions stating perceived facts must not be revised, even if we are presented with arguments that contradict them. If we are ever faced with such arguments, we must say that there is a flaw in them somewhere–either in the premisses or in the inference—because the conclusion must be rejected. If, for example, we are presented with arguments that conclude that all pleasures are bad, we know that something has gone wrong, because we have experienced pleasures, and know that some are good. Of course, *good* arguments would not have arrived at that conclusion, and the most desirable way of proceeding in ethical theory (as in any other subject) would be to consider only good arguments. But Aristotle's point about the need to rely on facts as a check against arguments shows that in his opinion no method that evaluates arguments without paying attention to facts is guaranteed never to produce a bad argument.

Aristotle's method of examining arguments is set out in the following familiar statement in *NE* VII.:

> *As in the other cases we must set out the appearances, and first of all go through the puzzles. In this way we must prove the reputable opinions* (endoxa) *ideally, all of them, but if not all, then most, and the most authoritative* (kuriotata). *For if the objections are solved, and the reputable opinions are left, it will be an adequate proof.*

Can we find in this anything that corresponds to his thesis that arguments must give way to facts, when they conflict? It might be thought that he is making precisely this point when he says that if we cannot prove all of the *endoxa*, then we should prove the ones that are most authoritative. I doubt, however, that this is the proper interpretation, and will soon present an alternative. But notice that even if we read *VII.* in this way, we should recognize that determining what the authoritative *endoxa* (i.e. the facts) are is not a matter to be settled by assessing the persuasiveness of competing arguments; rather, it is something that is already known to us, before we begin examining arguments. Otherwise, everything in Aristotle's methodology would be absorbed under the heading of argumentation, and he would have no way of making his point that arguments must be rejected if they conflict with the facts.

There is another way of reading our passage, however. We can say that in *VII.* Aristotle is not giving a complete account of proper methodology, because he thinks that, in addition to going through the puzzles and sifting through *endoxa*, we must check our results to make sure that they are in harmony with the facts. On this interpretation, the most authoritative *endoxa* are not to be identified with the facts, although both must be preserved. This, I think, is the better reading. Aristotle seems to be telling us how to examine arguments so as to come to a conclusion. What we seek to do when we study puzzles and *endoxa* is to find *proofs*: the passage twice uses this term. And of course a proof is a *logos*—something Aristotle contrasts with *erga*, facts. In considering puzzles, we typically examine opposing arguments and look for ways of salvaging what we can from the conflicting viewpoints. But an *ergon*, or fact, is not an argument or a conclusion arrived at by argument, but something that is to be used as a check on arguments.

Furthermore, the passage from *NE* X. That we considered earlier strongly implies that the *erga* are something that we perceive or in some way observe: arguments that 'clash with what accords with perception (*aisthçsis*)' that is, facts are to be rejected. But perception seems to be a way of ascertaining the truth that differs from the method advocated in VII. In that passage, we are told to ascertain the reputable opinions the views held by the many or the wise and to preserve as many of them as we can. To survey these beliefs is to listen to *logoi*; this is not the same process as perceiving the facts. For example, someone who has never experienced pleasure can still ascertain the reputable opinions about it; and similarly, someone who has experienced pleasure (a child, for example) might be ignorant about what is said about it by the many and the wise. Note that Aristotle's discussion of pleasure seems to separate these two processes—examining the *endoxa* and checking arguments against the perceived facts. He begins by remarking, in X. that those who condemn all pleasures are refuted by facts that we can perceive; and then in X. He begins his examination of the reputable opinions about pleasure. We already know, before we examine these conflicting views, that pleasure is not always bad, because we have experienced it. Similarly, in X. When Aristotle warns us that we should always make sure our arguments accord with 'facts and life', he clearly distinguishes between this way of finding the truth and the method of examining *endoxa*. For he makes his point about checking arguments against facts *after* he has assured us that his arguments about the good are in harmony with the opinions of the wise in other words, *after* he says that he has preserved the *endoxa*. The way he defends his own conception of happiness indicates that there is something more to be done in the study of ethics than work through puzzles and preserve reputable opinions; the conclusions one arrives at by these methods must also be checked against the facts.

There are two further points that should be noticed before we move on. The first is that on my reading Aristotle rejects a methodological thesis, sometimes called 'fallibilism', that is now widely accepted. To be a fallibilist is to hold that no matter how obvious or well founded our beliefs may seem, none should be held immune from revision. For there is always the possibility that new data or arguments will be discovered, and upon reconsideration the balance of reasons may require us to change our minds. So defined, fallibilism is embedded in Rawls's method of 'reflective equilibrium', a process of searching for general principles that cohere with more specific 'provisional fixed points', about which we feel confident. Rawls's idea is that some of our pre-theoretical judgements are relatively secure and can be used in theory construction, but that as our theory grows in strength, it might provide us with reason to give up some of the views we initially took for granted. The 'fixed points' we start with are none the less called 'provisional', because they are never so well grounded that we can make them immune from reconsideration. We cannot know with certainty that we will never be presented with arguments that require a revision in views that now seem assured.

Fallibilism in general, and the method of reflective equilibrium in particular, may seem so reasonable to us that we pay insufficient attention to those parts of Aristotle's philosophy that are incompatible with them. Perhaps that is one reason why a great deal of attention has been paid to the methodological passage of *NE* VII. for here Aristotle makes it explicit that although we would like to preserve as many *endoxa* as we can, we may in the end have to reject some of them. When we work through the arguments, some views that had some initial plausibility may have to be rejected. The point we must bear in mind, however, is that although Aristotle is willing to reject some of the *endoxa*, there are other initial assumptions the perceived facts that he says we should never reject.

The second point to notice is that Aristotle's doctrine that in ethics facts have priority over arguments is paralleled by similar methodological remarks of his about inquiry in other areas. For example, in *Generation of Animals III.* 10. 760b27-33 he says that the facts (*sumbainonta*) about the generation of bees have not yet been sufficiently ascertained, but that when they are, one should rely more on perception than on arguments (*logoi*), and should accept only those arguments that agree with what is observed (*phainomena*). Similarly, we are told in the *Prior Analytics* that it was only after sufficient astronomical phenomena had been grasped that demonstrations of the truths of astronomy were found; in general, Aristotle says, the principles (*archai*) of every science are given by experience. It is on these grounds that he criticizes, in the *De caelo*, the Platonic theory of elemental transformation: Platonists defend their theses at all costs, not realizing that a theory of nature must be accountable to what is observed. In the study of both nature and politics, there is a range of observations that the successful student must make initially, and the arguments that are constructed in each field must be kept in check by surrendering to the data when they conflict with them.

We should now turn to a question that will lead us back to the passage with which we began: according to Aristotle, what sort of person makes the ethical observations that serve as a check on ethical theory? Does every rational being perceive the moral facts? Or do only some have these perceptions—namely, those who have been well brought up and have started to acquire the ethical virtues?

Nearly every human being, including children, has experienced pleasure, and is therefore in a position to reject arguments that try to show that all pleasures are bad. So, clearly, Aristotle does not believe that virtuous people have a monopoly on the perceptions that control theorizing. None the less, he might think that some people—namely, those who develop bad moral habits perceive so few ethical facts that they cannot make a proper study of ethical theory. Notice how natural it would be for Aristotle to come to this conclusion. For ethical facts play the same role in political theory as do botanical or zoological phenomena in theories of nature; and it is only those who have made a special effort to perceive the phenomena in these fields who possess enough facts to proceed to theory construction. And surely, in Aristotle's opinion, not every human being has made a serious effort to ascertain all the moral facts.

Furthermore, if ethical facts were trivialities compatible with any possible ethical theory, they would not enable us to discriminate between rival theories. It would be no accomplishment for a theory to harmonize with the facts, and Aristotle's advice to test theories against the facts would be irrelevant. And since ethical facts must be significant truths, we can understand why it might be doubted that they are perceived by just anyone. We should not be surprised to find Aristotle saying that morally deficient people fail to perceive them. Rather, he must mean that it is the kind of life one lives that gives one the experience of facts with which arguments must harmonize. Here *bios* of course refers to a specific way of life; Aristotle does not mean that merely being alive gives one perception of moral facts. Furthermore, he cannot mean that the arguments he gives in defence of his conception of happiness are in harmony with the kind of life led by those who, like Thrasymachus and Callicles, advocate injustice. Rather, he must be saying that when those who had been well brought up judge his arguments 'from the facts and from life', they will accept his conclusions.

We can now return to the passage with which we started, for this provides the strongest textual support for supposing that it is only a certain kind of person who recognizes a sufficient number of moral facts. Recall the context: Aristotle distinguishes in *NE I.* 4 between two kinds of starting-points: those that are already known to us at the beginning of our study of ethics, which we use as the basis of our theorizing, and those that are not yet known to us at the beginning, but must be worked towards (1095a32-b4). Having said this, Aristotle next makes the point that students of ethics must have been brought up in good habits if they are to profit from their study of the subject. Clearly what he means is that it is *by* being brought up well that we acquire the starting-points of the subject. And there would be no point in saying this unless he were assuming that those who are badly brought up do not acquire these starting-points.

It is not clear whether the starting-points Aristotle refers to here are simply the facts he refers to later when he says that arguments must be tested against facts. Perhaps the class of starting-points is larger than the class of facts: it may include not only the facts one perceives by leading a certain kind of life, but also the *endoxa* the opinions of the wise and the many that ethical theory ought to preserve so far as possible. But in any case, the facts must be among the starting-points, because, as we have seen, they are acquired not as a result of argument but through perception and by living one's life in a certain way. One cannot acquire them by entering into argument, because they are the means by which arguments are tested. So it is plausible to take Aristotle to be saying that one must come to ethical theory already knowing moral facts: these are the touchstones of moral theory, since they must never give way to argument; and the ethically uneducated are handicapped students of the subject, because they fail to perceive them.

Aristotle's procedure may arouse this misgiving: by assuming from the start that ethical theory must harmonize with facts accessible only to the virtuous, is he not begging the question against those who doubt the value of the virtues? He assumes that in order to acquire the moral facts one must lead a certain kind of life, and then concludes, unsurprisingly, that one should lead that kind of life. Is he not moving in a circle?

I will return to this issue in the final section, but we can see the beginnings of a defence of Aristotle if we first raise this question: what facts does he have in mind when he says that they are perceived only by those who have been well brought up? I propose the following hypothesis: what those who are well brought up see is that the virtuous actions they perform are intrinsically desirable, pleasant, and noble. They do not experience good action as a burden, something to be undertaken solely for its external rewards. Just as all people feel the attraction of pleasure and do not need a theory to see that at least some of it is desirable, so those who are well educated recognize, by forming certain habits, that virtuous actions are in themselves appealing. By contrast, those who form bad moral habits fail to experience virtuous activity in this way, and treat it as a hindrance or a mere means to more important goods.

If this is what Aristotle means, then we can explain why one must have these data if one is to be a good student of ethics. Ethical theory is a search for the ultimate end, and one of the properties of an ultimate end is that it is desirable in itself. What Aristotle is proposing, then, is that one must come to the subject with an adequate conception, based on one's experience of life, of which items are desirable in themselves. It is not easy to see how someone who has an impoverished conception of intrinsic goods could cure this deficiency by engaging in reasoning. How, for example, could an argument prove to someone who does not feel the attraction of pleasure that it should be desired *for itself*? Someone who lacked this experience would rightly doubt any argument for this conclusion. Similarly, Aristotle holds that there is no persuasive argument for the conclusion that virtuous acts are in themselves desirable. That is why he thinks that those who are badly brought up make poor students of ethics. They come to the subject with too limited a conception of what is valuable; in fact, the very thing that will turn out to be the ultimate end is something they are unequipped to consider as a candidate, because they cannot recognize its intrinsic value.

This gives Aristotle the beginnings of a defence against the charge that he is begging the question against moral sceptics, and is merely presupposing what he needs to prove. He does start with the assumption that virtuous activity is good in itself, but that is a weak assumption, and falls far short of what he needs to prove. For many other items are desirable in themselves honours, amusements, pleasures, and so on. So the facts perceived only by those who are well brought up that virtuous activities are intrinsically desirable do not show that such activities have greater worth than many other sorts of goods. It is the job of ethical theory to move from the assumption that virtuous action is a good to the conclusion that it is *the* good; making that assumption by no means guarantees that one will find good arguments for that conclusion.

This does not completely rescue Aristotle from the charge that he is begging the question against the sceptic. For it may still be asked: why should ethical theory build on the experience of the good, rather than the experience of the bad? Might not the perceptions of the bad be accurate, when they report that they find virtuous activity to be unpleasant and burdensome? What entitles Aristotle to assume that when they say this, they are failing to perceive what is really there? I will return to this issue later.

What I have said so far puts us in a better position to understand a general theme that runs throughout Aristotle's moral philosophy. In many passages, he expresses the idea that in order to discover how to lead our lives, it is not sufficient that we reason well, since reasoning must always start somewhere, and it can only have a successful outcome if it manages to start in the right place. Where reasoning starts makes a great difference, and since it cannot be reasoning itself that determines where it starts, it must rely on something other than itself. Practical thought must therefore take its starting-point from ethical virtue, since that is the excellence of the part of the soul that begins its education before we have developed our ability to make reasoned decisions

This, I think, is the underlying idea behind the following well-known passage:

> *For virtue preserves the starting-point, but vice destroys it; and in actions, that for the sake of which is the starting-point, just as the hypotheses are the startingpoints of mathematics. In neither that case nor this does reason teach about the starting-points. Rather, it is virtue, either natural or habituated, that teaches correct belief about the starting-point.*

It is natural to be puzzled by this statement, because it seems at odds with Aristotle's own practice. When he reflects on the proper function of human beings, in *NE I.* 7, he appears to be giving an argument for adopting virtuous activity as our ultimate end; and similarly, in X. 7-8, he gives several reasons for identifying perfect happiness with contemplation. Why then does he say in this passage that it is virtue rather than reason that 'teaches correct belief about the starting-point'?

His meaning, I suggest, is that ethical inquiry does not give students a new end, but instead gives them a better understanding of an end they already have. Virtuous activity is already one of the things they find desirable in itself, and ethical arguments do not, and cannot, try to show that they are right to do so. The starting-point about which they have already acquired correct belief is ethical activity, and what they correctly believe about it is that it is good in itself. Just as the truth of the basic hypotheses in mathematics cannot be derived from other hypotheses (otherwise they would not be basic), so there is a truth about the highest practical principle that it is desirable in itself that cannot be demonstrated by showing how it leads to other goods. For obviously any argument that shows how it leads to other goods fails to demonstrate that it is good *in itself*.

The general theme that reasoning rests on unreasoned assumptions is also expressed by a statement Aristotle repeatedly makes about practical wisdom: 'Our function is achieved both through practical wisdom and through ethical virtue. For virtue makes the goal right, whereas practical wisdom makes what serves the goal right'. Here too one may raise the same puzzle: Aristotle himself has used reason to discover what the correct goal is, and surely in doing so he has exercised an intellectual virtue. Why, then, does he assign excellence in practical reasoning a more restricted role, giving ethical virtue something that does not reason the job of making the end correct, and leaving practical wisdom the subordinate role of finding what promotes the goal?

To these questions, we can reply: in order to acquire practical wisdom, one must already have perceived certain facts, and one must have been educated in the virtues in order to have these perceptions. Those who have been properly educated already have some knowledge of the end: they know virtuous activity and its intrinsic goodness. But it is because they have been brought up in a certain way, not because they have considered certain arguments, that they have this knowledge. So virtue makes their goal correct in the following sense: it is because they have been properly trained (not because they have reasoned in a certain way) that they come to ethical theory with virtuous activity as one of their goals; and it is because they already have this goal when they become students of ethics that they are able to conduct a proper examination of the ultimate end.

Aristotle must be taken to mean that the kind of virtue one has when one first approaches ethical theory—the kind that makes the goal correct—is not complete ethical virtue, because it has not yet been integrated with practical wisdom. Practical wisdom and complete ethical virtue are acquired only after one has finished one's ethical inquiry, and achieved a full understanding of the ultimate end. And even then it has not reached its fullest development. For practical wisdom is also a skill that enables one to see what best serves one's ends in particular circumstances; if one knows only what goals one should seek, but not how to achieve them, then one is not yet wise. This too is part of the point Aristotle is making when he says that 'virtue makes the goal right, whereas practical wisdom makes what serves the goal right'. The job of practical wisdom is to take us all the way from the initial material we have when we start our inquiry about the human good to the discovery of what to do in particular circumstances; it is not yet practical wisdom until it reaches that final stage. So it cannot be his intention in this passage to deny to practical wisdom the job of giving a reasoned defence of a specific conception of happiness. Rather, his implicit point is that if we have only done that, but have not yet filled out that conception in so much detail that we know how to act on it, then we have not yet achieved practical wisdom.

Aristotle's theory of moral education allows him to explain why his conception of happiness is not more widely accepted. He acknowledges that those who are misguided about the proper ends of human life are in some respects good at practical reasoning: by admitting that they can be clever, he concedes that they can skillfully use reason to achieve their ends. But that admission raises the question of why they use reasoning well to find means to their ends, but do not use reasoning well to discover what the right ends are. Since they are sometimes good at reasoning, why might they not follow and accept the arguments that Aristotle presents for his conception of happiness?

It may be tempting to reply on his behalf. 'They have no trouble following the argument, but when they reach the conclusion, they refuse to accept it, and claim that something must have gone wrong. And so they are biased against the conclusion, and refuse to give the argument a fair hearing.' This, however, cannot be Aristotle's diagnosis, because, as we have seen, he himself accepts a methodology that requires one to reject a conclusion when it contradicts what one has learned from one's experience of life. So he cannot count someone who does that as biased, and he cannot explain why his conclusions are rejected by saying that others are prejudiced against his position. Instead, he must say that his arguments are rejected because of the poverty of their experience and their moral perceptions. They are like people who theorize about astronomical phenomena without having made enough observations. When those who are inexperienced in this way fail to arrive at the right theory, we do not diagnose their failure as a lack of reasoning skill because that would imply that if they were smarter, they would have compensated for their lack of experience. Similarly, Aristotle holds that it is an improper early education, not a lack of skill in reasoning, that accounts for the fact that some people fail to discover what the goal of life is.

But he is not taking the general position that changing one's mind about moral issues is impossible, that one must for ever accept whatever moral beliefs one acquired at an earlier point in one's life. People can listen to arguments and be persuaded that the habits that they have acquired are bad ones; Aristotle acknowledges this in one of the passages cited at the beginning of this essay. Recall his statement in *Politics VII.* 13 that people 'do many things contrary to their habits and their nature, because of reason, if they are persuaded that it is better to do otherwise'. What we must now recognize is that this statement is open to a number of different interpretations. Aristotle might mean: (A) some who have been brought up well have been persuaded by bad arguments that they have overvalued the virtues; (B) some who have been brought up badly have been persuaded by good arguments that they have undervalued the virtues; or (C) both. But there is reason to doubt that he intends (B). For if he accepts it, then it is mysterious why he does not address his arguments to everyone, not just to those who have been well educated. If arguments have in the past made bad people realize that their habits were bad, then is it not worth continuing to make this effort?

There is no similar basis, however, for being doubtful about (A). Consider someone who has been well brought up and loves virtue for itself. When he starts to talk about ethics with others, and hears dialectical debates about ethical topics, there is no guarantee that he will not begin to question the moral beliefs he has acquired. And if he is the sort of person who follows the argument wherever it leads, he may be persuaded—if he reasons badly that the virtues exist only by convention, or that virtue is generally good for others, but contrary to one's own good. Of course, if he has been corrupted in this way by bad arguments, then he has failed to follow Aristotle's methodology; for, as we have seen, Aristotle holds that arguments must be rejected when they conflict with the facts one perceives. But it is certainly possible for people to be brought up well and to fall into error because they do not accept Aristotle's methodology.

Nonetheless, it may seem a curious asymmetry that Aristotle should hold (A) but reject (B). Why should he think that good habits can be undermined by reasoning, but not bad habits? I suggest the following explanation: Aristotle thinks that when people develop bad moral habits, they also develop a certain attitude towards reasoning: namely, that its proper role is that of an instrument for the satisfaction of one's appetites and passions. And so even if they listen to arguments about the proper ends of life, they do so as a sport, and they do not take seriously the possibility that reason can discover that some ends are more worthwhile than others. Their habits thus ensure that they will never seriously re-evaluate the worth of their ends. By contrast, those who have been well brought up have been trained to look upon reason not merely as an instrument to be used for other purposes, but as something that is worthy in itself. And if they have not reflected on the proper relation between arguments and perceptions, they are vulnerable to a certain error: they trust reason wherever it leads, even when it supports conclusions that clash with their moral perceptions.

The danger that one may be corrupted by argument is a familiar theme in ancient philosophy, for this is precisely the question raised by the activity of Socrates and the sophists. We should recall what Plato says about the issue in the *Republic*:

> *When young boys get a taste of arguments for the first time, they mistreat them, as though it were a game, and bring them into contradiction. And when they have refuted many, and have been refuted by many, they fall hard and fast into believing nothing that they believed before. The result is that they themselves and everything that pertains to philosophy are discredited by others.*

Here Plato seems to be implicitly criticizing Socrates for corrupting the young. If one introduces students to ethics at too early an age, and demands reasons for traditional beliefs, one taps a well of contentiousness, and all convictions are abandoned. To avoid this, Plato prescribes that in the ideal city the study of the good will be postponed to a later stage of life. But to anyone who is seriously concerned about the corrosive power of reason, Plato's solution may seem shallow. Intellectual belligerence is not found only in the young. And in any case, merely waiting for students to mature will not immunize them against the kind of intellectualism that makes some people follow the argument wherever it leads, even when it leads to absurd or repugnant conclusions. So it is a plausible conjecture that one motive that lies behind Aristotle's methodology is his desire to keep the philosophical study of the good from having a corrosive effect. In *his* classroom, the perception of moral facts always serves as a check on arguments, and so the danger that philosophy will be discredited as a destructive moral force is eliminated.

We have come to a surprising conclusion in our interpretation of Aristotle's statement that people 'do many things contrary to their habits and their nature, because of reason, if they are persuaded that it is better to do otherwise'. One's first inclination when reading this is to take him to be glorifying reason, by noting its power to rule over nature and habit. What we have learned, however, is that, on the contrary, he thinks something has gone wrong with reason when it rebels against both nature and habit. Our nature gives us the perception that pleasure is at least sometimes good; and if we have been properly habituated, we perceive the goodness, pleasure, and nobility of virtuous action. The task of reason is to build on these perceptions, because if it does not anchor itself in experience, it runs the risk of corrupting, rather than perfecting, us. We are not used to thinking of Aristotle as someone who harbours misgivings about argumentation; but his many statements about reason's need to rely on unreason provide abundant evidence of his fear that the intellect unaided will go astray.

We can now return to the passage with which we began and apply our interpretation to it. We have learned to avoid two errors that can be made about Aristotle's meaning when he says that 'we need to have been brought up in fine habits, if we are to be adequate students' of ethics.

First, we might take him to be admitting that it is impossible to find arguments that have persuasive force against people like Thrasymachus and Callicles, who question traditional moral beliefs. And this, it might be said, is because in his opinion there are no premisses acceptable to all rational human beings that lead to the conclusion that the best life must be ethical. Realizing this, Aristotle looks for premisses that are accepted by, or acceptable to, those who have the ethical virtues, and he shows that these premisses support the conclusion that their lives are good ones.

We should now be able to see that Aristotle is not limiting his arguments in this way. For the methodology we have ascribed to him places no restrictions on what sorts of premisses are to be used in ethical arguments. When he restricts his audience to the virtuous, he leaves himself free to use premisses that are, or ought to be, acceptable to anyone capable of following an argument. And if he can show from such premisses that the best life consists in ethical activity, then that conclusion ought to be accepted by everyone. Nonetheless, he assumes that those who have been badly brought up will not accept such arguments. They will steadfastly insist that there must be something wrong with the premisses or the reasoning, because the conclusion conflicts with the kind of life they lead. And in saying this, they assume a methodology that Aristotle himself accepts. But this still allows him to say that a personal deficiency underlies the moral sceptic's rejection of good arguments. The sceptic need not have the wrong methodology, but he does have too little experience of the moral facts, and this is why he is unable to recognize good moral reasoning when it is presented to him.

The analogy with the study of nature, used earlier, helps clarify the situation. Consider people whose false conception of the heavens is based largely on traditional myths, and who have made few observations of astronomical phenomena. Assume that they reject scientific arguments whose conclusions conflict with their picture of the universe, because they are not familiar with the facts those arguments presuppose. Our inability to reach them through argument ought to place no restriction whatsoever on the sorts of premisses we use in astronomy. We would not say that arguments in astronomy are limited to showing that certain things are true according to the perspective of astronomy students; there is no basis for such perspectival talk.

What we should say is not that Aristotle's *premisses* are restricted to those that are acceptable to people who have been well brought up, but that his *conclusions* are restricted in certain ways. If his arguments had led to the conclusion that virtue is at best of instrumental value, those who have been well brought up would rightly object that there must be something wrong with the premisses or the inferences, because the conclusion violates facts that they perceive. The arguments are restricted to the good because only they are in a position to test the arguments by appealing to the facts.

We have also learned to avoid a second way of misunderstanding Aristotle's statement that good students of ethics must have been brought up well. We might take him to propose this restriction because he wants an audience that is committed to accepting ethical arguments wherever they lead, and he thinks that those who are badly trained will be biased: when they listen to arguments that lead to conclusions conflicting with their way of life, they will not have an open mind and will not give them a fair hearing.

What this interpretation misses is that, for Aristotle, the construction and evaluation of moral theories requires something more than rationality, familiarity with common beliefs, and an open mind. In addition, one must have perceived the moral facts. So Aristotle cannot express his criticism of the morally uneducated too abstractly: he cannot say that because they reject arguments that conflict with their way of life, they are biased. Rather, his criticism must be that they fail to perceive the moral facts, and are therefore in a poor position to evaluate moral arguments. They are excluded from his lecture room not because their reason is weak (they can be extremely clever) or because they reject conclusions that do not harmonize with their experience (that is no deficiency), but because their experience is so limited that they wrongly reject good arguments.

Aristotle's lectures, then, are not addressed to all rational agents, because it takes more than rationality to assess ethical arguments, just as it takes more than rationality to assess theories about the heavens. They are addressed to those who are not only rational but also ethical, because only they have perceived the facts by which ethical arguments are tested.

There is one final issue that must be addressed. It may seem that if my interpretation is correct, then Aristotle has assumed without argument that ethical activity is good in itself, that those who experience it as such are right, and that those who have no such perception are missing something. Does this not simply beg the question against the moral sceptic? Why should we not take seriously the possibility that the intrinsic goodness of virtue is just a prejudice of the virtuous, and that those who see virtue as a mere means are the ones who perceive the moral facts?

I suggest that Aristotle would have this to say: if the perceptions of the good were not perceptions at all, but false appearances, then we would find some indication of this when we construct an ethical theory. As it turns out, a theory can be developed that fits the ethical facts well; the *Nicomachean Ethics* is just such a theory. When we look for arguments that show that an ethical life is best, we find them, and those arguments survive our best methodological tests. It is no trivial matter to construct such a theory, and our success entitles us to be confident that when we approached ethical theory with certain assumptions, we were moving in the right direction. Since all has gone smoothly, there is no reason to doubt that what we take to be perceptions of the facts really are perceptions, and not misapprehensions.

All this would be put in doubt if those whom Aristotle regards as bad people were to develop their own successful arguments and theories—theories that differed from Aristotle's and that matched the appearances with which they began. In that case, he would have to face the difficult problem of evaluating two rival theories, each backed by what are claimed to be facts. But as he saw the situation, those who are badly brought up have no such theories. They have no interest in the difficult intellectual task of developing systematic conceptions of goodness, character, friendship, pleasure, constitutional design, and the rest of practical philosophy. All that they have are their appearances: some things seem good to them, others bad or indifferent. Aristotle has no reason to be concerned with opponents who have nothing more to say than this. Theories must fit the perceived facts or be rejected, but successful theory construction allows us to answer those who claim that the facts are whatever appears to them.

8

Aristotle and The Uses of Logic in Philosophy

Introduction

Aristotle was rightly proud of his discovery, and so it is not surprising that he greatly overestimated its power, apparently thinking that syllogistic would be sufficient to represent the deductive structure of demonstrative sciences, including geometry or mathematics in general. It is only natural that the modern logicians who vindicated Aristotle's position in the history of their subject should have gone on to find Aristotle also pursuing other interests of his modern successors, such as proof theory and other parts of logical theory. For example, Jonathan Lear in his *Aristotle and Logical Theory* sets out to show that Aristotle was 'not only the father of logic, but also the (grand)father of metalogic'; and an article by Robin Smith describes "'Aristotle as Proof Theorist'". I do not wish to deny that these subjects can be found in the *Analytics*, but it seems to me that some of his more recent commentators have been inclined to ascribe to Aristotle an interest in the formal theory of deduction independent of the wider purposes of the *Analytics*, thus painting him as more of a logician in the modern sense than he probably was.

Just as there was a dispute in late antiquity over whether logic was a part or merely an instrument of philosophy, So there is some uneasiness today about whether logic properly belongs to philosophy or not. Logic has developed into a formidable technical discipline that may perhaps better be seen as a branch of mathematics—certainly one needs to be a trained mathematician to do any significant work in the field. But most philosophy departments still require their students to take at least a course in elementary logic. Even if the connection between informal argument and formal logic has become harder to see, it is still the case that we need a clear understanding of such notions as consistency, inference, and validity; and though philosophical arguments usually are not deductive proofs, they had better not be logical fallacies. Furthermore, formalization can often help us to clarify distinctions that are hard to detect in ordinary language, even if we do not believe that formalized languages are in some way better or more scientific than natural ones. So a part of logic, at least, continues to be an instrument of philosophy or rather, of any discipline that makes use of reasoning and argument.

Aristotle was interested both in logic as a theory and in its more humdrum uses in philosophical, or indeed everyday, argument, and more than half of the text of the *Prior Analytics* is concerned with the uses of logic in argument, rather than with either the exposition of a formal system or what we would call logical theory. This is what one should expect, since Aristotle invented formal logic for the purposes of his general theory of argument, not just as a formal theory of deductive proof or an 'underlying logic' for demonstrative science. In order to show how the perspective of a general theory of argument differs from that of logical theory, I will argue that although syllogistic can be shown to be complete in the modern logician's sense, it was not considered by its author to be complete in the sense relevant to his project. A deduction system is complete in the modern sense if it allows one to deduce all (and only) the valid formulae. What Aristotle had in mind when he set out to show that 'every deductive argument (*sullogismos*) is in one of the (syllogistic) figures'

(A23. 40b20-2) was the claim that every valid deductive argument can be formulated as one or more syllogisms in the narrow sense. This, as Aristotle recognized, is not the case (A44. 50b2-3). However, I will also argue that he thought syllogistic captured at least a necessary component of every valid deductive argument, and perhaps that it was indeed sufficient as an account of the logical form of scientific demonstration. Finally, I will illustrate the role of formal syllogistic in the theory of argument by a few examples from the second half of book A and from book B.

The system of syllogisms is introduced in *Prior Analytics* A4 as part of a general theory of valid deductive argument, more general than the theory of scientific proof, which is set out in the *Posterior Analytics*. Formal logic is only a part of such a general theory, and that is why, after presenting the system of syllogisms as an account of the valid forms of deductive argument, Aristotle goes on to discuss heuristics how to find premisses for theses that one wants to prove and what he calls analysis—that is, how to discover the syllogistic structure of premisses and terms in arguments formulated in ordinary language. The title of the whole work, "'*Analutika*'", refers to this part of the treatise, not the formal theory set out in its opening chapters. Much of book B can be seen as concerned with argumentative strategies and the detection of fallacies, and its last five chapters contain the sketch of a theory of rhetorical argument. So although the introductory lines of the *Prior Analytics* describe the treatise as a preliminary to the treatment of demonstrative science, the general theory developed here should serve the practitioner of dialectic and rhetoric as well as the scientist or philosopher.

In the context of such a general theory, the system developed in A1-22 is only a beginning, not the complete account of valid deductive argument that Aristotle in his more optimistic moments claims to have found, and that too many of his later followers have taken it to be. We do not have to think that Aristotle would have agreed with the arguments which Alexander of Aphrodisias presents for not pursuing the subject of valid inference for its own sake. But it may be that Aristotle developed his formal theory only to the extent that he thought he needed it for his account of demonstration, leaving many loose ends that seem to have been picked up by his students Theophrastus and Eudemus. That may be the reason why, for example, he did work out a system of modal syllogistic, but did not try to offer a formal account of the second type of valid deductive argument he recognizes in A23 what he calls 'argument (syllogism) based on a hypothesis' although he saw that it was not covered by the system of the syllogistic figures.

The point that Aristotle himself considered his formal logic as incomplete may have been obscured by the fact that he actually purports to offer a completeness proof, and that the first half of this proof can be read as a completeness proof in the modern technical sense. In order to show in what sense formal syllogistic was not complete, then, I have to draw attention to some differences between the system of syllogisms as described and developed by Aristotle in *Prior Analytics* A1-7 and its best modern models.

I take it to be generally agreed by now that formal syllogistic is best represented as a system of natural deduction, rather than an axiomatized theory. Aristotle explicitly introduces all the elements of such a system, and several scholars have shown that within its limits it is complete—that is, allows one to deduce all and only the valid formulae. None the less, I think it is misleading to assume that Aristotle regarded formal syllogistic as a system of deductive inference. Although it would be correct to say that he uses such a system, it is not what he is talking about when he sets out to prove completeness, or when he shows, in A7, that all syllogistic moods can be reduced to the two universal moods of the first figure, rather than the four he had introduced as perfect in A4.

This is so because Aristotle is focusing on the notion of valid argument, not logical consequence or valid inference in general. His definition of 'syllogism' stipulates that a syllogism must have at least two premisses, and that the conclusion must not only follow, but also be different from the premisses. This shows, I think, that he thought of syllogisms as arguments or argument forms, not just valid deductions or inferences. The notion of a valid deductive argument may be hard to define precisely, but it is clear that it is narrower than the notion of a valid deduction. For example, any proposition can be validly deduced from itself, but no one would wish to present an inference of p from p as an argument. When Aristotle says, as he does several times, that nothing follows of necessity from a single proposition, he should not be taken to deny that any proposition implies itself, or to maintain that nothing can be inferred from a single premiss. After all, in A2 he actually proves the validity of four types of single-premiss inference: the conversion rules he is going to use in his proofs in A5 and 6. But he apparently thought that such inferences could not be used as arguments, because their conclusions would not state anything different from their premisses and hence they would be question-begging. The syllogistic moods *Barbara* and *Celarent* have a different status, and when it comes to showing that the two particular moods of the first figure can be reduced to them, Aristotle does not mention any of the other rules of his system, but speaks as though all syllogistic moods could be derived from *Barbara* and *Celarent* alone. So he is not trying to establish the minimal number of primitive rules of inference for the system he uses, but the number of primitive forms of argument presupposed by it. What he thought about the deduction rules—conversion, *reductio, ecthesis* we do not know, since he never discusses their status.

Again, the first half of the completeness proof in A23 takes the form of showing that any direct deductive argument with two or more syllogistic premisses can be transformed into a chain of two-premiss syllogisms which will therefore consist entirely of arguments in one of the syllogistic figures. This can be read as a completeness proof in the modern sense, but it is actually only one half of Aristotle's own purported proof. The second half sets out to show that all arguments 'based on a hypothesis' and most importantly, all *reductio* arguments will also fall into the figures; and this part is a failure. Aristotle first offers an analysis of hypothetical arguments according to which such arguments consist of a syllogistic deduction plus one more step, which he describes as 'based on a hypothesis'. This is the step that distinguishes hypothetical arguments from normal direct syllogisms. In the *reductio* arguments discussed almost exclusively in A23, the step would appear to be the move from '*p* implies a falsehood' to '*p* is false', and hence to the assertion of not-p. In the direct hypothetical arguments analysed in A44, the step seems to be, in modern parlance, an application of the rule of *modus ponens*. In any case, the hypothetical arguments are clearly not complete without the last step which leads to the conclusion, and so it is astonishing to see Aristotle assert, at the end of A23, that these arguments too will be in one of the figures. The most he can say at this point—and he has not proved that either is that such arguments must contain a syllogism in one of the figures. And at the end of A44 he does acknowledge that this type of argument cannot be analysed as a syllogism in the narrow sense.

With regard to the modern formal models of syllogistic, this should show that although the natural deduction system Aristotle uses can indeed be shown to be complete, Aristotle's syllogistic as a formal theory of valid deductive argument is not complete, and Aristotle did not think it was. The divergence between Aristotle and his modern commentators was, I think, because they treat *reductio* as a deduction rule, the validity of which need not be proved within the system. Aristotle so uses it himself in A2, 5, and 6, but in A23 he considers reductio as a distinct type of argument, and he is right in pointing out that it is not covered by the syllogistic moods. This is not a minor omission in Aristotle's projected theory. For it appears from A44 that the class of hypothetical arguments is supposed to contain most, if not all, of the argument forms treated in the *Topics*, and Aristotle emphasizes that these need to be investigated and clearly distinguished (50a39-40). But it seems that he left this task to his students.

Now the explicit recognition that hypothetical argument is not syllogistic comes much later than the completeness proof in A23, and so one might be tempted to fall back on a developmental explanation, saying that Aristotle believed what he claims in A23, and came to realize only later that hypothetical argument will not fit into the figures. But speculation about chronology should obviously be a last resort, and it would seem particularly implausible in this case. The *Analytics* are among the works that Aristotle himself cites by their traditional title, and though they obviously do not constitute a polished treatise, and do seem to contain sections (such as modal syllogistic) that were inserted into already existing drafts, there is good reason to think that it was Aristotle himself who put together the materials collected in the four books. Moreover, the argument of A23 actually shows that hypothetical arguments are not strictly speaking in the figures. Hence it seems more plausible to suppose that Aristotle was content with the weaker claim that every proof or every valid deductive argument must at least contain a syllogistic deduction. If this were true, then anyone who tried to produce a formally valid argument would need to rely on the syllogistic moods, even if the argument consisted of a hypothetical step in addition to the syllogism.

But why did Aristotle think that hypothetical arguments had to contain a syllogism in the narrow sense? This assumption appears unargued in both A23 and A44, and that in spite of the fact that the example Aristotle gives in A44 might actually be taken to show just the opposite. I think that the reason why Aristotle still thought he did not have to argue for his claim has to do with his conception of syllogistic necessity: he thought that the necessity that forces one to accept the conclusion of a hypothetical argument depends upon the necessity of the preceding syllogism.

Aristotle did not have the notion of a propositionally complex sentence or proposition. He thought that one should in principle be able to reformulate any given valid argument as a series of categorical propositions in which 'one thing is said of one thing'. Simple sentences are not contrasted with complex ones formed by logical connectives, such as conjunctions, conditionals, and so forth, but with sentences that express more than one categorical predication. For Aristotle, what we would call a 'conjunction' appears to be a set of two propositions, and similarly for the other complex sentence forms. An Aristotelian syllogism in one of the figures consists of at least two categorical premisses and a categorical conclusion which is said to result of necessity, because what is asserted in the premisses is (supposed to be) the case. But the premisses assert that some one thing holds or does not hold of all or some of some other things, and so the conclusion will follow necessarily only if the term relations asserted to hold in the premisses necessitate the term relation asserted in the conclusion.

In a hypothetical argument, on the other hand, it will indeed be necessary to accept the conclusion, but not because one has asserted some premisses such that the term relations asserted necessitate the term relation in the conclusion. The conclusion is accepted because its contradictory has been shown to be false, or because some other proposition has been proved and one has agreed beforehand to accept a proof for that proposition in lieu of a proof for the conclusion. Aristotle contrasts the two sorts of necessity in A44, saying that 'it is necessary to agree [sc. to the conclusion]; not on the basis of (ek) a syllogism, however, but on the basis of a hypothesis' (50a25-6). An anachronistic way of describing the difference would be to say that in the strictly syllogistic case, the inference is justified by the term relations asserted in the premisses, while in the case of hypothetical argument it is justified only by the (assumed) relations between the truth-values of the propositions involved. Aristotle did not realize that truth-value relations could in fact be asserted in complex propositions such as conditionals, and so he thought that the conclusion of a hypothetical argument, though validly established, had not been reached in the same way as the conclusion of a proper syllogism.

This does not yet show, of course, why a hypothetical argument would have to contain a syllogism; but one can see why Aristotle would have thought so from looking at his description of the two types of hypothetical argument he recognizes. One type is described as follows. One begins with an agreement to the effect that a proof for a proposition q will be accepted in lieu of a proof for another proposition *p*, the original demonstrandum. One then produces a proof for *q*, and because of the initial agreement, the interlocutor will have to agree that *p* has been proved as well. An example of this type of argument—no doubt the paradigm case that accounts for the label 'hypothetical'—would be Socrates' argument 'from a hypothesis' in the *Meno*. Socrates and Meno agree that if they can show that virtue is knowledge, they will have shown that virtue can be taught. Socrates then sets out to find a proof for the thesis that virtue is knowledge, and it is clear that if he had found such a proof, he and Meno would have been satisfied that virtue is indeed teachable. Aristotle calls the proposition for which a proof is to be offered the 'substitute' (*metalambanomenon*)—the thesis that virtue is knowledge is substituted, as it were, for the original demonstrandum and he claims that it must be proved by a direct syllogism. Now unfortunately his example in A44 does not bear him out, for he clearly envisages an indirect proof for the substituted thesis, as the ancient commentators already point out. But this will not invalidate his general claim that every valid deductive argument must contain a syllogism if it can be shown that every *reductio* argument contains a syllogism; so we must look at the other type of hypothetical argument.

A *reductio* is an argument in which one derives a falsehood or absurdity from the contradictory of the demonstrandum, and then concludes that the demonstrandum must be true because its contradictory has been shown to be false. In order to derive the absurdity, one cannot use another indirect argument, since presumably nothing absurd can be derived from the thesis to be proved. Given that all premisses are assumed to be categorical, it would seem that the absurdity can only be deduced by a categorical syllogism, as Aristotle maintains. For since Aristotle does not recognize the possibility of a direct *modus ponens* argument, he cannot consider the option of deriving either the so-called substitute proposition or the falsehood in a *reductio* from a conditional together with the proposition that forms the antecedent. The necessity involved in hypothetical argument thus seems to be parasitic upon syllogistic necessity in the narrow sense, because the final step can only be reached if a proof has been given, either for the falsity of the contradictory or for the substitute thesis, and that proof cannot itself be hypothetical, on pain of a regress.

So much for Aristotle's claim that every valid deductive argument must contain at least one syllogism. It would assure him that he had established the indispensable core of a general theory of argument, and although he could not in fact prove the ambitious thesis of A23, the first half of his argument there the completeness proof for direct syllogistic deductions retained its importance as a proof that the core theory was indeed complete.

Furthermore, he may have thought that this part would provide all that was needed for scientific demonstration, even if it did not adequately cover the wider field of dialectical argument, or indeed scientific reasoning in general, because demonstration in the strict sense would not have to rely upon hypothetical argument. Though both forms of hypothetical argument recognized by Aristotle may have been taken over by the philosophers from Greek mathematics, Aristotle may have thought that they belonged to a heuristic or preliminary stage of scientific investigations. Plato's Socrates claims to have learned the hypothetical method of reasoning from the mathematicians, although the geometrical example he uses to explain the method is notoriously much harder to understand than the dialectical procedure it allegedly serves to illustrate. It seems clear, however, that the example does not illustrate a method of proof, but a heuristic strategy. The *Meno*'s argument about virtue and knowledge appears, together with another geometrical example (not Plato's), in *Prior Analytics* B25, the chapter dealing with 'leading away' (*apogôge*). This procedure clearly serves a heuristic purpose: namely, to 'lead away' from a given problem that appears for the moment intractable to another one that can be more easily solved. Aristotle describes the *Meno* example as follows: 'let A be teachable, B stand for science, and C justice. That science is teachable, then, is obvious, but it is unclear whether virtue is a science. It seems that this will bring us 'closer to scientific understanding' because it shows us that if we can find a proof for the minor premiss (BaC), then we will have a (syllogistic) proof for the desired conclusion, 'virtue is teachable' (AaC). It is interesting to note that the argument considered here is not 'hypothetical' in the sense of A23 or A44; the additional assumption is simply the minor premiss in a regular syllogism. What was earlier described as a hypothesis or agreement—'If (we can prove that) virtue is knowledge, then (we have shown that) virtue is teachable' turns out to link the minor premiss and conclusion of a proper syllogism. The hypothesis, then, was by no means arbitrarily chosen, and the example invites the consideration that in the direct case, at least, one might try to eliminate the need for an agreement by finding an additional premiss that will turn the hypothesis into a syllogism. Thus direct hypothetical argument might be thought to figure in scientific reasoning only as a preliminary to the discovery of syllogistic proof.

That still leaves indirect argument, and Aristotle obviously knew that this was in fact quite common in Greek mathematics; his own example of a *reductio* argument is the proof for the incommensurability of the diagonal with the side of a square. Nevertheless, he maintains in several places that any indirect argument can be replaced by a direct one, so that *reductio* could in principle be dispensed with. The argument for this claim, as far as I can see, comes from his treatment of syllogism 'through an impossibility' (*dia tou adunatou sullogismos*) in B11-14. There he describes indirect argument as an argumentative strategy, to be employed if an opponent is not willing to accept a premiss one needs to derive the conclusion one is aiming at. An indirect argument, Aristotle explains in B14 (62b29-31), is one in which one assumes what one wants to refute, and leads on from there to an agreed falsehood. So if the opponent will not agree top, you ask him to accept its contradictory he can hardly refuse to do that if he has rejected the original proposition and then try to derive an obvious falsehood from this assumption together with some other, already accepted premiss. This will serve to show that the contradictory of the premiss you tried to introduce must be false, and hence allow you to use the desired premiss after all.

In the simple cases Aristotle considers in B11-14, it is also true that the desired proposition could have been derived from the contradictory of the 'obvious falsehood' together with the other accepted premiss, and so Aristotle concludes that the same terms can (always) be used to construct either a direct or an indirect argument. When one tries to discover a scientific proof, as opposed to refuting an opponent in a dialectical debate, one will presumably not have to resort to such stratagems, and hence indirect proof will be dispensable. Since the difference between direct and indirect argument thus seems to be merely strategic, and the same terms will be used in both cases, Aristotle thinks that the heuristic devices used for constructing direct syllogistic deductions will be sufficient to cover indirect argument as well. The hitch is, of course, that not every indirect argument will be as simple as the ones Aristotle analyses in B11-14. The examples he has in mind there probably do not come from mathematics, but from the indirect proofs he himself had offered in A5 and 6, where the 'impossibility' arises in each case because the contradictory of one of the assumed premisses has been derived from the 'hypothesis' (i.e. the contradictory of the conclusion that follows from the premisses). It is probably significant that Aristotle does not seem to distinguish between deriving an 'obvious falsehood'—that is, a patently absurd but not logically false proposition and deriving a contradiction. Only belatedly, in B15, does he acknowledge that one might need more than one syllogism to derive a contradiction (64b17-27) namely, in those cases where one has not assumed the contradictory of the derived proposition in advance. But it is not clear that this would have led him to revise his view about the dispensability of indirect proof. He knew that such proofs were common in mathematics, and hence he found it important to show that his theory could deal with them; but he probably did not try to derive, for example, the incommensurability theorem from the premiss 'no number is both odd and even' together with other mathematical truths.

Aristotle may also have thought that in a truly scientific system of demonstrations, indirect proofs *should* be replaced by direct ones. He thought that direct arguments were preferable to indirect ones for epistemological reasons: as he points out in *Posterior Analytics* A26, when one derives a falsehood in an indirect argument, the premisses of the syllogistic deduction one uses will not state the facts on which one's eventual conclusion is based, and hence will not be 'prior to the conclusion' in the way required for demonstration. Only when the argument has been transformed into a direct syllogism which uses the contradictory of the 'obvious falsehood' as a premiss will the correct order of epistemological priority be restored. I suspect that what Aristotle disliked about indirect proofs was that they do not do what an Aristotelian demonstration is supposed to do: namely, explain why the conclusion must be true. The incommensurability proof does show that the diagonal in a square cannot be commensurable with the side; but one can hardly say that it explains or states a reason why the diagonal must be incommensurable, least of all by providing an appropriate middle term. So perhaps Aristotle hoped that in principle, at least, demonstration could proceed without indirect proof.

However that may be, even if formal syllogistic did not provide the comprehensive theory Aristotle had promised at the beginning of A4, the system of the figures would be the foundation of all valid deductive arguments, whether scientific or not, and its applications in heuristics and analysis would be as important for dialectic or rhetoric as for science or philosophy. In the rest of the *Prior Analytics* after A26 and before he turns to his official treatment of demonstration, Aristotle is concerned to show how formal syllogistic should be used to construct or to criticize arguments, and his main focus appears to be on dialectic.

In *Prior Analytics* A27-31, Aristotle describes an ingenious method for finding premisses for any given categorical conclusion. Once one has the complete list of valid syllogistic moods provided in A4-6, one will no longer have to collect and memorize long lists of propositions about various fields, as Aristotle had recommended in the *Topics*. Instead, one can construct lists of terms that either follow or are followed by a given term. The thesis under discussion—the *problçma*, as Aristotle calls it here, using the terminology of the *Topics*—will have to contain two terms; hence by looking for terms that occur in the lists for both of the requisite terms, one will be able to find an appropriate middle term to construct one's syllogism. Alexander of Aphrodisias illustrates the procedure by a delightful example: lists of terms one can use to argue that pleasure is or is not a good, as the occasion demands. Aristotle's system is more efficient and economical than Platonic division, which is therefore demoted to 'a small part' of heuristics in A31; and Aristotle insists that his method is the only one guaranteed to locate all the premisses that can be used to construct valid syllogisms. At the same time, it may also show, depending on the exhaustiveness of the lists, where a syllogism can not be found.

Another advantage, not emphasized by Aristotle himself, is that it is arguably more general in its scope, and certainly much easier to use, than the system of the predicables that Aristotle had used to organize his materials in the *Topics*. It is hard to imagine an orator holding forth about questions of genus, species, and definition, while it is clear that she would be interested in the quantity or quality of her premisses—whether some predicate is or is not true of some or all members of a given class. Syllogistic shows that the formal validity of an argument can be established or checked regardless of the specific type of predication that occurs in its premisses and conclusion. Hence special conditions regarding the different types of predication can be treated separately from a general account of deductive validity. This certainly simplifies the task of the orator, who can now just study the system of the syllogistic moods (she might, indeed, memorize them with the help of mnemonic verses, as the medievals did), instead of delving into the arcane metaphysical questions that fill so many pages of the *Topics*.

It is not surprising that Aristotle seems to replace references to dialectic as a general theory of syllogisms by references to the *Analytics* in the chapters that deal with argument in the *Rhetoric*: for syllogistic provides all that the orator needs in order to construct valid arguments; she does not have to study up on the predicables. This does not mean that the orator will have to learn about scientific proof instead of dialectical argument, of course. The syllogistic figures will have to be part of the equipment of the dialectician as well; and given that the *Analytics* do not offer a detailed account of hypothetical argument, the *Topics* may still be needed as a handbook for the orator. What is missing from the *Analytics* is an account of the so-called general, or subject-neutral, *topoi*. In the framework of the classification of argument forms Aristotle uses in *Prior Analytics* A23, these should probably be described as general types of 'hypothesis' that one might expect one's interlocutor or one's audience to agree to. (An example might be: 'what holds of one of two similar things, will hold of the other also'.) The sketch of a formal treatment of arguments concerning things preferable to their opposites in *Prior Analytics* B22 may show that Aristotle at some point planned to work out a formal theory of such arguments, but he evidently did not get around to this project. However, it invites the suggestion that a revised handbook for dialecticians might have paid less attention to the predicables than the *Topics* does.

The *Topics* as we have it is largely a handbook for *Academic* dialecticians; a manual based on the syllogistic moods, by contrast, could equally well have been used by people who had no special interest in genus, definition, or proprium. Hence the method of heuristics introduced in *Prior Analytics* A27-31 is at least as important for dialectic and rhetoric as for the theory of scientific proof. In fact, although Aristotle does briefly discuss the use of his method in the context of science in A30, it seems rather obvious to me that lists of terms are more likely to be used by a dialectician than by a scientist. A science, as Aristotle says (46a22-8), will have to begin by assembling, as completely as possible, the observed facts about its subject-matter. These will have to form most of the premisses and conclusions of its demonstrations, and at this stage it may be helpful to look for common terms in order to find out what can or cannot be derived from what. But as the *Posterior Analytics* shows, this will hardly be enough to establish, for example, the correctness of a proposed definition, or the claim that a thing's being F is to be explained by its being G rather than the other way around. Alexander was right, I think, to illustrate the use of heuristics by an example from the dialectician's repertoire.

Aristotle declares at the beginning (47a5-8) that his previous claims about the universal scope of the syllogistic figures will be confirmed if it can be shown that it is indeed possible so to analyse any given argument. This is no doubt correct, but unfortunately the following chapters do not in fact confirm Aristotle's optimism. Since it is already clear how one has to deal with explicitly categorical propositions, this section concentrates on difficult or recalcitrant cases examples of obviously valid arguments that are not syllogistic in form, or fallacies that appear to be formally valid syllogisms but are not really so because, as Aristotle wants to maintain, their premisses have not been correctly analysed. Aristotle never shows any serious doubt about the adequacy of the syllogistic moods to capture the form of all valid arguments, but he often emphasizes the difficulty of uncovering the proper structure, and the need for more detailed investigations.

From a modern point of view, several of these chapters could almost be read as collections of counter examples to demonstrate the inadequacy of syllogistic. But Aristotle evidently did not see things this way. A36 may show most clearly why he was so confident: there he declares that the technical term '*huparchein*' (belonging) covers much more than straightforward cases of predication. It appears that his method of analysis allows him to treat just about any sort of proposition as a categorical premiss. In other words, he thinks that he knows what the 'logical form' of an argument has to be, and does not consider formalization, as modern logicians might, as a way of exploring or discovering different logical structures. The shortcomings of syllogistic as a way of representing complicated arguments are too well known to need spelling out in detail. With respect to the possible usefulness of syllogistic, however, it seems more important to emphasize that in spite of the difficulties so candidly discussed by Aristotle himself, analysis or reduction to syllogistic form can be very useful in cases where the form of the premisses presents no problem.

This comes out most clearly, perhaps, in the discussion of rhetorical arguments from 'signs' (B27) and the *Rhetoric*'s brief treatment of *lusis*-dissecting an opponent's arguments which refers back to the *Analytics*. Aristotle shows that all but one of the customary types of sign argument are formally invalid, so an orator who has studied the *Analytics* will know exactly how to show that the argument, even if it has some merit, will not be sufficient to establish its alleged conclusion. Also, given some acquaintance with modal premisses, one may be able to show that an apparently cogent objection is not in fact conclusive. For example, if an orator has used what appears to be a universal premiss, say, ' Those who walk around late in the night are thieves', and the objection is raised that the generalization does not hold without exception, one can retort that what one was actually claiming was only that all those who walk around late at night are likely to be thieves—a proposition much harder to disprove, since one might have to show that the alleged suspects are in fact more likely not to be thieves than to be thieves; Aristotle does not give an example in this passage). Despite its limitations, then, syllogistic can be used quite successfully at times to identify types of invalid argument, and in this respect it can serve an important function that modern logic also fulfils: namely, to spot faulty inferences or gaps in arguments. I should admit, however, that Aristotle's attempts to trace fallacies to faulty ways of rendering the supposedly categorical structure of premisses do not look like an improvement on the treatment of fallacy in the *Sophistici Elenchi*.

Now the use of syllogistic as a diagnostic instrument to discover weaknesses or faults in arguments seems, as in the case of heuristics, more important for those who engage in debate or in courtroom pleading than for those who try to construct scientific proofs. Presumably a serious scientific researcher will carefully try to avoid fallacious inferences, and therefore use only forms of argument that she knows to be valid. Given Aristotle's preconceived notion that proofs just *have* to be syllogistic in form, it is not likely that the chapters on analysis were meant to persuade the reader that mathematical proofs, for example, could be presented in syllogistic form. Aristotle's examples tend to be of the sort known from the Topics, and what is being confirmed, to the extent that anything can be said to be confirmed here, would seem to be the claim that the syllogistic figures are adequate to deal with all sorts of arguments *beyond* the field of scientific demonstration.

The sections on heuristics and analysis in Prior Analytics A complete a project to which Aristotle briefly adverts in the opening paragraph of A32. The three parts he mentions there are probably the system of the syllogistic moods, heuristics, and analysis. The contents of book B are more difficult to classify, partly no doubt because the book contains some notes or sketches that do not cohere very well with their context. For example, the book begins with a chapter that seems to offer some corollaries to formal syllogistic, and in effect bring in the syllogistic moods that were later classified as belonging to the fourth figure. At the beginning of B23 Aristotle makes a remark that indicates that he has so far been dealing with dialectical and demonstrative syllogisms, and is going to extend his investigation by applying the doctrine of the syllogistic moods to rhetorical argument as well; but he does not indicate precisely what was the point of the preceding chapters. Still, it seems fairly clear that these chapters belong to the general theory of argument as opposed to the special theory of demonstration. They either try to establish metatheorems regarding deductive argument in general, or deal with questions of argumentative strategy.

I have already mentioned the unfortunate theorem to the effect that an indirect argument can always be replaced by a direct one. But there are better examples as well. One theorem of which Aristotle was understandably proud is proved in B2-4; namely, that a true conclusion can be validly derived from false premisses. One may find it pedantic and tedious that Aristotle goes through all the syllogistic moods to show how this is possible in each case, with one or both premisses false, when two examples would have sufficed to establish the general claim. But this should not divert our attention from the fact that Aristotle's proof is a considerable achievement. It is one thing merely to assert that the truth of the conclusion tells us nothing about the truth of the premisses, another to offer a rigorous proof to show that this is so. Aristotle also shows that if a false conclusion is derived from apparently true premisses, then either one or more of the premisses is false, or the conclusion does not follow. These are points that may appear trivial to readers trained in modern logic, but they still need to be made in any introductory class on reasoning and argument, and Aristotle was the first not just to state, but to prove, them.

The chapters on the so-called conversion of syllogisms (B8-10) may look like a debater's exercise: showing how a given set of propositions and their negations can be combined in different ways to deduce different conclusions. But once again it is important to note that formal syllogistic enables Aristotle to prove his claims, not just to tell his students that they should try out various combinations to see if anything follows. Finally, as Myles Burnyeat has pointed out, the last section (on rhetoric) shows how syllogistic enabled Aristotle to distinguish clearly between two sorts of things that would ordinarily be called proofs, by Aristotle as well as his contemporaries: namely, valid deductive arguments and formally inconclusive but relevant evidence used to support or corroborate a given thesis. Although Aristotle did not go on to develop a theory of evidence, he obviously recognized that not every thesis can or should be justified in the same way, and even that formally inconclusive evidence may be just as convincing as an elaborate deductive proof.

Despite its obvious limitations as a general theory of deduction, formal syllogistic allowed Aristotle to establish a number of fundamental points in the theory of argument. The crucial step, of course, was his discovery that the validity of an argument depends on the form of its premisses and conclusion, not their content or the peculiarities of the subject-matter under discussion. For a general theory of argument, the distinction between formal validity and truth may well be more important than the notion of a deductive system or an axiomatized theory. I hope to have shown that Aristotle's formal logic need not be seen exclusively as an attempt either to provide the underlying logic for axiomatized theory or to develop a system of deductive inference. It is at least as much a contribution to a theory of valid argument in general, and in this role it was correctly described by the ancient commentators as a tool of philosophy.

9

Philo's Plans for Program in Philosophy

Introduction

Forbidden sexual activity includes certain kinds of fornication as well as other kinds of sexual activity marked as rebellion against God, whereas religiously compliant sexual activity shows no such insubordination. This distinction between permissible and forbidden sexual conduct is simple in its structure, opposing as it does obedience and disobedience to a deity. This leading concern of biblical sexual morality, however, differs from those that inform the sexual principles of Plato, the Stoics, and the Pythagoreans. The Greek philosophers do not organize their primary sexual dictates by whether or not sexual and reproductive conduct shows obeisance to a god who requires exclusive worship. The ancient Greek populace did not do so either. The polytheistic organization of Greek culture precludes this requirement, even among philosophers who exalt the monarch of their rehabilitated Olympian pantheon as "God".

Despite the outward simplicity of the biblical dichotomy between the sexually permissible and forbidden, neither the

Septuagint nor Paul presents a straightforward explication of the specific contents of these categories. Paul's ominous warnings against sexual fornication make this particular activity seem the worst of deviance, but what does the practice involve, and how should it be prevented? If, for example, a Christian man copulates with a woman, a man, and an animal, is he a fornicator in any, some, or all cases? Questions such as these have been of pressing concern within Christianity at least since the second century, when Tatian, Clement, and other supporters of Paul started fleshing out what sexual activity was permissible for Christians, if any, and denying flesh to the forbidden. A long prescriptive tradition has developed since their efforts. To name but one much later instance, a seventeenth century *Treatise of Fornication* begins with the query *"What the Sin is,* which the Apostle [Paul] here exhorts to fly, and that is Fornication." First on the author's agenda is to "define the *Thing* to be avoided," so that Christians might flee from its perils. This endeavor goes back again and again to Paul's letters for the answers, and his starting point was the Septuagint.

In this chapter I too explore fornication and other sexual rebellion against God in the Septuagint and Paul, as well as the sexual behavior that they designate as safe and permissible. Unlike preachers of old and today, though, my interests are at a remove from the pulpit. I explore why Paul and his supporters have for centuries been urging Christians to run from the Thing like deer from all-consuming flames. What motivates and sustains this imperative? To answer this and related questions, I examine the Septuagint in order to understand what Paul, Philo, Tatian, and Clement adopt and modify from it. The Greek Pentateuch, Prophets, and Paul are here treated as sexually grounded blueprints for a reformed social order, just like the Platonic, early Stoic, and Pythagorean reforms, for they similarly work toward social change and begin with reforms in sexual and reproductive mores. Despite the differences between the philosophical and biblical sexual principles of social reform, they all start off as ambitious programs at odds with current conventions, and they make genitals, wombs, and minds the center of regulatory change. This is not to suggest that the Septuagint is only political theory, for the Pentateuch, Prophets, and other books were part of a diverse living religion among Jews and God-fearers in Hellenistic culture, and Paul's Septuagint-based ideas were eagerly taken up by Christians of Greek and other Gentile backgrounds. As read by Philo, Paul, and their supporters, however, the Septuagint allows new sexual and reproductive mandates of social order to emerge, and these are my primary interest. I attempt no exploration of the religious history of ancient Israel and Judah, let alone make broad claims about what the Bible really means in any universal sense. My plan is to account for the religious sexual principles that Paul, Tatian, and Clement advocate from Septuagint and leave as their legacy for Christianized society to contend with.

As stated in the introduction, my findings from the Septuagint and Paul do not apply to Hebrew-based rabbinic Judaism. There are myriad thematic connections between the Greek and Hebrew aspects of Israel's heritage, and no rigid barrier separated Hellenistic and Palestinian Judaism from each other. Nonetheless, the adaptations that Paul makes to God's sexual program have a distinctive edge to them that contributes to ecclesiastical reasons for segregating Jews from Christians on religious and sexual grounds by the late fourth century. To understand these developments and the social divisiveness to which they led, we must not regard the Greek and Hebrew exegetical traditions as though they were unanimous in the sexual norms they promote.

Septuagint Principle of Sexual Rebellion or Apostasy

The Septuagint Pentateuch forbids God's people from engaging in acts of religiously alienating rebellion, or apostasy, as one of its main underlying rules. Certain kinds of sexual activity are marked as apostasy, and these fit into two groups. First, sexual activity constitutes rebellion against God if it occurs while worshipping gods other than or in addition to the Lord. When members of God's people engage in such sexual relations, they transgress the premier commandment to worship God alone and no other gods. One cannot be devoted to the Lord alone and at the same time make love in a polytheistic or other-theistic way, regardless of whether the sexual activity is sedately marital with a religiously alien spouse or the most unruly cultic practice imaginable.

Second, sexual activity is rebellious if it is a specific kind of defiling act, a sexual "abomination" (bdðñïéÝóèùlugma) in the eyes of God. This classification is ambiguous, however, for the Pentateuch is not forthcoming about the criteria by which the sex acts in this group are considered abominations. Perhaps they were considered inherently repellant to God, or possibly their association with the worship of other gods sufficed to taint them. If the former, it is likely that priests or prophets who projected this opinion onto the biblical God regarded such sex acts as polluting, deviant, contrary to the natural order (such as a human being copulating with an animal), a breach of a man's and family's property rights (such as adultery), or some combination of these and other possible factors. Some of the sexual abominations, however, are portrayed as ugly emblems of polytheistic rituals the sort of thing those Canaanites routinely do in thrall to false gods. Even though the blight associated with alien worship does not necessarily explain why certain sexual practices are marked as abominations, their association with other gods is still a significant part of what makes them seem repellant. One function of labeling the sex acts as abominations, then, is to persuade God's people to turn from the worship of other gods and to devote their sexuality and reproduction strictly to the Lord. By the letter of Pentateuchal law, then, sexual activity is off-limits to the extent that it involves worshipping alien gods or is classified as an abomination. There is significant overlap between the two categories, because some sexual abominations are named as such partly because they involve the worship of other gods.

The Greek Pentateuch attributes fearsome risks to sexual and non-sexual rebellion, especially when the disobedience involves other-theistic worship. First, apostates forfeit their standing in the religious community, for they have abandoned the core principle of biblical monotheism inscribed in the First Commandment. Second, the rebels in theory also give up their lives. The religiously obedient should put them to death even if they are kin by blood or marriage. "If your brother on your father's or mother's side, your son or daughter, the wife in your embrace, or a friend as dear to you as your own life secretly appeals to you, saying let us go and worship other gods, ... you will not consent or listen. You will make a public proclamation about [the offender], with your hands set to kill him [or her] first, and the people's to do so last. They will stone [the offender], who will die because he [or she] sought to bring you into apostasy from the Lord. " Stories in Septuagint history amply reinforce this violent mandate. Thus the rule against religiously alienating behavior is not minor etiquette. It is critical to monotheistic social order so critical that persons in principle must surrender themselves or close kin to retributive death for engaging in sexual or non-sexual rebellion.

In the Septuagint sexual fornication consists of sexual intercourse between men and women that transgresses the criteria of religiously acceptable copulation. Its heterosexual specificity is made clear from examples. Male Israelites, for instance, fornicate with Moabite women at the festival for Baal-peor. Similarly, Jacob's daughter Dinah is subjected to fornication when Shechem rapes her at a festival. The sexual activity would be an abomination but not fornication if Shechem's victim were a son of Jacob or if any son or daughter of Israel were to engage in autoeroticism or sexual activity with an animal. It is important to appreciate this heterosexual specificity of the rule against fornication; it is not vaguely against sexual irregularities of any sort, but against men and women engaging in sexual intercourse outside of God's ordinance system.

Fornication in many instances involves sexual apostasy against God. Members of the Lord's people are implicated in religious rebellion if they engage in adultery, incest, or acts of sexual intercourse partly or fully in devotion to gods other than the Lord. For example, Israelite wives commit adulterous fornication and must be stoned to death if they have male lovers, regardless of whether the adultery occurs in a ritualistic setting or not. Male Israelites, further, must abstain from sexual intercourse with women in other-theistic rituals or else they too must be put to death. Finally, the men and women alike must not marry religiously alien persons, for this leads the couples and their children to worship other gods. These kinds of fornication are marked as apostate defiance of God and his covenant, and perpetrators of these activities must in principle be destroyed as rebels.

The Septuagint, however, does not present the position that fornication is unconditionally rebellious behavior that warrants death. The Pentateuch adopts a more lenient stance under several circumstances toward fornication within the community of God's people. If, for example, an unbetrothed woman is raped or seduced, neither she nor the man involved is to be put to death. Also, if a betrothed woman is raped, not she, but her rapist, is to die. Further, occasional sexual relations between female prostitutes and males among God's people are in several instances portrayed as an acceptable custom on the part of the men, not as flagrantly disobedient fornication. Hence in Septuagint terms persons do not become apostates marked for death simply by virtue of fornicating. They do, however, rebel against God and should be eliminated if their sexual fornication implicates them in devotion to alien gods, in adultery or incest, or if they are males who rape betrothed females in the community.

The Septuagint does not limit its notion of sexual apostasy to forbidden kinds of intercourse between men and women, even though these are its predominant concern. Also included are male homoerotic sexual relations, at least in certain positions, and sexual activity between humans and animals. These prohibitions, however, are mentioned sparingly. Leviticus refers to these acts as abominations and prescribes a capital punishment against transgressors. "Let them be put to death." The main concern of the Septuagint is to outlaw practices of adulterous, incestuous, or other-theistic sexual intercourse between women and men. This is a significant point. The Septuagint primarily strives to enforce the rule that God's people practice sexual intercourse and reproduction strictly in its image of religious sanctity. Only secondarily does it try to root out male homoeroticism and sexual activity of humans with animals. This insistence stems to a considerable degree from the desire of priests and prophets to draw God's people, their offspring, and their children's children toward the Lord and away from other gods, like iron filings toward one numinous magnet and away from others, despite their attraction.

The Quid Pro Quo Attributed to the Biblical God

In order to understand the sexual prohibitions attributed to the Lord, it is pivotal to recognize that the Septuagint imparts a layer of religious significance to ancient concerns about sexual defilement or pollution. In the Pentateuch sexual defilement and dishonor are incorporated into a new order of wrongdoing disobeying a deity who requires unconditional obedience and devotion. For example, even before the Septuagint's "Yahweh-aloneist" religiosity was a glimmer in the eye of Moses and his followers, the dishonor of females being raped by male foreigners was already offensive. When Dinah is raped by Shechem, her brothers retaliate against him and his people because this outsider with a foreskin defiled their sister and ruined her reputation, not because Dinah stands ruined and repellant for betraying the First Commandment (albeit inadvertently) by having sexual contact with a male who worships alien gods. However, once the Pentateuch identifies various kinds of sexual activity as forbidden by the Lord, the sexual activity is also a betrayal of God and the strictly monotheistic society being commissioned in his name. The order of wrongdoing expands to include the factor of covenant-breaking defiance, especially, but not only, on the part of willful agents. We cannot readily appreciate the Pentateuch's implacable requirement of capital punishment for certain kinds of sexual activity without appreciating the religious treason being associated with them. For example, adultery in the Pentateuch is never wrong simply because it transgresses a man's or family's property rights, even though this criterion of disapproval remains at work. In Septuagint terms adultery is wrong primarily because it constitutes defiance toward one of God's commandments, and keeping the commandments is a required part of worshipping the Lord alone. The same holds true of other sexual transgressions. Within this religious system, further, a genuinely new sexual transgression appears on the scene, one that presupposes, and hence does not antedate, biblical monotheism as a norm: the danger of men or women making love and reproducing with partners who worship gods other than the Lord. Prior to the formulation of Yahwism, such non-Yahwist practices of marriage and procreation were the status quo in the ancient world.

The Septuagint offers a potent and disturbing rationale for eliminating agents of religious rebellion: If apostates remain alive in the community, God will disinherit and destroy the community or a substantial portion thereof. This danger is portrayed as a live threat, given its precedent in the fate that the Lord is said to have dealt to the sexually abominating Canaanites and others. "If you forget the Lord your God and proceed after other gods to worship and bow to them, I bear witness to you today by the sky and earth that I will destroy you, just as I destroyed the other peoples because of their irreverence". It is as though the Canaanites were culpably remiss in failing to anticipate and conform in advance to the way of the Lord, and God responds by uprooting their religious culture, the sexual mores that were part of that culture, and a number of the people themselves. He then grants and guarantees their land to Israel, but with a formidable stipulation: His people are to remain keepers of the new dominion only if they unconditionally obey his laws. The prohibition against worshipping other gods sexually and reproductively is crucial, for the degree to which biblical monotheism becomes a reality correlates with the theistic orientation shown in the people's acts of sexual intercourse, procreation, and religious patterns of childrearing. The people must not continue to devote their sexual and reproductive energy to other gods, as their ancestors used to do, for the biblical God now claims them exclusively as his own. In case the people lapse, they must atone for their failings and renew their commitment to worship God alone. Otherwise, God will see to it that they and their patrimony face a similar demise through genocide, exile, and slavery, with its sexual and other abuses.

The covenantal proviso in the Septuagint functions rather like a Faustian bargain. God grants his people inviolable access to prosperity, protection, and hegemony, but only so long as they surrender the other-theistic rituals and sexual practices that they used to enjoy. A veritable heaven on earth is theirs, but the cost is the very soul of religious and sexual pluralism. The people must relinquish in perpetuity the ability to act on their own cognizance religiously and sexually, for in order to have no other gods but God, they must make love, reproduce, and raise children for the Lord alone. And while Faust could have turned the devil down, God's terms are imposed in the Pentateuch as an already binding contract that the Israelites cannot reject without being annihilated. The Israelites thus become a collective of tragic heroes who must comply with their assigned fate if they wish to live, to receive God's blessing instead of his curse. The Lord has warned them of the calamity to come if they disobey—the same disinheritance and destruction that God has already dealt to the Canaanites at their hands. Deuteronomy reaffirms the quid pro quo by expressly reminding the Israelites that they must never think they are above God's laws simply by having been chosen as his people. The Lord esteems obedience more than he esteems any particular people, for he takes equal joy in helping the obedient to flourish and in destroying the rebellious. It would thus be utter folly for the Israelites to defy the strictly monotheistic sexual mores to which they have been appointed.

Given the Pentateuchal terms of God's protection, agents of religiously alienating sexual and reproductive practices are public enemies. In the interest of community security, the dissidents in principle must be purged through stoning or some other method to contain the religious treason and avert God's retaliation. Members of God's people who abide by this biblical teaching have ample scriptural grounds to kill sexual transgressors of God's laws. Even if they do not resort to violence, they have grounds to harbor intense loathing and intolerance toward the transgressors. Tolerance is reprehensible, for to turn a blind eye elicits retribution from a deity who already has a formidable record for brutalizing peoples because of their sexual devotion to alien gods. The force of this doctrine comes through in the chilling openness with which rebels are targeted for destruction, as though they were carriers of a plague rather than family members, friends, or neighboring tribal groups.

In conjunction with annihilating deviants, the people claimed for the Lord must also eliminate polytheistic mores and sacred sites from God's domain. "You will neither bow down to their gods, nor worship them, nor carry out their rites. You will destroy and lay them low and tear down their monuments". Once the obedient do away with these rituals and the condemned sites, the other-theistic competition declines and makes way for the people to be safe and sovereign in the Lord.

The moral of Numbers' composite story about Moabite and Midianite women highlights the danger of sexually fornicating rebellion. When Israelite men engage in sexual ceremonies with Moabite women devoted to Baal, the men must be killed. As Moses tells the judges, "Each one of you put to death your kinsmen who have been initiated into the worship of Baalpeor". Though the narrative has a break where we would learn whether the Israelites carried out these orders, it would appear that initially they did not. In response God unleashes a scourge that kills twenty-four thousand Israelites, until God's ardent supporter Phineas rises up to prevent total extirpation. Phineas observes that an Israelite man, Zimri, has taken a Midianite woman, Cozbi, as a lover and, perhaps, as a wife. He encapsulates God's anger in his own indignation and impales the two of them together, making sure that his spear runs "through the woman's womb" in the Septuagint version. This death-bearing thrust prompts God to relent. At least one man, Phineas, has unquestioningly obeyed his orders, and God thus spares the remaining Israelite people. Thanks to Phineas, he declares, "I did not utterly wipe out the Israelites in my jealous anger", and in reward God grants Phineas a priesthood to be passed down in his male lineage. The Lord's killing field through which Phineas picks his way toward priesthood is made up of public enemies who ostensibly deserved to die.

The Septuagint version of the Numbers incident specifies the anatomical locale of Cozbi's slaughter for a didactic reason. Even though Zimri is the transgressor, not Cozbi, Phineas skewers her through the womb in order to show that his people must cease dissipating the Lord's claim to power by producing and rearing children for gods other than or in addition to the Lord. The spear through her religiously alien womb declares that once and for all there is to be no more fornicating sexual rebellion in the Lord's community networks of kinship and marriage, no more syncretistic religious diversity borne through the children across generations. So pressing is this rule that the people must even surrender their disobedient kin in order to prove their loyalty to God alone.

Jeremiah succinctly indicates the difference between the defilement of rebellious sexual fornication and pollutions that do not involve apostasy. Defilements of the customary sort have a simple and relatively unproblematic purification, such as ritual washing or periods of isolation. These acts of purification cleanse the defilement and restore persons to the social order of the Lord. By contrast, Jeremiah asserts, no amount of soap washes away the defilement of fornicating rebellion and the defiance associated with it. As he declares in the assumed voice of God, "[Israel,] your rebellion will teach you; and your wickedness will betray you. You declared 'I will not be your religious slave. Instead I will go upon every high hill and under every shady tree and there I will be dissipated through my sexual fornication.' 'You are defiled by your wrongful actions,' the Lord states, 'even if you wash with cleansing soda.' When the defilement derives from religiously alienating sexual fornication, not even an ancient equivalent of lye or detergent gets out the stain. Bloodshed is the only effective method of purging sexual apostates, and it must be used to keep the community clean and secure. To all appearances, this violent religious principle meets with valiant resistance time and again. In terms of the Septuagint quid pro quo that Jeremiah supports, however, the principle is right and the resistance is wrong.

Septuagint Principle of Religious Endogamy

The biblical notion of sexual fornication conjures up images that outrage Jewish and Christian conventions of decency men and women pulsating in acts of cultic intercourse while glassy-eyed idols play the voyeur. While the Septuagint does denounce orgiastic sexual rites, the more critical problem comes from reproductive intercourse in syncretistic intermarriages. Though more mundane, this marital fornication is more problematic precisely because it is woven into the everyday life of the community and affects the religious character of the offspring. "You must not intermarry with [the nations whom I am driving out before you]. You will not give your daughters to their sons nor take their daughters for your sons; if you do, they will draw your sons away from me [the Lord] and make them worship other gods. Then the Lord will be angry with you and will destroy you straightaway." The occasional orgiastic festival is of more sporadic concern and easier to keep at bay.

Members of God's people who marry persons of an other-theistic orientation and share in their spouses' religious mores engage in no trivial breach of the First Commandment. They enter into alien worship through their wedding, marriage customs, and childrearing, and so do their relatives who participate in the wedding, condone the marriage, and celebrate the children's religiously mixed coming-of-age ceremonies. The transgression of the spouses, moreover, has an unavoidably sexual aspect, for in the ancient world marital sexual activity was partly devotional, just as the wedding was. In antiquity, sexual arousal, activity, and reproduction were in part immanent divine powers, not simply human forms of energy. Sexually aroused persons who make love and women who give birth share in and honor gods of sexuality and procreation, such as women in childbirth who cry out "Hera help me! Save me, I beg you!" The gods who motivate, control, and have their presence in sexuality and reproduction vary by culture, such as Aphrodite, Eros, Zeus, and Hera for the Greeks, or Yahweh for the Jews. Since the practice of religiously diversified intermarriage is not for the Lord alone, it incompatible with obeying the First Commandment. When persons within God's community intermarry, they defy a core feature of the covenant, because their action impinges on the religiosity of future generations. Religiously mixed marital sexual activity therefore ranks high among the kinds of rebellious fornication to drive out of the community and to keep out in perpetuity.

Let us consider an example so as to better appreciate why religiously mixed marriages take precedence over orgiastic rituals and prostitution among the kinds of sexual fornication to eliminate. If a male member of God's people takes a religiously alien woman as a wife, she, depending on her background, would worship the queen of heaven, Ishtar, Aphrodite, or other deities of sex and marriage, such as Hera and Zeus. She would also practice domestic religious ceremonies of a sort alien to her husband's religion, such as rituals of birth and puberty for her children. She would teach her daughters and sons to follow her example (which by then is likely to be somewhat syncretistic with her husband's) when they marry and have children. She might also encourage her husband to follow her lead. And if her husband tried to be the autocratic Hosea in her household, she might resist or persuade him that their family is better off and better protected by continuing to worship the gods of her heritage, such as the queen of heaven, than by worshipping Yahweh alone. In defiance of Jeremiah, diaspora women in Egypt openly declare such a preference for Ishtar with the full support of their husbands, leaving the prophet to retort ominously, "We will see whose word will prevail". By contrast, a male Israelite who visits a prostitute or secretly takes part in an orgy in an outlying town does not enter into the same degree of religious danger that the syncretistic husbands and children do, so long as he goes back home to his family and religion of biblical monotheism and teaches his children to do likewise.

The Septuagint prescribes two measures to remove the danger of syncretistic marriage from the midst of the Lord's people. First, marriages between members of God's people, such as the Israelites, and persons who belong to seven specific religiously alien groups in the promised land, such as the Amorites and Canaanites, are in principle absolutely prohibited. The punishment for this apostasy, according to Deuteronomy, is a swift punitive death. The status of these seven ethnic groups is distinctive, however, because they are in active dispute with the Israelites over the patrimony of land. Unlike them, members of religiously alien groups that have no connection to the land claim of the Israelites are not untouchable as prospective spouses, but are to be accommodated by the second measure. These Gentile outsiders may marry into God's people, provided that they willingly convert to the Lord alone and agree to impart the ways of biblical monotheism to their children. The Moabite Ruth illustrates this point well. Since the Moabites are not one of the seven prohibited tribes in Deuteronomy, a Moabite woman may convert and, like Ruth, vow, "Your people are my people and your God is my God". With this declaration, the woman is no longer alien in the sense that matters for biblical monotheism. Once converted, she is rehabilitated from a biblical perspective and can be accepted as a wife and mother among the Lord's people. If, however, Ruth has a sister who continues to worship the gods of her ancestral heritage, the sister remains dangerously alien. Were she to marry an Israelite, she and her husband would know no peace if the likes of Phineas and Jeremiah were in their neighborhood, for her husband has rebelled against God by joining with her in marriage, and he relegates his children and parents to the same alienated standing. Hence, intermarriages are acceptable only when they are no longer "interfaith" in the ancient sense of worshipping gods other than or in addition to the Lord. The principle of biblical endogamy is thus elastic, for it is open to many Gentiles, so long as they convert and sincerely vow to abide by the First Commandment. I hereafter refer to this principle and practice as "biblical" or "religious endogamy," for its criterion of the eligible marriage pool is whether the prospective spouses already follow or agree to follow the way of the Lord alone. Other kinds of endogamy practiced in the ancient world were more fixed and culturally closed. They tended to restrict eligible spouses by characteristics that persons have by birth and cannot change, such as ethnic status or Athenian citizenship, not by religious conduct that one can change through conversion. The community of the Lord alone uses its marriage rules to balance the requirement to be impervious to the polytheistic sexual mores that surround them without becoming entirely closed as a group.

The production and rearing of religiously mixed children poses a special danger to the norm of biblical monotheism. To the extent that the children become polytheistic, God's share of compliant worshippers declines in future generations, and with the reduced populace, God's social recognition diminishes. The Pentateuch and Prophets are dedicated to counteracting this trend. By their teaching, if monotheistic devotion wanes through syncretism or secularization, cultural suffering will occur as divine retribution for such dissolute tendencies. This retribution can and should rekindle atonement and monotheistic ardor among the surviving people. The Prophets rebuke the syncretistic offspring, in an effort to gain them as devotees of the Lord alone. Hosea labels them "children of fornication" and "religiously alien children," and urges them to renounce the religiously mixed ways of their parents. He inveighs against the influence of religiously alien mothers in particular, and some of the offspring apparently include his own children by Gomer, Hosea's wife, who preferred to worship Baal and continued to do so. Hosea's vituperative exhortations are meant to stigmatize and sting the offspring into turning wholly toward the Lord. In addition, the Prophets pointedly remind the people about the Lord's conditional terms of protection God will destroy them if they turn a blind eye to the religious diversity growing up in their midst. The Lord will either render mixed unions barren or kill any children born to Israel from them. Ezekiel draws attention to the same problem. The former denizens of the sacked city of Jerusalem had wrongly turned a blind eye to the presence of Amorite and Canaanite spouses and parents in their communities, who were unconditionally off-limits as marriage partners. As Ezekiel sees it, God rightly brought about Jerusalem's destruction because of this forbidden mixing of peoples and religious customs. The offspring are an impure alloy of several metals, which the Lord will have to melt down to regain the pure silver. Thus the procreation of children who worship gods other than or in addition to the Lord are at the heart of sexually fornicating danger, for this practice corrupts the Yahwists' brightest hope, the purely monotheistic generations of the future.

Divergent Responses to the Biblical Mandate Against Sexual Rebellion

The biblical dictate that God's people must eliminate sexual fornicators who are implicated in apostasy appears primitive and brutal, stemming from days when the Lord's adherents were too busy lashing out at competing gods to develop the Lord as a deity of forgiveness and mercy. A benevolent god, though, is more appealing and sophisticated than a deity who outdoes the stomping ogre of folklore in his dealings with his own and other peoples. Numerous devout teachers, such as Jesus and other rabbis, have accordingly tried to get beyond the violent terms of the covenant. They highlight alternative biblical passages, such as the tenet that God is "compassionate and gracious forgiving iniquity, rebellion, and sin, and not sweeping the guilty clean away". Though they strive to leave behind the use of terror to inculcate the worship of God, other proponents of the Lord, such as Paul and Philo, continue to promulgate the violent terms and have a divided conception of God. On the one hand God is providence or agape, but the other hand is the Lord's fist clenched in wrath against agents of sexual rebellion and the community that fails to root them out. Persons who internalize the Pentateuch's ineluctable quid pro quo have a compelling motive to restrict permissible sexual activity and reproduction to marriages that comply with biblical endogamy and to demand the same protectionist standard of sexual conduct from all community members. This is not to claim, however, that they are necessarily so Phinean as to kill religious sexual deviants, be it in vigilante style or by verdict of biblical law. Nonetheless, ardent followers of the Lord have solid Pentateuchal grounds for urging some form of violent and in principle deadly action against sexual apostates, so strong is the biblical abhorrence of allowing religious syncretism to seep into the Lord's domain through fornicating intercourse and procreation.

Paul's Religious Sexual Ethic and Its Adaptation of the Septuagint Pentateuch

The apostle Paul is a highly innovative advocate for the protectionism of an Israel that knows no cultural boundaries. He treats some basic tenets of the Septuagint Pentateuch and Prophets as variables open to change: The peoples to be claimed for the Lord become humanity at large, the biblical God is conjoined with Christ, and the promised land of pure dominion partly becomes a kingdom at the end of time. Paul's core rules for Christians to gain and retain hegemony in this domain, however, remain focused on eliminating practices of rebellious sexual fornication in the Gentile lands of the ancient Mediterranean. As argued here, Paul in his Christian mission strengthens the Pentateuchal prohibition against rebellious sexual fornication in three ways. He streamlines the prohibition into an unconditional format for all humanity to follow; he elevates its importance while setting aside other major aspects of biblical law; and he considers sexual intercourse in honor of other gods to be worse than non-sexual aspects of othertheistic worship or idolatry.

For two reasons, Paul's fervid sexual morality should not be regarded as a typical product of his being from a Hellenistic Jewish background. First, his zeal for the Lord was already extreme prior to his conversion to Christianity. On fire to uphold the Pentateuch in full, he persecuted Christians for deviating from it. Second, as a Christian he sustains and broadens his devotional zeal by reclassifying Gentiles as Israel and bearing an antipathy toward their polytheistic sexual mores that is modeled on the antipathy that the Prophets show toward the historical Israel's behavior of sexually fornicating in honor of other gods. These two features are key to understanding why Paul is severe and innovative in his insistence that sexual fornication must be driven from Gentile lands.

Paul believes that the violent terms of the Septuagint pact are true and apply universally to Gentiles as well as to God's historical people of Israel, Judah, and their descendants. God's realm is the known world, for all human beings are Israel, Gentiles and Jews alike. God is destined to bring his wrath against other-theistic sexual mores in the entirety of this domain. The Canaanites were but the first altercation in a much bigger battle about how human beings are to conduct themselves as religious agents sexually, reproductively, and in non-sexual respects. Paul accordingly teaches formerly Gentile Christians that they must abandon their hitherto traditional sexual worship of other gods. He tells the Corinthian Christians that God killed twenty-three thousand Israelites because of their sexually fornicating worship of alien gods and other acts of disobedience. The Corinthians must take heed of this example and abandon the gods to whom they used to direct their energy sexually, reproductively, and in other respects. They also must remain vigilant to prevent others in their community from participating in such practices. If the Corinthian Christians are negligent, they too are destined for a horrible demise, just like the Israelites. Paul issues the same message to the Thessalonian Christian community. They must abstain from sexual intercourse in worship of other gods in order to avoid "the avenging Lord". The community in Rome receives notice as well. Paul states that God's wrath is emerging against some or all Gentiles for the sexual worship that they devote to their gods. The Roman community must refuse to have further dealings with such sexual practices or they too will be destroyed.

Paul does not recognize the Pentateuch's distinction between rebellious and non-rebellious sexual fornication. Christians on his view must unconditionally "flee from sexual fornication", especially in the context of worshipping other gods. He emphasizes this imperative by according fornication a prominent place in lists of vices that Christians must always avoid. In order for sexually active Christians to comply with this imperative, they must make love strictly within the marriages that Paul deems to be sufficiently in the Lord, the parameters of which are demonstrated in the next section. Otherwise, they succumb to Satan. Paul is especially outraged by sexual fornication, as he indicates by his condemnation of the Christian man who makes love with the wife of the man's father. Even without involving incest or adultery, sexual fornication constitutes surrender to Satan, and as such is unconditionally forbidden and rebellious. As Paul unequivocally declares, a man who sexually fornicates severs himself from the body of Christ. Paul does not distinguish between degrees of disobedient sexual fornication, as the Pentateuch does, because he is struggling to teach Christians that they must protect themselves and their children at all costs from the sexual and reproductive conduits of other-theistic worship that pervade their social world. To remain free of such Satanic influence, Christians must flee sexual fornication altogether and make love solely within the bounds of religiously acceptable marriage.

Paul goes so far as to support the biblical principle of eliminating rebellious sexual fornicators in order to protect God's Christian people from divine retribution. His position about how to administer a death penalty is ambiguous, but undeniably harsh. In First Corinthians Paul judges that the man who fornicated with his father's wife must be sentenced to die. As Paul makes clear, the sentencing applies to the man as an agent of sexual fornication (porneðåñßïéa), not as an adulterer or agent of incest, even though the man is both. Thus Paul's death sentence here cannot be regarded as a rare measure that applies only in the extreme case of incest and adultery. His judgment would be as stern were he to catch Christians sexually worshipping Aphrodite. The terminology Paul uses in his death sentence, however, is ambiguous. The Corinthians must hand the man over to Satan "for the destruction of his flesh". Paul perhaps means that the Corinthians must surrender the man to be put to death through supernatural and Satanic forces. By this interpretation, the Corinthians must summon superhuman powers to bring about this end, but they themselves do not lay a violent hand on him.

It cannot be ruled out, however, that Paul aims to stir up zealots in the community to kill the man outright, problematic though such a procedure might be if Roman authorities were to find out. Deuteronomic precedent requires the death penalty, which Paul cites in delivering his condemnation. "Eliminate the wicked man from your midst".

¸Ejaðåñßïérv is the Septuagint euphemism for killing sexual apostates by human agency, such as stoning. In other sectors of Hellenistic Judaism, further, the elimination of sexual apostates is required, just as the Pentateuch stipulates, and in several instances the prospective executioners are human rather than supernatural. Finally, in Paul's phrase "the destruction of the [man's] flesh," the term used for "destruction" is Üleyrow, which has the same word root as the name Paul gives his angel of destruction in 1 Cor 10:10, ü òloyreutÞw, who sees to the massacre of the rebellious Israelites. Regardless of whether Paul has in mind a supernatural or conventional death penalty, and whether the Corinthians would have carried through his sentencing in any form, he unambiguously believes the Pentateuch's teaching that the man ought to be killed to avert the divine retribution to which the man has subjected the Christian collective through his sexual fornication. Paul is therefore deeply imbued with the Pentateuch's teaching that God's obedient people must take preemptive action to eliminate rebellious sexual fornicators in order to keep the community safe. Motivated by this antipathy toward agents of sexual defiance against God's will, he introduces this preemptive measure to Christianity as an unavoidable necessity for the collective good.

Paul, moreover, makes the Corinthian man's death sentence sound like a merciful and prudent measure for everyone concerned, the fornicator's included. In this respect he offers a radically different version of Deuteronomy's offer to choose monotheistic life over retributive death. So long as the Corinthians hand the man over to Satan for his destruction in the flesh, they do so to ensure that the man's "spirit be saved on the day of the Lord" at the resurrection. Their action provides the same assurance for themselves. To Paul, Christians would be negligent fools to throw away eternal life by tolerating fornicating sexual deviants among them. The life that matters most starts with the resurrection, unlike this transient life of the flesh, in which death is mere sleep until the grand awakening. The Pentateuch, by contrast, does not suggest that the sexual apostates themselves benefit by their death, for it does not share Paul's conception of the resurrection. In the Pentateuch the advantage falls strictly to the community through the people's restoration to God. The corpses of the sexual apostates lie there for the benefit of the repentant survivors, not of themselves. Paul therefore renews and strengthens the mandate that God's people must bring about the demise of sexual apostates. Among Christians in Gentile lands, the only good fornicators are dead ones, and it is good for them to be dead. Paul thus makes it possible, in theory, for Christians to wish with a clear conscience that fornicators in their midst meet their redemptive demise, and possibly even to take action to make that wish come true. Regardless of whether the death-bearing agent is demonic, human, or both, by Paul's teaching the hooded executioner is an angel of mercy.

Even though Paul deplores the sexual abominations condemned in the Pentateuch, such as homoeroticism on grounds that he elaborates from Leviticus, the danger of sexual fornication has much higher priority in his mission. He inveighs against homoeroticism but once in his letters, [64] while he repeatedly denounces fornication. This is because Paul's pinnacle of religious sexual danger remains, as in the Pentateuch, a heterosexual deviance a male among God's people making love to a biblical harlot, as Paul describes her, not a man making love to another man or a woman to a woman, though these also offend his conception of God's sexual mandate.

Paul elevates his prohibition against sexual fornication by his screening of other Pentateuchal rules. By the time he comes to avow that Jesus is the Christ, or savior, and takes this distinctive message of the Lord to the Gentiles, he regards fundamental features of the Pentateuch as not binding on formerly Gentile Christians, such as the dietary laws and male circumcision. Extensive sections of the Pentateuch, in fact, do not carry over into the regulations that he presents to Christians in his letters. Paul does not relent at all, however, regarding monotheistic sexual obedience. Thus the liberty Paul thinks Christians have gained from following biblical law he does not extend to sexual and reproductive behavior. Instead he intensifies this prohibition by repeatedly presenting it in unconditional terms. Paul's letters consequently portray God more as though he were the monotheistic chief of an antifornication vice squad. The Pentateuchal God, by contrast, is not quite so fixated on his people's sexual behavior, because he has numerous matters of holiness to oversee: diet, war, circumcision, the Sabbath and other holy days, the arts of proper sacrifice, tabernacle-building, and so forth. The God whom Paul reshapes for Christians to follow has fewer regulatory functions. Central among God's remaining tasks is to keep watchful surveillance on Christian patterns of sexual and reproductive conduct.

Paul uses strong imagery to stress the threat that sexual fornicators pose for the security and integrity of the Christian community. Christian bodies, he states, are the temple of the holy spirit and fornication is a sin "against the body", not unlike the desecration of a temple. Non-sexual transgressions do not bear this pivotal danger. Even though non-sexual sins are wrong, they are less intimately threatening because they are "outside the body," such as the transgression of Christians litigating in a pagan court. Further, if Christians are lax about allowing fornicators in the community, then a pollutant permeates the whole community, which Paul visualizes as a yeast that pervades the entire loaf of bread. If, however, Christians show no tolerance toward sexual fornicators in their midst, they will be a pure, unleavened bread that no yeast as foreign ingredient can pervade. Like the Prophets, Paul makes free use of metaphors to teach the norm of biblical monotheism. Flee from sexual fornication or else you desecrate your body as temple, and the community becomes an impure bread of death rather than the pure bread of life.

Paul's hostility toward other-theistic sexual fornication and its putative dangers is all the more noteworthy insofar as the biblical prohibition against idolatry does not adequately explain it. He regards sexual intercourse and procreation for other gods to be far worse than other non-sexual aspects of other-theistic or idolatrous worship. Though he continues to forbid Christians from worshipping other gods, just as the Pentateuch and Prophets do for God's historical people, he adopts a divergent stance on two equally idolatrous practices: dining on food and drink in worship of alien gods, as opposed to making love in worship of them. Regarding sacrificial food and drink, Paul maintains in principle that Christians must not dine "at the table of demons", yet he tempers this stance considerably. Christians may partake of food offered to idols, but only so long as they are not expressly informed about its identity as a religiously alien offering. If they are so aware, they should abstain, but the matter is not a critical concern. As he responds to the Corinthian Christians, "Food will not dedicate you to God. We are neither left behind if we do not eat nor do we prevail if we do eat" food offered to alien gods. When it comes to sexual intercourse in worship of other gods, however, Paul's stance differs radically. Christians under no circumstances are to politely ignore whether their sexual relations are in honor of gods other than the Lord, for to do so would be a reckless eliciting of divine retribution. Though "food is there for the belly and the belly is there for food, " he contrasts this dictate by adding that "The human body, though, belongs not to sexual fornication but to the Lord, and the Lord belongs to the human body". To Paul, then, it is a comparatively minor matter whether Christians occasionally dine on sacrificial food devoted to other gods, but it is a pressing concern that their acts of sexual intercourse never be devoted to gods other than or in addition to the Lord. Hence, regarding the worship of other gods, heterosexual copulation perturbs and provokes him far more than the dining does, even though both are of the body and other-theistic. Since both practices are equally idolatrous, the danger of idolatry per se does not sufficiently explain Paul's alarmist stance against fornication. Why he singles out and elevates the danger of other-theistic sexual intercourse as he does is an important topic that remains to be explored in the following chapter.

Paul's Principle of Religious Endogamy

Paul upholds the Septuagint principle of religious endogamy and its strict protectionism, though he imparts an inchoate Christian direction to it. He also pragmatically adapts this principle in First Corinthians to accommodate a common situation in his early Christian mission the religiously hybrid union that develops when one Gentile spouse converts to Christianity before the other spouse does.

Paul distinguishes between two kinds of married couples in his missionary communities. There are couples who are fully married by virtue of both being in the Lord, and there are those who are not yet in this preferred devotional class of marriage. In the second group only one spouse per couple has thus far converted to Christianity from a pre-existing condition of being polytheistic worshippers of Greek and other gods. Only the first group receives Paul's more honorific label "the married"; the others are "the rest". In the case of "the rest," because the couples were Gentiles at the time they wed, ancestral gods recognized their marriage and any childbearing done so far. These domestic partnerships remain at risk, for one spouse in each couple remains polytheistic and may teach his or her children to carry on this tradition. To Paul's mind, the families in question nonetheless show considerable promise of becoming fully rehabilitated, for the Christian spouse is obliged to make an effort to save the unconverted spouse and children. Paul accordingly considers "the rest" to be in transition toward full Christian marriage. In the interim, however, he makes a hierarchical division between the two groups of couples. Only "the married" are fully married in the Lord, so only they must heed Jesus' absolute prohibition against divorce. The marriages of "the rest," however, are not unconditionally binding, for their marriages are not yet fully genuine to Paul's mind, infiltrated as their sexual and domestic life still is by other gods of sex, birth, the household, and the public sphere. If the Gentile spouses do not consent to remain married to their Christian partners, then Christians have Paul's permission to let that union dissolve. Finally, Paul sees need to reassure the Christian spouses among "the rest" that the religious danger emanating from their partners is defused by special dispensation. In these already existing marriages the Christian spouse sanctifies the Gentile spouse and thus neutralizes the danger that the intimate yet alien partner would otherwise pose to the Christian spouse and community at large. The bona fide "married" couples, by contrast, require no such reassurance, for these marriages fully meet Paul's standard of genuine marriage. There are no alien deities stirring the sheets of their marriage bed.

Though Paul extends a special dispensation to already formed Gentile marriages that become halfway Christian and promise to do so fully, he does not allow Christians to marry unregenerate Gentiles. Paul commands that many Christians "marry". By this imperative he means, as his own phrasing suggests, that they should join the preferred ranks of "the married" by avoiding polytheistic partners and marrying a co-religionist in the Lord. First, Paul presumes that single Christians who marry must find the right balance between engaging in devotional prayer to the Lord and in marital sexual relations. The sexual activity serves the cooperative purpose of keeping Satan at bay. If Christians marry Gentiles, however, the Gentile spouses cannot carry out either of these two tasks. The couple can neither pray together in Christian monotheism nor ward off Satan through practices of sexual intercourse dedicated to God through Christ. Gentiles would not have heard of Satan, let alone vest the enormity of importance in keeping him at a distance that Paul and his fellow believers do. Only Christians who marry fellow constituents of God's people can pray and make love in the manner Paul requires of newly made marriages. Second, Paul expressly states that Christian widows may remarry "only in the Lord," that is, only with a man whom her religious community recognizes as belonging to their group. Paul therefore makes it clear that the marriages he allows Christians to make must abide by his transformative conception of biblical endogamy: The marriages must be indissoluble unions of Christians married to Christians (or possibly to other members of God's people) or else to Gentiles who convert to being in the Lord. Single and widowed Christians who wish to be sexually active must marry only within this Pauline branch of biblically monotheistic faith, make love only with their spouses, and rear children devoted to God alone. The sanctions against transgressive mixing are great. If Christians willfully pair off with unregenerate polytheists, they commit sexual fornication by reverting to polytheistic religious mores, and they and their children are damned. Religiously defiant marriages of this sort are unacceptable in the Christian community because they provoke the wrath of "the avenging Lord," if not immediately, then at the more pivotal end of time.

A passage in Second Corinthians shows the fervid anger early Christians could summon against Christians marrying Gentiles. Paul likely wrote this passage, but its authorship remains disputed. Regardless of whether he wrote it, borrowed it, or someone else inserted it, its marital principle is substantively the same as the one Paul promotes in First

Corinthians: Be Christian and marry a fellow member of God's people if you plan to marry. Second Corinthians 6:14–7:1 forbids "believers", who are members of God's people, from "entering into alien unions with unbelievers". The unions of primary concern are religiously pluralistic marriages that lead to the syncretistic worship of alien gods. "The believers" and "the unbelievers" are portrayed as though they were different religious species that must never be paired off together to copulate and reproduce hybrids. The participle Ýterozugoýntew refers primarily to the making of marriages, as opposed to other kinds of unions, for it applies a rule against mixed animal breeding in Leviticus 19:19 to spouse selection. Leviticus 19:19 prohibits the mating of unlike animals. 2 Cor 6:14–7:1 recasts and extends this rule to mean that Christians should no more pair off with unconverted Gentiles than, say, sheep should mate with horses. Other striking imagery in 2 Cor 6:14–7:1 reaffirms this resolute marriage restriction by separating Christians from the lower species of idolatrous beast: Christians are vessels of righteousness, light, Christ, and the temple of God, while unbelievers are carriers of lawlessness, darkness, Beliar, and idols. Second Corinthians thus brings the fervor of Ezekiel or Hosea to the nascent social norm of Christian endogamy. Paul in 1 Corinthians 7 endorses the same substantive marriage rule, though 1 Corinthians 7 uses less excitable rhetoric and is written more in the tone of marriage counseling.

It is consequently a mark of deep historical confusion to portray the formative Christian idea of sexual fornication as though it refers simply to acts of sexual intercourse outside of marriage and classifies such relations as immoral because they are extramarital, such as premarital sexual activity among adolescents in the modern day. Paul's conception of sexual fornication refers to sexual intercourse that is for the most part marital but outside of the institution of marriage in the Lord, aside from the pragmatic dispensation he allows for transitional marriages that become mixed through the Christian conversion of one Gentile spouse before the other. He finds such relations immoral because they are religiously diversifying, not because they are extramarital. Paul's stance on marriage is consequently one of fierce religious protectionism on par with the Prophets' own, albeit on different theological terms and in open new Gentile terrain.

Paul's norm of biblical endogamy proves revolutionary in relation to the traditional domestic and political culture of the Greeks and other Gentiles. In ancient Greek society, each city and its households provided the foundation, maintenance, and cultural existence of the gods and heroes. Central to these cities and their gods were the established local religious patterns of procreative relations among the citizens. As Plato states, "one ought to beget children, for it is our duty to leave behind, for the gods, people to worship them". Women and their reproductive bodies played a pivotal role in the household center of this Greek political system. Paul in his antifornication program aims to convert their bodies, domiciles, and cities into a new religious sphere with a far more centralized and exclusive focus on worshipping the biblical God alone through Christ.

Paul on Forbidden Desires against God's Will

Paul lends a psychological dimension of forbidden desire to the prohibitions he adapts from the Septuagint, such as his rule against sexual fornication. Transgressions against God do not simply include disobedient actions, but also the desire to commit such actions—the impulse itself, quite apart from whether one actually partakes of the forbidden activity. On this topic Paul is part of a broader Hellenistic Jewish and early Christian trend that stresses the danger of rebellious impulses very stringently. In Matthew's Sermon on the Mount, for instance, adultery is no longer only an act of disobedient sexual behavior. When a man looks with desire at a woman who is forbidden to him as a sexual partner, he commits adultery "in his heart", even if he does not make love to her. Paul as a missionary to the Gentiles, however, narrows the range of forbidden desire in the Hellenistic Jewish sense, which signifies that it is wrong to want to transgress any of the rules in biblical law, sexual and non-sexual alike. He thinks, as noted previously, that Christians must uphold but a few key Noahide rules from the Pentateuch (such as the prohibition against fornication), and not the Law in its entirely. The way Paul psychologizes sin is important to understand, for its anguished coloring plays a significant role in shaping the hairshirt ethos of ecclesiastical sexual morality.

Paul's understanding of wrongful "desire" or wrongfully "desiring" is thoroughly informed by a Hellenistic Jewish variant on the Septuagint Tenth Commandment. The variant is a two-word imperative oýk ÝpiyumÞseiw, which he cites and stresses in Romans 7:7 and 13:9. The Tenth Commandment in the Septuagint has the familiar lengthy form, which begins with the two-word imperative, oýk ÝpiyumÞseiw, followed by its complete set of direct objects, the neighbor's wife, house, field, servants, ox, and plow. This commandment in full prohibits men from coveting the people and goods belonging to other men in the community. It primarily protects the ownership privileges of male heads of the household. The persons and goods, wife included, are marked as inviolably a man's own insofar as other men must refrain even from wanting to take, let alone actually taking, any of them. In Hellenistic Jewish and early Christian exegesis, however, the phrase oýk ÝpiyumÞseiw occasionally stands on its own, as attested, for example, by Paul and Philo. In this twoword form, the Tenth Commandment takes on a significance that subsumes and goes beyond coveting in the sense of "strongly desiring to possess." The newer prohibition teaches that it is wrong or sinful even to desire to act contrary to God's will. Adherents of the Lord must refrain from wanting to disobey God's laws in any respect, be it a coveting of another man's wife or plow, a longing to worship other gods, a yearning to toil on the Sabbath, or any inclination to transgress Pentateuchal regulations, whether or not the rebellious inclination involves coveting.

Paul's Christian didacticism is imbued with the Hellenistic Jewish sense of Ýpiyumßa as a wrongful inclination or impulse to transgress God's will. In 1 Thessalonians 4:3–5, he sternly reminds Christians that it is "the will of God" for them to refrain from sexual fornication. If they disobey, then they succumb to being "in the passion of desire". The Thessalonian Christians suffer this sinful "passion of desire" not merely because they are heated with arousal, but because their sexual inclination is contrary to what God requires of them. They still want to engage in customs of sexual intercourse that the Lord forbids Gentile Israel to take part in, such as other-theistic copulation in the way of their ancestors.

In First Corinthians Paul likewise discloses that wrongful desire in his sense signifies an impulse to act contrary to his conception of God's will. He warns the Christians in Corinth not to be "those who desire wicked actions," by which he means the select Pentateuchal rules Christians must avoid: sexual fornication, idolatry, and resisting God's prophets or messengers. In this passage he teaches Christians these rules by drawing upon incidents in the Pentateuch that elicit divine punishment against disobedient Israel: the Israelites worshipping Aaron's golden calf, the Israelite men engaging in sexual fornication with the Moabite and Midianite women and the Israelite soldiers opposing Moses' orders. Christians, as Paul's Israel, must learn to fear God from the negative example set by biblical Israel and its retributive suffering. They must worship no gods but God, abandon practices of sexual fornication, and obey Paul's commands. In the Septuagint, however, the Israelites rebel against God only if they engage in the actions forbidden by the Pentateuch, while the Corinthians rebel against God simply by wanting to transgress Paul's more sexually specific compendium of Pentateuchal interdictions. The men sin against God if they even desire a forbidden woman, just as Flaubert's St. Antony later sins with desire despite himself when the Queen of Sheba captivates his gaze.

The same principle holds true for Christian women in their desires for the forbidden. According to Paul, then, Christians who even want to make love in the religiously alienating wilderness outside of marriage in the Lord relegate themselves to the outer darkness of apostasy and destruction.

Paul also blames Ýpiyumßa in the sense "desire to disobey God" for sin that takes the form of rebellious action. In Septuagint Psalm 105, Paul notes, the apostate Israelites "felt wrongful desire in the wilderness" and thereupon "tested God in the desert" by their acts of transgression. Their foolish testing of God's resolve then led to their destruction by his hand. To Paul this incident reveals two fundamental points: God means what he says in his vow to destroy the disobedient and save the obedient alone, and in order to avoid disobedience, God's people must avoid the stimulus of wrongful desire altogether. In short, they must obey Paul's aphoristic commandment oýk ÝpiyumÞseiw. Paul enforces this commandment by making wrongful desire itself a sin.

In Romans 7:7–25, however, Paul expresses disbelief that mortals can obey oýk ÝpiyumÞseiw through their own willpower. As he sees it, the desire to transgress God's will is an overwhelming kind of contrary law in the bodily limbs of human beings, which struggles against the obedient "law of the mind" that worships God. The greater force of thc bodily law enslaves human beings to the sin of wanting to defy God. Paul accordingly expresses considerable angst about the human condition, for he is convinced that these persistent wrongful desires subject God's people to a punitive state of being alienated from God, which he vividly describes as "the body of death". Human beings are severed from God and hence dead because obeying oýk ÝpiyumÞseiw is simply out of their reach, even if their actions may achieve an outward show of piety. Paul sees only one route to freedom from this plight. Through Christ the Lord alone, people can be rescued from their servitude to the desires that Gods forbids. Thanks to Christ, Christian Israel is uniquely gifted to live by this commandment without any opposing impulses. Genuinely devoted Christians do not even want to question Paul's teachings. They submissively obey them in full.

Paul's conviction that human beings are utterly unable to obey oýk ÝpiyumÞseiw by their own will and discipline sets him apart from his Hellenistic Jewish background. No other known Jew or early Christian concurs with Paul on this matter. The cardinal tenet of Judaism is that God is an eminently reasonable legislator whose laws both can and should be upheld in their entirety. As Deuteronomy states, "This set of commandments that I give to you today is not over burdensome or far from your reach". According to Paul, by contrast, people are uniformly abject slaves to the desires God forbids them to have, so much so that Christ has had to intervene in order to make obedience and salvation possible. As signs of such enslavement, Paul's Christian communities have not yet submitted totally to his teachings. They still yearn to worship their native gods, to make love outside of marriage in the Lord, and to question Paul's authority. Still, as Christians, they have a decisive advantage over other branches of God's people, for they at least have received the interventionist grace that Paul considers necessary to obey oýk ÝpiyumÞseiw to the full. Only as obedient Christians will God's people finally drive desires for religious pluralism and sexual freedom far, far away from their formerly Gentile lands.

Paul's conception of wrongful desire, as I have argued, is grounded in his Greek biblical background and the Hellenistic Jewish goal to refrain even from wanting to transgress God's laws. It is consequently misguided to continue the Greek patristic habit of explicating Paul's notion of Ýpiyumßa as though it were directly informed by Plato's idea of the irrational appetite, the Stoic passion of excessive desire, or some combination of the two. Paul gives no indication of using or even knowing Ýpiyumßa in the Platonic or Stoic philosophical senses. His conception of Ýpiyumßa as culpable desire is fully intelligible in terms of the Greek biblical background that informs his urgent concern to curtail the inclination to act contrary to God's will.

The Septuagint Pentateuch offers a potent but morally problematic rationale for eliciting compliance with the First Commandment and its corollary of biblical endogamy across generations. God is said to promise his people security, prosperity, and dominion in the land he gives them as their patrimony in exchange for their exclusive devotion. The land of milk and honey is theirs in perpetuity so long as they cease to partake of polytheistic mores, especially in their sexual and reproductive behavior. If they fail to comply, however, especially by the marital sexual worship of other deities, God vows that he will disinherit and destroy many of them, just as he did to the Canaanites. Though many today would find this teaching misguided and dangerous if taken seriously, Paul found it true and too dangerous to ignore.

Paul regards the Greek biblical quid pro quo to be as indubitable and universal as the law of gravity. If members of God's Gentile Israel persist in the sexual worship of other deities, they will fall as surely as the apple that landed on Newton's head. The suffering instigated by "the avenging Lord" occurs either in this life, as the Prophets maintain, or in the even more permanent and precious afterlife, as Paul teaches. It would be hard to imagine a more potent formula for inculcating monotheistic sexual obedience, for it is fear-inducing; works at the formative social level of marriage, reproduction, and childrearing; and connects these sexual customs with dire consequences for deviating and with unsurpassed glory for compliance.

Paul reworks the Pentateuch's religious sexual program into his own highly restrictive code. Christians, he contends, must unconditionally "flee from sexual fornication," and this is the first and foremost of all the sexual and non-sexual transgressions they must avoid. Paul's antifornication marital principle, further, is easy to learn and the reward he promises is great: Christians who choose to be sexually active must take as a spouse a fellow member of God's people and then engage in marital sexual relations only. As their reward they and their children will be saved at the end of time. Paul allows only one grandfather clause to his nascent Christian rule of religious endogamy the transitionally Christian marriage of "the rest". Christians who defy Paul's sexual rules, however, must in principle be extirpated by some ambiguous means for the putative good of all. If the community is so foolish as to turn a blind eye to sexual scofflaws, then they too are complicit in the defiance and are marked for judgment day.

According to Paul, it does not suffice for Christians to abstain from sexual intercourse in the worship of other gods and yet long for such ancestral mores. They must fully comply with his understanding of the commandment against forbidden desires. Christians alone, further, have received the ability to bend their will entirely in compliance with the Lord. Thanks to Christ's saving grace, obedient Christians do not look with desire even once, let alone twice or a third time, at the temples and rituals of the people they used to be, for there lies the dreaded way of fornication.

At this point we have come far in understanding the innovative gestalt of Paul's sexual morality, which is driven by his insistence that Christians must run away from sexual fornication foremost of all other-theistic dangers. The Pentateuch's sexual regulations on their own, however, fail to adequately motivate the emotive intensity of the restrictive sexual principles advocated by Paul and his patristic followers. To understand this extremely important dimension of early Christian sexual morality, we must turn to the sexual poetics of the Pentateuch, Prophets, and Paul.

Philo and his Double Set of Laws

Only the *Timaeus* is fully appreciated thus far for the formative role Plato's writings play in Philo's Middle Platonist thought. The cosmological *Timaeus,* however, readily assimilates only to the first couple of chapters in Genesis. After Genesis 3 cosmology yields quickly to the rules and normative tales concerning what members of Israel should and should not do as a society open to proselytes, such as worshipping God alone and not coveting another man's property, as well as dietary regulations concerning clean and unclean food, and many other matters impinging on the daily life of men, women, and children alike. The *Laws* of Plato provides a suggestive companion piece to Moses' *Law* or, more descriptively, *Laws*. Beyond the virtually identical title of the two works in Greek, Plato's *Laws* covers the same regulatory terrain, albeit with different rules: what the members of Magnesia should and should not do as a closed city 5,040 families strong, such as worshipping Plato's rehabilitated Greek gods and refraining from unnecessary desires for private property, as well as dietary regulations meant to eliminate appetitive indulgence on a community-wide basis, nowhere more so than in the sexual sphere.

Despite the differences in the specific laws of Plato and Moses, Philo and the Christian Platonists such as Clement (who built upon Philo), found it irresistible to regard Moses' *Law* and Plato's *Laws* as part one and part two of the same dispensation. They assimilated the two works, where feasible, and included some features of the *Republic* in the mix. They interpreted roughly similar themes in the Septuagint Pentateuch and Plato as evidence that Plato had learned from Moses, and used allegory to smooth the rough edges of the synthesis.

Plato's and Moses' laws seem to agree on three general points. First, sound legislation originates from a single god within a culture, God or ü yeüw, who sounded like the same deity, or close enough, to synthesis-inclined readers in Alexandria. Plato makes this argument about the legislative role of God in the opening of the *Laws,* while in Genesis 1:1 God speaks as lawgiver for nature; and then for mortals later in the Pentateuch, through Moses as intermediary. Second, Plato's conception of the theocratic state in the *Laws* arguably captures the gist of Moses' envisioned social order in the Pentateuch, as Josephus maintains. Third, Plato delivers his regulations in the *Laws* with a firm and assured hand, as the Pentateuch does, though the Pentateuch does it in a more stern and fixed manner. To Philo and the Christian Platonists, consequently, it was clear that Plato's *Laws* in its own way bore God's social mandate, and this conviction facilitated their amalgamating of Plato's and Moses' dictates for social order.

A biblical piety nonetheless prevails in Philo's (and Clement's) melded laws of God, for the Pentateuch comes first and Plato respectfully second to Hellenistic Jewish thinkers, at least as a matter of religious principle. The Pentateuch thus regulates the hermeneutic relationship to a considerable extent. Passages in Plato must show some *prima facie* congruence with the Pentateuch to be eligible as a borrowing, while aspects of Plato's thought that do not fit with the

Pentateuch are left aside, such as Plato's conviction that communal sexual reforms and rehabilitated Greek polytheism are both necessary and desirable in order for human beings to live like the gods. In practice, however, Plato is as much Moses' teacher as his student, especially in Philo's reworked program to restrain sexual desire.

Philo's sexual principles are part of an innovative agenda for social order that borrows from Plato and the Pentateuch, makes sense only in relation to both, and yet represents neither without noteworthy transformation. This is especially true for Philo's reinterpretation of the problems Plato sees with sexual desire, which Philo presents in his take on the aphoristic version of the Tenth Commandment: "You will not desire". In Philo's synthesis, forbidden desire in the Hellenistic Jewish sense, which signifies any inclination to defy God's will, becomes primarily sexual in light of Plato's conviction that uncontrolled desire for sexual pleasure is the single biggest source of individual and social corruption. Conversely, the biblical problem of spiritual fornication, or "screwing with" God's laws, is recast as an affliction that is caused primarily by sexual desire in the appetitive part of Plato's tripartite soul.

Though not a Christian, Philo is a major figure in the development of early church ideas about permissible sexual conduct. He in effect revisited Mt. Sinai and brought down a tenth commandment with a freshly minted meaning, one that Plato helped inscribe. Philo's innovative sexual agenda greatly helps explain why Christian Platonist church fathers later strive to quarantine sexual desire. The church fathers' sexual restrictions and related notion of forbidden desire develop from Philo's synthesis and are not understandable without it. Previous scholars on Philo's sexual ethics, however, have studied its Jewish and Middle Platonist components, not the utterly new sexual program that he produced from these components and bequeathed to the church through Christian Platonism. Philo's major role in the making of Christian

Platonist sexual asceticism has not yet received the recognition it deserves.

As argued here, Philo has two main criteria by which he distinguishes morally impermissible from permissible sexual activity: First, is the sex act practiced "for pleasure" rather than "for procreation"? The Pythagoreans and Plato are Philo's sources for this procreationist criterion. Second, does the sexual activity entail rebellion or apostasy from God? The Septuagint Pentateuch is the source for Philo's conception of sexual apostasy. He assimilates these two criteria to a limited degree. The uncontrolled sexual appetite for pleasure, Philo contends, is the primary motivator of rebellion against God, both directly and through the many vices it propagates. He does not, however, grant the reverse, that all sexual activity for pleasure, rather than for reproduction, constitutes apostasy from God. He nonetheless comes close to maintaining the latter position in various ways, and in response to Philo, Christian Platonists such as Clement later take up this position and put it at the center of their highly restrictive sexual dictates. To understand this development, we must begin with Philo's understanding of the desires that God forbids.

Philo's Revolutionary Conception of Forbidden Desire

Philo's Jewish Middle Platonist notion of forbidden desire combines two Hellenistic ideas that are philosophically distinct and originate in different cultural milieus. The first is the Hellenistic Jewish concern about the desire to disobey God's laws, which we have previously explored in connection with Paul. The second is the Middle Platonist problem of excessive physical appetites for the pleasures of food, drink, and especially sexual activity, contrary to reason's judicious sense of moderation. In Greek biblical terms, the desire to disobey God's regulations is wrong on theological and pragmatic grounds, theologically because the rules in principle derive from a divine being who is beyond fallibility, pragmatically due to the fearsome repercussions associated with transgressing, such as disinheritance and destruction. In Platonic terms, the uncontrolled sexual and other physical appetites are wrong because of the myriad psychological and social vices to which they ostensibly lead. Philo makes the Middle Platonist problem of the excessive sexual appetite a dominant concern of the Septuagint Decalogue, for he regards the sexual appetite as the most fiendish instigator of spiritual fornication. He does so by synthesizing the Hellenistic Jewish and Middle Platonist problems in his explanation of the abbreviated Tenth Commandment.

In branches of Hellenistic Judaism and early Christianity uninfluenced by Plato, the abbreviated Tenth Commandment taught that God's people must refrain even from wanting to disobey the Pentateuchal laws. Paul, as we have seen, understands it in this non-Platonic way, though he reduces the number of biblical rules for Christians to follow, while intensifying the rules against sexual fornication and religiously diversifying procreation. Philo's approach to sexualizing Pentateuchal law differs markedly from Paul's because he brings Plato's sexual ethics and political theory into the picture.

Philo accepts Plato's theory of the irrational physical appetites as well as his position that the sexual appetite is the most domineering and recalcitrant of the lot. Philo concurs with "those philosophers who researched the nature of the soul and found that its nature is tripartite: reason, spirit, and the irrational appetite". He further agrees that the appetites are an unavoidable part of our human and animal nature: "Nothing escapes from the irrational appetites completely". These inborn urges, however, are miscreant drives. Contrary to reason, they are insatiable in their primary desires for too much sexual pleasure, food, and drink. As Philo puts it, the soul's irrationally appetitive part "dwells [near the navel and diaphragm,] farthest from the royal abode of reason, for it is the most insatiable and unrestrained of beasts and is fed in those regions where digestion and copulation are located". Human beings must keep their appetites under rational guard by curbing their wild sexual desire through restricting the intake of food and drink.

Uncontrolled sexual desire, or eros, is especially problematic for Philo and his predecessor Plato. Sexual eros on Plato's view comes into its own as a raging tyrant once surplus nutriment fuels its voracity. The combined sexual appetite and reproductive urge, when fattened and left to their own devices, are the main root of depraved minds and social mores because they stimulate a proliferation of other passions. Philo fully agrees with Plato on this matter. Sexual eros is "the passion at the origin of wrongdoing". To prevent it from spawning other corrupt passions, people must keep it under strict control.

Philo transfers and attributes Plato's plans for appetitive and social reform to Moses and God through his gnomic Tenth Commandment. As he observes in *Special Laws* 4, oýk ÝpiyumÞseiw makes God speak with terse ambiguity and "deliver an oracle" in the mode of Apollo. Moses brought this commandment down in order to free God's people from intemperate sexual relations, feasting, and wine-drinking, as well as their many progeny, such as acquisitive greed and political tyranny (*Spec* 4.87–91, 95– 6). To underscore this point, Philo cites, directly from *Republic* 575b6–9, a list of the proliferating vices that he attributes to breaking his version of the Tenth Commandment. In God's social order these iniquities would become a thing of the past, so long as the people heed the commandment oýk ÝpiyumÞseiw by getting their appetitive urges under control, especially sexual desire.

Restricting diet is an important part of taming sexual desire for both Philo and Plato. Philo regards Moses' dietary laws as the one sure regimen that reduces sexual desire and thereby subdues its offspring of vices. Moses established the dietary prohibitions in Leviticus because he knew that the prohibited types of animal flesh, such as pork, are particularly laced with an aphrodisiac surplus. Insofar as "eros has often filled the known world with unspeakable disasters," Moses strove to cut off this appetitive proliferation at its nutritive source. By prohibiting the listed meat, poultry, and fish from the people's diet, he "contrived the putting out of appetitive desire, as though he were withholding wood from a fire".

Moses thus "began to train and chastise the appetite centered on the belly", because he knew God's people needed to put their "love-mad" sexual behavior on the right kind of diet. Thanks to Moses' foresight, virtuous social order is readily within reach, on their lips and at their hands. So long as they keep the forbidden food off their plates, sexual restraint will follow, and with this control in place the many other vices die off. Philo consequently sees no mystery behind the obscure reasons why Leviticus prohibits the eating of animals that, for instance, have cloven hooves but fail to chew the cud. Moses clearly had Plato's appetitive reforms in mind.

Philo's commandment oýk ÝpiyumÞseiw would mean "you will not have appetitive desire," if he were to interpret it at face value. He adopts no such literal reading, however, for he concurs with Plato that persons neither can nor should try to extinguish the appetites altogether. Though the appetites are incorrigibly wicked when given free rein, to escape them completely would be as undesirable and unfeasible as trying to remove the liver, the appetites' central locale, for they are what motivate us to stay alive and to produce the next generation. Philo thus softens an otherwise impossible oýk ÝpiyumÞseiw into a feasible rule you will not have excessive appetition. To heed this rendering of the Tenth Commandment, God's people need the sage scriptural guidance of God, Moses, and Plato, combined with their own human effort to exercise moderation. They do not need anything like the extraordinary intervention that Paul thinks mortals must get from Christ in order to obey his distinctive and non-Platonic rendering. Paul's rule requires the extirpation of desires that conflict with his conception of God's mandate for Christians, such as the desire to practice polytheistic sexual intercourse and procreation. Philo's Platonic rendering of this commandment does not involve such extirpation, at least in relation to the physical appetites.

Philo, however, does not simply transfer Plato's appetitive program unchanged to the Pentateuch. He reinterprets Platonic appetition and sexual desire foremost in light of the Hellenistic Jewish prohibition against the desire to disobey

God's will. Though Philo likely is not the only proponent of Jewish Platonism to reevaluate the Platonic physical appetites in this way, he is the only one known to do so. On his view, the sexual and other physical appetites are inherently bad because their inborn proclivity to be unrestrained is also a proclivity to transgress God's will as written in the Pentateuch. "The irrational appetite", and the sexual appetite in particular, "is the beginning of wrongs and violation of the Law". Physical appetition in general is "the origin of unjust acts", "a great and excessive wickedness, truly the origin of all wrongdoing," and "most shameful and cause of the most shameful deeds". The sexual appetite, though, is the worst of the lot given its persistent itch for the illicit, which for Philo means that its most deep-seated urge is to sexually defy biblical social order and to spawn myriad other wrongs in rebellion against the Lord. Moses consequently "cast the irrational appetite off with loathing" to the fullest extent possible and he taught his community to do likewise, most pithily through the oracular Tenth Commandment. The sexual appetite must be bridled, as Plato urges, but for Philo it must be bridled because it is at core an impulse to stimulate sexual behavior that shows religious defiance toward God.

Philo's Tenth Commandment is innovative as a Decalogue rule because it valorizes sexual desire as the main source of all wickedness. The Hellenistic Jewish Tenth Commandment in its two more traditional forms does no such thing. The commandment in its complete Septuagint form prohibits covetousness on the part of male property owners for the property and persons belonging to other men. Though forbidden coveting includes a man's desire to sexually arrogate for himself another man's wife or servant, this coveting is no worse than wanting to steal the ox and plow or to displace another man's family from his home. Further, the shortened form of this commandment is not sexually specific, for it prohibits God's people from wanting to transgress any of his laws, non-sexual and sexual alike. Philo's version however, prohibits unrestrained sexual desire as the primary origin of all religious defiance and corruption in the city of God. As Plato states, “Human sexual desires are the source of countless woes for people individually and for entire cities”. God’s people accordingly must make every effort to impound their sexual desire. The other two versions of the Tenth Commandment require nothing of the sort.

Philo, however, differs dramatically from Plato by insisting that sexual and other appetition is a “great and excessive wickedness, truly the origin of all wrongdoing”. Influenced as he is by the sinfulness of desiring to disobey God in Hellenistic Judaism, such as we see in Romans 7 on Ýpiyumßa, Philo loses touch with Plato’s central point that appetitive sexual desire is valuable within reason and beneficial when exercised to the necessary degree required for good health. For Philo it has no redeeming merit because there cannot possibly be any merit in wanting to act contrary to God’s will. Philo’s poetic imagery highlights the unconditionally negative value that he associates with eros and its feeding grounds. Just as no fuel escapes being consumed by fire, nothing gets away from the appetites. They function like poison and poisonous animals, such as snakes. The appetites sack and burn down the soul if one lets them, for appetitive passions are a “city-destroyer of the soul”. The appetites, though part of human nature, are inherently poisonous, shameful, evil, and snake-like, because they are a deep inner affliction to rebel against God, nowhere more so than the erogenous zone. Further, though Philo and Plato concur that unrestrained eros is the leading source of wrongful actions, Philo’s conception of right and wrong is biblically based. For Plato, people who give free rein to sexual desire primarily transgress the greater wisdom of human reason, not a god who requires unconditional obedience to him. Philo reworks Plato’s moral problem of the appetites in a Hellenistic Jewish mode that intensifies and alters the dangers that sexual desire poses. Sexual desire is inherently wicked and its primary yearning is to break away from the regulatory confines of the Pentateuch.

Philo markedly revises the traditional Greek biblical idea about the root of wickedness against God by vesting grave danger in sexual desire and its fricative pleasures. In Hellenistic Judaism and early Christianity, the primary danger of wickedness and rebellion against God is the desire to follow alien gods. The Wisdom of Solomon states this position most succinctly. The worship of alien gods or "idols" is "the beginning and end of all evils.". Though religiously diversifying sexual behavior is central to this danger, the fundamental problem is still the alien or syncretistic worship, not the sexual activity itself. Acts of sexual fornication are the secondary fallout of such worship, for without alien gods and forbidden patterns of worship, there can be no sexual fornication. In other words, "the invention of idols is the beginning of sexual fornication". In biblical terms, consequently, God's people must concentrate not on curtailing sexual desire per se, but on eliminating the worship of other gods in their midst in order to ensure the security of biblically monotheistic marriage and reproduction in the Lord. As the Pentateuch states, God's people must tear down the sacred sites of other gods and ritual practices in the promised land, for there lies the purported origin of wrongdoing, especially in the sexual domain of human behavior. For Philo, however, the "origin of wrongdoing" and "of violation of the Law" is innate sexual desire and its tendency to excessive pleasure, as Plato argues, not the worship of competing gods in the vicinity. Eros is what needs dismantling. Religiously alien sexual worship is simply one venue invented to accommodate the nefarious ways of eros.

Philo, however, does not leave behind the alarmist biblical stance toward the worship of other gods. Eros becomes the baneful idolatry of the soul. Philo identifies sexual desire as a kind of spiritual fornication against God that implicates the soul in psychologically worshipping Aphrodite in her inborn guise as the harlot Pleasure. Philo loosely explains this biblically grounded notion of soul fornication by putting the Stoic terminology of soul passions to an entirely new use.

On Philo's view, the inborn appetite to defy the Lord is inherently culpable and as such fit to be described with the terminology and definitions that the Stoics use for excessive desire (Ýpiyumßa) in the sense of a culpable soul passion. Sexual and other appetition is intrinsically, as the Stoics define soul passions, "an unmeasured and excessive impulse" (Ümetrow kaß pleonÜzousa ürmÞ) and "an irrational and unnatural movement (kßnhsiw paró fæsin)" of the soul. As such its very function is culpable, for "every passion is blameworthy (Ýpßlhmpton)." The substance of Philo's notion of appetition, however, is not at all Stoic. Appetition is inherently wicked on the grounds that it strives to disobey God, starting with the sexual urge against the Tenth Commandment and transmogrifying from there to a full-scale assault on biblical social order. It is in this Jewish Platonist sense that irrational appetition is a passion, for the impulse to go against God is "unmeasured, excessive, unnatural, and culpable."! In Stoic thought, by contrast, excessive desire (Ýpiyumßa) as passion has nothing to do with forbidden desire in the Hellenistic Jewish sense. The Stoic passion of excessive desire is "unmeasured, unnatural, and culpable" in the sense that it is a faulty evaluative decision and impulse that conflicts with right human reason and should be corrected through Stoic education, not in the sense that it is an innate, irrational, and inherently wicked affliction that strives to defy a supreme deity and can only be suppressed. In Philo's writings, further, the four canonical Stoic passions, desire, pleasure, fear, and remorse, become a canon of two: the irrational appetite and its pleasures. The Stoic definitions of the passions that Philo uses are thus like a label that at first glance looks Stoic, but the contents have changed. The innate sexual appetite is an excessive passion because it itches to defy a god who requires full compliance with his rules.

Philo appropriates the Stoic terminology of the passions to recast the biblical danger of spiritual fornication in psychological terms. For the Stoics, the passions cause a soul "disease" (nüsow), but for Philo, the soul becomes "fornicated" (peporneumÝnh) and thus "defiled" through its appetitive desire and pleasure. The new malady that Philo ascribes to the appetite dominated soul presupposes the Pentateuchal metaphor of spiritual fornication and its didactic message. This metaphor serves to deter God's people from insubordination by casting the opprobrium of sexual fornication on transgressions in general. Philo is doing the same thing here in a Platonizing psychological vein, for he is utilizing the Pentateuch's sexual slur quit "screwing with" God's laws to depict appetitive eros as the source of all such spiritually fornicating transgressions, which for Philo starts with religious sexual defiance of the Lord and generates countless other vices from there. Philo situates spiritual fornication and its defilement in the soul (the soul's third part in particular) because that is where he, following Plato, locates sexual desire, hunger, and thirst. This new religious affliction of soul fornication further underscores the non-Stoic nature of Philo's passions of desire and pleasure. Even if the sexual and other appetites do not successfully provoke God's people into rebellion, that is what these snakelike and fornicating passions of the soul hiss to do. Similarly, the irrational sexual and other appetites are "shameful idols of the soul", like inner psychic icons of alien gods luring God's people to turn away from the Lord and to worship the appetites instead. If the idolatrous enticement succeeds, the soul succumbs to fornicating against God, first sexually and then in many other ways spawned by eros. Once a soul succumbs, human regimens of purification are worthless at restoring it. Even the strict Pythagorean regimen fails. Only the Lord God can save the soul that is fornicated beyond human remedy. Though Philo draws upon the Stoics and Plato to articulate this notion of soul fornication, neither the Stoics nor Plato would recognize Philo's religious sexual ethic as their own, for Philo's presupposes the Pentateuch and its didactic metaphor of spiritual fornication.

Through imagery of the biblical harlot, Philo elaborates his position that the sexual appetite strives to fornicate against God's will. To understand this imagery, one must realize that Philo, like Paul, presumes that the biblical innuendoes about harlots are true: Such women embody the seductive and largely sexual lure to abandon the Lord.

Appetitive Pleasure, Philo asserts, is a biblical whore. She gives alluring looks, walks suggestively, and boldly holds her neck upright. Likewise in the Septuagint, women labeled as harlots use the same stereotype gestures of enticement to lure male members of God's people to their religious ruin. Pleasure is Philo's preeminent biblical whore because appetitive sexual pleasure is what lures God's people to transgress the aphoristic Tenth Commandment and other biblical laws. Philo, through his claim that Pleasure is a biblical whore, emphasizes the danger of disobeying God that he associates with excessive appetitive pleasure. He also perpetuates the stereotype that the woman unconstrained by biblical monotheism embodies religious anarchy, be she a flesh and blood Jezebel or Philo's Jezebel, Pleasure.

The biblical whore Pleasure as Philo conceptualizes her, however, is no ordinary woman and the pleasure that he fears is not generically appetitive. She is the goddess Aphrodite and her pleasure is sexual. The cosmic force of Pleasure, Philo states, instills sexual arousal and sexual pleasure in living creatures, including human beings. "Pleasure is a mighty spirit throughout the world." The creatures of "the air, water, and land" eagerly copulate when stimulated by her powers. Here Philo is simultaneously describing and debasing the power of Aphrodite by way of literary allusion, for the mighty spirit of sexual arousal that he ascribes to the whore Pleasure is Aphrodite's main attribute as presented in the *Homeric Hymn to Aphrodite*. Aphrodite as awesome goddess in the *Hymn* likewise stimulates all creatures of "the air, water, and land" to become aroused and eagerly copulate. The sexual dominion she wields over animate beings is a central part of Greek religious and world order. For Philo, by contrast, Aphrodite as Pleasure is not a genuine goddess who merits reverence, as she was for the Greeks. She is the cosmic madam of religiously alienating sexual desire. God's people must avoid Aphrodite's strong attraction and sexual power for the same reason that Jeremiah commands the Jewish women and men in Egypt to drive Ishtar from their religious lives. Insofar as sexual pleasure is an alien yet alluring deity, her force is inimical to upholding the commandment to worship God alone.

Philo, though, regards Aphrodite as a goddess whose power and presence are much more pervasive than her statues in various temple precincts indicate. He locates her in sexual desire, genital contact, and orgasms, just as the Greeks themselves did. For Philo, though, Aphrodite wields her sexual power in the soul's appetitive zone in an effort to lure God's people into her realm of hedonistic sexual rebellion, just as Septuagint harlots try to draw Israelite men into fornicating rebellion. Pleasure gives the provocative "glance and nod" of the biblical harlot, and she even "whinnies" like the male adulterers whom Jeremiah likens to stallions in heat. The peoples and animals in her thrall barely wait for her imperious glance and nod before copulating in recognition of her power. Persons devoted to God must protect themselves as much as possible from her indwelling hold on the soul. If they fail, they revere Pleasure rather than God. Their fornicated souls become the domicile of the "shameful soul idol" par excellence, Venus de Milo herself. By this revolutionary understanding of the origin of transgressing God's laws, the very nature of human eroticism becomes the pursuit of the inner whore goddess who incessantly nods and winks and whinnies come on over, seek sexual pleasure, abandon God, and worship me.

Despite his Platonism, Philo differs greatly from Plato in the central danger that he sees in sexual arousal and pleasure. Though Plato is his source for the idea that uncontrolled eros is the taproot of all wrongdoing, Philo instance, Philo portrays the biblical patriarchs as exemplars of the strictly reproductive sexual behavior that God's people must emulate in order to keep sexual desire under tight control. Abraham's sexual relations with Hagar are strictly for reproduction, not for pleasure. Abraham further thinks that Isaac should make love to Rebecca only for the procreation of children, not for pleasure. Joseph too fends off the advances of Potiphar's wife by declaring his procreationist virtue: "Before acts of legitimate marital intercourse, we do not know other women, but come as chaste males to chaste females, not with pleasure as the end, but for the production of legitimate children". Moses as well remains oblivious of sexual pleasures except insofar as they are necessary for "the sowing of legitimate children". According to Philo, therefore, the patriarchs lived by the procreationist rule and thereby set the example of properly restrained sexual devotion to the biblical God.

Philo's reputation as "the Pythagorean Philo" among the early church fathers is borne out by the austerity of his sexual ethic, which is Pythagorean in origin. He objects to married couples engaging in sexual intercourse for any purpose other than reproduction. Husbands who exceed the limit with their wives make love "licentiously, not with other women, but with their own wives". Philo rules out the possibility that married couples may reasonably engage in sexual relations for other purposes, such as fostering mutual friendship, as the Stoics argue, or keeping Satan at bay, as Paul maintains. Philo belongs fully to the later Pythagorean tradition of Ocellus and Charondas, who likewise maintain that sexual relations can only be rightly for procreation or reprehensibly for pleasure. Philo also learned the procreationist dictate at least in part from Ocellus, for he read "the treatise of Ocellus Lucanus, titled 'On the Nature of the Universe'" and found its teachings eminently valuable. Philo's thought shows other Pythagorean tendencies as well, such as his conviction that overeating or eating the wrong foods makes one oversexed. His endorsement of procreationism is therefore but one aspect of his broader endorsement of Pythagorean ideas, which is true of Seneca and Musonius as well. Philo's procreationism, however, differs in a noteworthy way from its Neopythagorean and Roman Stoic counterparts. He regards the sexual dictate as the formal mandate of the biblical God.

Procreationism gains greater breadth and normative force once Philo incorporates it into the Pentateuch and makes it the only acceptable way to be sexually active in worship of

God. Leviticus 18:19, for example, prohibits a man from having sexual relations with a menstruating woman in order to avoid uncleanness. Philo ascribes a new motive to this law. The husband is meant to be strictly a "good farmer" of his wife's womb, and as any farmer knows, flooded fields cannot be successfully planted. The husband must not make love with his wife during her period because he knows she is at flood stage. The procreationist husband, moreover, fears his seed will perish in his wife's menstruating womb, for deliberately non-reproductive ejaculation destroys "the seed of one's children," as Charondas asserts, and it thereby helps destroy humanity, as Plato earnestly maintains in the *Laws*. Once the wife's menstrual period ends, however, Philo exhorts the husband to take courage and sow as he sees fit to help produce a flourishing crop of children in the Lord. Philo thus provides a new rationale for the prohibition in Leviticus against a man copulating with a menstruating woman. The husband is not avoiding uncleanness, he is following God's procreationist rule. Pythagorean reproductive technology has now joined forces with the biblical God.

Philo similarly recasts Leviticus 18:22, which prohibits a man from lying with a man "as though with a woman," and refers to such activity as an abomination. To Philo, male homoerotic lovers are foolish and reprehensible farmers in the reproductive agribusiness God requires of them, for they labor over fields known to be sterile at the expense of fruitful ones. These men also deliberately make cities desolate by emasculating their inherently procreative seed. Philo thus justifies Leviticus 18:22 on the same grounds that Plato gives in the *Laws* against male citizens copulating with one another during their time of reproductive service to the city. If the male citizens transgress this rule while they are on procreative duty, they are destroying the human race. Plato in the *Laws*, however, does not disallow male homoerotic relations once the men are retired from duty. Philo's anti-homoerotic procreationism is binding throughout a man's lifetime. The biblical God would not have it otherwise on his view, for to make love for any reason other than reproduction within marriage is to fall into fornicating pursuit of Aphrodite as Pleasure.

Philo reinterprets the Septuagint Pentateuch in a striking way by maintaining that it supports procreationism. The Pentateuch promotes the value of reproducing families devoted to the honor and glory of God, for this is central to biblical ideals, as the Pentateuch shows in numerous ways. This biblical directive is not procreationist, however, because it does not limit religiously acceptable sexual behavior to marital reproduction alone; while this is the restriction that Philo instates under the rubric of God's law. Philo's procreationist conception of God's sexual mandate sets his sexual ethic apart from the sexual rules one can reasonably claim are contained in the Law. Not surprisingly, then, his Pythagorean-based views are incompatible with those of Paul and the rabbis, whose principles of sexual conduct remain closer to their respective biblical backgrounds in Greek and Hebrew.

Though Philo's reading of procreationism into the Pentateuch is innovative, it is not arbitrary. On his view, God's Law and philosophical conceptions of natural law "are in mutual accord." Persons who adhere to the Pentateuchal rules live "according to nature's intent". Philo's sense of natural law, further, is infused with the Pythagorean stance that human sexual conduct should be strictly procreationist. As he states, "Servants of God fulfill the law of nature" by practicing strictly reproductive sexual relations in marriage. Given that God's law and Philo's procreationist idea of natural law are in mutual agreement, proper sexual obedience to God's law must meet the procreationist standard. Philo's Jewish Middle Platonist exegesis thus serves not to distort the Law as he sees it, but to uncover the hidden wisdom of its procreationist norm. This is not to diminish the fact that his hermeneutic effort transforms biblical sexual principles in light of Pythagoreanism. Philo's procreationist conception of biblical law is one of the revolutionary results of interpreting the Pentateuch as a document of normative nature.

There is a major difference in religious tenor between Philo's procreationism and that of Greek and Roman advocates of the rule. The norm of strictly marital and reproductive sex is Philo's key way to harness sexual desire in strict devotion to the Lord and to prevent it from following its inherently lawless tendency to pursue alien gods, be they Baal, Ishtar, or the soul-dwelling harlot Aphrodite or Pleasure. Greeks and Romans who favor procreationism, by contrast, are not biblical monotheists and do not regard sexual activity and its pleasures as a hostile divine power. Plato, Musonius, and the other Greek and Roman advocates of procreationism regard reproductive sexual relations as an intrinsic and obligatory part of worshipping their gods. This polytheistic piety is one of their arguments in favor of procreationism. As Musonius and Plato argue, citizens egregiously shirk their religious and civic duties unless they produce restrained children in order to foster Aphrodite and other gods of the city and to sustain the symbiotic relationship between gods and mortals. The First Commandment rider of Philo's sexual ethic, however, segregates procreationists married in the Lord from the polytheistic social world surrounding them. Once this procreationist norm is in place, the hitherto elusive attainment of untroubled monotheism and prosperity will belong to the Lord's people in perpetuity. Philo's Pythagorean and Roman Stoic counterparts share neither his theological separatism nor his belief that procreationism is the way to the promised land.

In addition to his procreationist dictate, Philo has a second criterion for distinguishing impermissible from permissible sexual activity. This criterion, which adheres to the letter of Pentateuchal law, is motivated by the Septuagint's unconditional requirement for religious and sexual obedience to God. In the Septuagint, sexual and non-sexual actions that break the covenant rules elicit a death penalty in some form so as to avert God's wrath against the community. Philo concurs. If, in his estimation, a sex act constitutes apostasy from the Lord, it is absolutely forbidden and its agents should be put to death.

In ardent support of the Pentateuch, Philo urges that agents of sexual rebellion within the community be killed in the interest of public security. If an act of sexual fornication implicates the agents in adultery, it warrants the death penalty for both parties. "[Adulterers] are common enemies of the entire human race and must be punished with death." For the same religious reasons Philo rigorously upholds what he regards as the blanket Levitical death penalty for agents of male homoerotic and human-animal sexual relations. Men who make love to other men are "worth killing by those who obey the Law". Men and women who copulate with animals like wise "must die" along with their four-footed sexual partners. In the Pentateuch, these three kinds of sexual activity adultery, male homoerotic sexual relations (in some, many, or all positions), and sexual activity of humans with animals are unambiguously marked as rebellion and the penalty of death is their purification. Philo advocates this code with a Phinean spirit in word if not deed for his Hellenistic Jewish community.

Philo further believes that when a sex act is marked as an abomination in the Pentateuch, it counts as rebellion and its agents deserve to be put to death. He accordingly extends a death penalty to several kinds of sexual activity that the Pentateuch classifies as an abomination but does not assign a specific penalty. Philo thinks, for example, that it is an abomination for female members of God's people to become prostitutes. He bases this rule loosely on Deuteronomy 23:18–19, which prohibits the women from becoming a specific kind of cult functionary and states that women who transgress this rule commit an abomination. This functionary is interpreted in the Septuagint as being a "female bearer of fruit" or temple "harlot", for her cult and sexual standards deviate from the way of the Lord as defined by Deuteronomy. Deuteronomy leaves the question open as to how the people should respond to women who take on this forbidden temple role. Philo would have them killed. He takes the opprobrious term "abomination" in Deut 23:19 as a signifier that women in the community who become prostitutes are in rebellion against God. Such women are a source of "communal defilement" as well as "a pest and a bane," and thus must be stoned to death. Neither the Pentateuch nor the rabbinic tradition supports a death penalty for prostitution. For Philo, however, the women must be killed because the abomination of their presence imperils the security of the people.

Philo likewise shows his chilling severity toward agents of sexual abominations in his support of a Deuteronomic rule against reconciling after a marital separation. This rule states that a woman and her first husband commit an abomination when they reconcile if the woman has had a second husband during the separation. Though Deuteronomy does not state what measures the religious community should take, if any, against this transgression, Philo declares that the couple must be put to death for the abomination. He believes that the woman transgresses "ancient and divine sanctions" by cohabiting with a man while her first husband is still alive. Further, if the first husband takes the woman back upon her return, he commits "two of the worst transgressions, adultery and pandering". Philo's disposition against the perpetrators of sexual abominations is exceedingly harsh as a cautionary measure to keep his community on the safe side of religious obedience and God. He does not want to risk letting sexual abominations go unpunished given the grave threat that they pose for the community according to the Pentateuch.

Philo, following Leviticus, maintains that acts of incestuous fornication are also dangerous and must be avoided. He considers a sex act to be incest if it transgresses the heterosexual relations among kin prohibited in Leviticus 18. Philo finds the first Levitical prohibition, incest between a mother and her son, to be particularly dangerous: "No unholy act is more impious than to bring a father's bed to shame". He refrains, however, from advocating that agents of incest be put to death through human agency, but asserts that divine Justice takes action of her own accord against agents of incest, as shown by the examples of Oedipus and Persian royalty. Dßkh is the Greek force of cosmic justice best known for righting such imbalance. Philo therefore thinks that incestuous transgressors are doomed, but he does not urge the people in the community to strike them down as a preventive measure.

Philo makes his uncompromising position against sexual rebellion clear in his creative retelling of Numbers 25, where some Israelite men fornicate with Moabite and Midianite women during rituals in honor of Baal. The men commit apostasy on two counts, disobeying the First Commandment and making love to religiously alien women. Philo reveals the security danger that he associates with rebellious sexual fornication by attributing a conspiracy to the women. The Moabite women, he asserts, deliberately passed themselves off as prostitutes in order to seduce and weaken their enemies, the Israelite soldiers, as though the women knew that the Israelites remained powerful only so long as the men stayed untouched by their religiously alien sexuality. The Moabite women accordingly had "sexual intercourse with whomever they wished" among the Israelite soldiers, like guerrilla versions of Delilah behind enemy lines. By copulating with the men, they unleashed a "communal defilement" (koinün mßasma) that tainted the community and threatened its security because of God's vow to retaliate against his defiant people. To ward off the disaster, the Israelite Phineas takes on his vigilante role. Filled with "righteous wrath", he kills an Israelite and a Midianite woman. Other Israelites zealously follow suit and carry out violent purification on a mass scale. "They cleanse the defilement of the [Lord's] people" by massacring twenty-four thousand of their kinsmen who had sexual relations with the Moabite women. This purge, on Philo's view, is the plague mentioned in Numbers 26.1. The Israelites responsible for slaughtering their kinsmen remain "pure" and Phineas is a hero who rose to the defense of the Lord. The surviving Israelites are bloody but pristine because the slaughter of rebellious kinsmen is necessary to preserve the way of the Lord.

In agreement with the Pentateuch, however, Philo recognizes that there are kinds of sexual fornication that are not apostasy and do not warrant the death penalty. As stated in Exodus and Deuteronomy, if a man rapes an unbetrothed virgin, she is corrupted and her father should redress the problem in one of the two ways. The father must either marry his daughter to the rapist in the interest of social purity, or take a dowry from the man without marrying his daughter to him. If, however, a man rapes a virgin betrothed to another man, the rapist should be stoned to death but the woman should be spared, provided that she demonstrates through outcries, when demonstrable, that the act is against her will. Furthermore, Philo states that if a man rapes a woman separated from her husband or widowed, "there is to be no death penalty". Since the woman is no longer owned as the wifc of a spccific man, this act of rape does not implicate her attacker in adultery. Philo considers this sexual crime to be only half as grave as adultery, and he would subject the rapist to a flogging or a fine. He therefore still recognizes the Pentateuchal position that there are gradations of wrong when it comes to sexual fornication not all sexual fornication is outright rebellion. On this topic Philo differs from Paul, who urges Christians to flee sexual fornication unconditionally or else suffer divine wrath en masse when Christ comes to claim them.

Philo likewise concurs with the Pentateuch that marriages between members of God's people and foreigners are acceptable, so long as the foreign spouses have converted to the way of the Lord. It is misguided, Philo thinks, for his religious community to restrict eligible spouses only to persons born as members: "Inter-marriages with foreigners lead to new kinships that are not at all inferior to blood-relationships." Such marriages are to be commended, for their religious outreach makes the way of the Lord more widespread and welcoming. Philo sternly reminds his community however, that conversion must not proceed in the other direction, away from the Lord into religious diversification. If foreign spouses bring othertheistic practices to the marriage and God's community, then their marriages and families fall away from God and the community is imperiled. Such religiously deviant marriages are "the beginning and end of the utmost suffering" for God's people in the future. Philo therefore endorses the Pentateuchal idea that membership in the Lord's community is to be measured more by its monotheistic code of behavior than by its bloodline. He praises the marriage that supports this code, for it brings more persons to the light of God, while he deplores the marriage that abandons the code and plunges the family into the abyss of religious alienation.

Philo's conception of sexual apostasy and the social peril he links with it are based on in his exegesis of the Septuagint Pentateuch, not on his Middle Platonist learning. Regarding which sex acts are apostasy, he adheres to the strict letter of the Law, and in several instances he is more extreme. For instance, both Philo and the Pentateuch maintain that sexual fornication is apostasy if it involves a man making love to another man's wife, but not if it involves a man raping an unbetrothed virgin. Similarly, male homoerotic and human-animal sexual relations put their agents beyond the pale in their disobedience toward God, but raping a widow does not. Philo, however, would stone prostitutes for their abomination, which the Pentateuch does not countenance. Despite Philo's greater stringency, the Pentateuch provides the basis from which he develops his ideas about sexual rebellion against God, its grave social dangers, and the types of sexual activity that he classifies as rebellion.

Philo's Limited Synthesis of his Criteria of Impermissible Sexual Activity

Philo could easily have argued that married couples commit rebellious idolatry anytime they make love for pleasure rather than for procreation, given the procreationist cast he imparts to biblical law. As he clearly states, God's mandate is that sexual activity should be marital and only for procreation. To experience the pleasurable end of sexual desire is to succumb to the soul harlot and idol Aphrodite. With a sweeping gesture, then, Philo could have regarded all sexual deviance from procreationism as the defiant and fornicating pursuit of Aphrodite. He nonetheless stops short of this uncompromising position.

Philo does not grant that sexual activity constitutes rebellion against God simply by occurring for pleasure rather than for reproduction. He distinguishes between two degrees of sexual wickedness. On the one hand there are "the great evils" of sexual licentiousness. Sexual behavior is licentious when it exceeds its strictly reproductive function within marriage as ordained by God and nature. This behavior reveals that eros is ready to spring into lawlessness. Beyond this wickedness, however, lies the "even greater evil" of eros successfully defying God through formally rebellious sexual activity, such as adultery, male homoerotic relations, and reconciled marriages of the sort Philo abhors. His assimilation of Pythagorean procreationism to the Pentateuch therefore remains incomplete. Sexual activity for pleasure rather than for procreation is apostasy only in circumstances where the Pentateuch outlaws it on a literal level or stigmatizes it as an abomination.

Philo sees two degrees of sexual transgression at work in biblical history and in his own society. If husbands make love with their wives for non-reproductive pleasure, he recommends the regimen of Moses' dietary laws, not death, for this class of sexual offenders. Philo likewise remains content to rebuke men who seek out as wives women already known to be barren. These men are "adversaries of God" because they wish to "destroy their procreative semen," contrary to God's will and natural law. Verbal opprobrium suffices for spouses who exceed the procreationist limit in their marital sexual relations. Even though the men are at grave risk of becoming apostates, they do nothing to stir Philo's Phinean ire so long as their wantonly non-reproductive sexual practices do not yet succeed in breaking out of the marriage bond.

By contrast, the Sodomites were drawn into religious rebellion due to the lawless proclivity of appetitive sexual desire. When they succumbed to their unrestrained sexual appetite for pleasure, they "threw off the yoke of sexual restraint" and committed "lawless acts of copulation", for they broke the unconditional law against male homoeroticism that Philo sees in Leviticus. The Israelites likewise rebelled against God out of unbridled sexual desire when they fornicated with the Moabite women. The Sodomite and Israelite incidents show eros fulfilling its deepest lust to defy God, which in turn leads the transgressors to be destroyed, in accordance with God's quid pro quo. These admonitory examples show Philo that God's people must adopt the norm of procreationism to prevent sexual desire from ever getting its rebellious way again.

Philo thus assimilates his two criteria of impermissible sexual activity together only to a limited extent. He does not identify all non-procreationist sexual activity as apostasy, even though he regards biblical law as procreationist and identifies sexual desire as idolatrous soul whoredom working its way against God. Philo nonetheless refrains from categorizing "love-mad" husbands and wives as apostates earmarked for destruction by the Lord. So long as the spouses' erotic madness stays marital, the community is not endangered and the couples may remain alive.

Summary

Philo reaches this position by identifying the Platonic notion of sexual desire with the Hellenistic Jewish concern about the inherently wrongful impulse to transgress God's laws. He makes this identification most notably through his Jewish Middle Platonist explanation of the commandment against forbidden desire. Appetitive sexual desire is the leading threat against the security and hegemony of God's people because its aim of unrestrained pleasure transgresses Philo's aphoristic Tenth Commandment and presses toward greater lawlessness licentiousness within marriage today, sexual abominations tomorrow. To emphasize this point, Philo adapts the biblical metaphor of spiritual fornication. Sexual desire and pleasure are fornicating soul passions. The lure of pleasure, and genital sexual pleasure specifically, emanates from the cosmic harlot Aphrodite. To pursue her beyond the procreationist limit is a kind of psychological idolatry, and this experience is fiery, poisonous, and snake-like fit for abhorrence, never enjoyment.

To counteract the dangerous powers of Aphrodite, God via Moses sternly limits sexual desire among his people to the strictly reproductive and marital outlet. The patriarchs solemnly lived by this rule and the people at large must heed it as well. This procreationist dictate is a sure way for God's people to finally transcend the religious sexual rebellion that has burdened them in biblical history. Husbands who fail to show strictly reproductive prudence with their wives are reprehensible because they allow sexual desire to slither closer to its goal of striking out against God, but they activate Philo's pre-emptive alarm only by transgressing the Pentateuch on a more literal level.

Philo lays the ground for a paradigm shift in biblical sexual norms, but he remains relatively conservative himself. He gives Christian Platonist writers ample reason to find any transgression of procreationism an act of hedonistic defiance of God, even within marriage. Philo himself, however, stops short of maintaining this position. Even though he asserts that God's law is procreationist and blames acts of sexual apostasy on the excessive sexual appetite, he does not think that persons commit apostasy simply by transgressing procreationism. Sexual relations within marriage for pleasure rather than for procreation are the major exception he allows. Philo's conception of sexual rules thus turns out to be more traditionally Pentateuchal than his adventurous exegesis would initially indicate. Despite his venturesome ideas that the Pentateuch is procreationist and that the aphoristic Tenth Commandment is inspired by the dangers Plato sees in appetitive sexual desire, Philo reserves the pre-emptive death penalty for transgressors who commit sexual abominations. Only agents of abominations pose the threat of God disinheriting and destroying his people.

Clement of Alexandria, as argued in chapter nine, completes Philo's paradigm shift, for in response to Philo he identifies any deviation from God's procreationist law as sexually hedonistic rebellion against God. Clement adopts this position, however, partly in an effort to defuse the even more extreme argument in favor of sexual renunciation offered by his formidable predecessor in patristic sexual morality, the encratite Christian Tatian, to whom we now turn.

10

Plato's Apologies and Socrates in Ancient Philosophy

Introduction

Dramatically, the reported conversation of the *Sophist* takes place on the day following that of the *Theaetetus*. But this dialectical continuity, highly significant though it is, scarcely papers over such striking differences between the two works as the *Sophist*'s avoidance of hiatus, the reduction of Socrates in that dialogue to a bystander, and the apparently solid findings concerning collection and division, metaphysics, and language arrived at by the Eleatic Stranger, who masterminds the discussion. For all we know, a number of years may have intervened between Plato's initial draft of the *Theaetetus* and his composition of the *Sophist*. If the *Philebus* is a still later work (as most scholars assume), Socrates makes one important return, to set against his virtual silence in the Statesman, his minor role in the *Timaeus* and *Critias*, and his total absence from the *Laws*. But the *Philebus* is a dialogue that has no setting in time or place. As such, and also in its dialectical austerity, it differs sharply from the *Theaetetus* and from most of the dialogues where Plato, in his maturity, casts Socrates as the principal discussant.

Why does Plato drop Socrates? Or rather, why does Plato make the Eleatic Stranger the principal discussant for the *Sophist* and *Statesman* after giving Socrates the leading role in the *Theaetetus*? The best approach to this question that I have read was advanced long ago by Julius Stenzel in studies widely known under the title *Plato's Method of Dialectic*. For Stenzel, the transition from Socrates to the Eleatic Stranger is a sign 'that Plato's philosophical interest has entirely changed its direction'. Prior to the *Sophist*, Stenzel suggests, ' Plato thought, as he made each new discovery, that he had simply found some new side to the main Socratic question some other consequence of the critical, yet productive logical method which the master had practised.' Stenzel's thesis is bold and complex. Rather than elaborating it here, which would take up all my space, I mention it because of its partial resemblance to the position I want to develop. In working on the *Theaetetus* recently, I overlooked or forgot Stenzel's work for a while, only to discover later a good measure of agreement between his views and what I was trying to say.

Yet neither Stenzel nor anyone else to my knowledge has focused the question as sharply as the material warrants. To achieve that focus, we need first to recognize that the Socrates of the *Theaetetus* has a vividness, wit, and existential presence which are the dramatic equal of anything Plato created in earlier dialogues. Not only that. This Socrates clearly recalls, but equally clearly revises, his previous literary incarnations. He presents himself, for the first and only time, as a philosophical midwife. He uses a great contemporary, Protagoras, to give himself a strict lesson in how philosophical discussion should be conducted if it is to be peculiarity of this Socrates, when it is acknowledged at all, is commonly explained along these reductive lines: we are invited to regard him as a direct reflection of Plato's own philosophical problems at the time of composition. So, according to David Bostock, ' Plato feels himself to be in much the same situation as when he wrote the early dialogues.' Hence Plato returns us to an aporetic and utterly inconclusive Socrates, incongruous though that Socrates is with the Socrates of the *Republic*'s positive proposals, and so on. It is true, of course, that Plato's Socrates in the *Theaetetus* emphatically insists on his own ignorance. However, that dominant characteristic is not peculiar to this Socrates among every later Socrates; it recurs in the *Phaedrus*, to say nothing of Socrates' frequent disclaimers even in the *Republic*. In addition, during his so-called digression in the *Theaetetus* Socrates makes ethical, ontological, and theological pronouncements which allude unmistakably to views he advances in the *Phaedo* and the *Republic*. There are different ways of interpreting the 'digression'. But on any interpretation, the digression complicates the representation of Socrates and what he stands for in the *Theaetetus*. Apart from all this, we presume to know much more about Plato than we are entitled to do when we assume that he himself, or even his Socrates in the *Theaetetus*, is committed to the dialogue's negative conclusions concerning the definability of knowledge.

I entirely agree with Bostock that the considerations which primarily influence Plato's representation of Socrates in the *Theaetetus* are philosophical. This pertains to all his images of Socrates and, *a fortiori*, to his reasons for discarding Socrates from the discussion in the *Sophist* and *Statesman*. In Plato, however, up to and including the *Theaetetus* (but importantly excepting part 2 of the *Parmenides*), philosophy is generally construed as an interpersonal dialogue where the theses discussed are not detachable from the beliefs, or at least the more than perfunctory admissions, of all the participants. In the *Theaetetus*, as generally before, Plato draws no distinction between philosophical activity and the life and interpersonal discourse of Socrates. That is what makes the dropping of Socrates so remarkable, especially after his appearance in the *Theaetetus* as the paradigm philosopher yet again. Up to this point, Plato has forged a virtually continuous link between his method of presenting the philosopher to the public and his own representations of Socrates. He has repeatedly defined the philosopher, ostensively, via these representations. Yet in the *Sophist* Plato chooses another philosopher, the Eleatic Stranger, to mastermind a conversation which has the object of distinguishing between the sophist, the statesman, and the philosopher.

Here, then, we have another remarkable fact. Not only does Plato, in the *Sophist*, drop Socrates from the main conversation of the day dramatically following that of the Theaetetus. Having in that earlier dialogue presented his readers with the very powerful and attractive Socrates I have described, he writes the *Sophist*, a dialogue which starts from the problem of identifying the genuine philosopher and eliminates any contribution to that problem by Socrates himself Is it that Socrates cannot define himself? Is his genuineness as the paradigm philosopher not self-evident from his self-descriptions and dialectic in the *Theaetetus*? Is Plato suggesting that there is more to philosophy and to the philosopher than he can convey by any representation of Socrates? Are the technical topics and dialectical method treated in the *Sophist* and *Statesman* the primary reasons why Plato keeps Socrates silent—even if Socrates has already outlined collection and division in the *Phaedrus*? I shall touch on all of these questions, but the one I shall eventually pursue the furthest concerns the identification of the philosopher independently of Socrates.

Before getting into further details, let me try to show why this question has a great deal to do with Plato's philosophical methodology. Prolific authors sometimes tire of the characters they create over a long sequence of words—one thinks of R. G. Wodehouse's Jeeves, or a detective storywriter's replacement of one favourite sleuth by another. But in Plato's case such a simple explanation can be firmly excluded. His Socrates is never a mere character. Plato constantly reminds his readers that his representation of Socrates is a representation which includes biographical reference to the historical figure. Plato's Socrates, as I have said before, is an existential presence in the dialogues. Throughout most of Plato's writings this figure embodies and expounds what must be Plato's conception, at the time of writing, of the best way to engage in philosophical inquiry. In those same works Socrates is represented as the living paradigm of what it means to be a philosopher a person uniquely committed to an interpersonal search for knowledge and to practices that never deviate from this commitment. It does not follow from these points that Plato endorses every question or answer, every doubt or thesis, he assigns to Socrates. As many scholars have recently urged, we cannot simply read off Plato's thought from the words that Socrates utters, or from the conclusions that he draws, or even from the myths to which he gives expression. What do follow, I suggest, are two inferences concerning Plato's philosophy in its written form.

The first inference is that his Socrates is generally the vehicle or personified representation of his author's methodology and philosophical ideals. However, because Plato's Socrates is both the author's imaginative construction and the historical figure, the role that he plays in the dialogues is extremely complex. My second inference is that in using Socrates as his philosophical vehicle, Plato is also commenting on and *interpreting the significance for philosophy of* Socrates' *life*. On this construal, the Socratic dialogues are never closed. The real Socrates is, as it were, an existential quantifier bracketed on to the conversations Plato has devised. Hence Plato's representations of Socrates' life typically include salient features of his actual biography, but it is above all a literary life, a life that Plato confers on Socrates in order to make philosophical sense of the figure Plato takes Socrates to have been. The point, as I would like to develop it, is that Plato, up to and including the composition of the Theaetetus, never stops rewriting the *Apology*. With the *Theaetetus* Plato completes that task, lets his former Socrates go, and moves on.

Before justifying the point about rewriting the *Apology*, I should make it crystal clear that I am not taking a view on the authenticity of anything Plato attributes to Socrates as documentary evidence of what the historical Socrates said and thought. In saying that Plato's Socrates regularly includes reference to the historical figure, what I mean is that Plato continually intends his readers to think of the Socrates of the *Theaetetus* and earlier dialogues as the philosopher who was tried and executed in 399 BC. This does not imply that Plato credits that man, or expects his readers to credit him, with the exact thoughts of Plato's Socrates. Where scholars have often gone wrong, in my opinion, is in supposing that the main question to ask about Plato's Socrates is the historicity or non-historicity of what that Socrates says. This, of course, is the key question if we are interested in the historical Socrates. But, so far as Plato is concerned, the principal issue is how he uses his own Socrates from start to finish; or, as I would prefer to put it, how the figure that Plato began to create in the *Apology* shapes Plato's philosophizing. Unlike Burnet and Taylor, for instance, I want to detach that figure from 'actual Socratic thought', both in the early (so-called Socratic) dialogues and in the works, starting with the *Meno* and *Phaedo*, in which Plato is often thought to be beginning his radical departure from the historical Socrates. But I sympathize with their belief that Plato's Socrates is never a mere mouthpiece of Plato's own philosophy or merely an imaginary ideal. An image of the real man, the existential figure, is always or almost always part of the representation, in my opinion.

Always, if we exclude the latest dialogues. Or, allowing that claim to stand, but including the *Parmenides*, should we say almost always? I have already declared my belief that this dialogue is prior in composition and thematic order to the *Theaetetus*. I have no doubt too that the philosophical content of both works, to which I would add the *Phaedrus*, reflects radical transitions in Plato's own reflections. The compositional order I find most plausible for these dialogues is *Parmenides*, *Phaedrus*, *Theaetetus*, an order that corresponds to Socrates' youth, maturity, and final year. Each dialogue, I think, exhibits Plato grappling with problems and proposals which he finally synthesizes in the *Sophist*; which is not to say that the compositional order of those dialogues precisely charts the stages of Plato's actual thought. (Like a number of scholars, I incline to the view that Plato wrote the Theaetetus with much of the *Sophist*'s methodology and doctrine already firmly in mind.) In the *Parmenides*, Socrates is 'very young', not yet firmly gripped by philosophy, as *Parmenides* says and mistaking Zeno's youthful contentiousness for a more mature ambition. In the *Phaedrus* Socrates is represented as a full-fledged philosopher, but in an unwonted rural setting. In the *Theaetetus* he is about to go on trial, and is situated in a context which is as close as Plato ever comes to giving an image of the Academy The point I want to derive from the three ages and settings of Socrates is that Plato marks his own transitions by linking them to a final representation and defence of Socrates' philosophical life in its entirety. In that case, the *Parmenides* can be accommodated to the picture I am sketching.

The farewell to Socrates, on this view, begins in the *Parmenides,* and ends in the *Theaetetus.* What motivates the farewell, I shall argue, is not simply the inappropriateness of having Socrates expound the doctrines and methodologies of the *Sophist* and *Statesman.* Nor is it mainly, though it surely includes, Plato's devotion to his own image of Socrates. The primary motivation, I believe, is a gradual but profound change in Plato's conception of philosophy and the philosopher. Signs of this change are already evident in the three transitional dialogues. By the time he wrote the *Sophist,* Plato discards Socrates because his own Socratic figure, many-sided though Plato has made him out to be, cannot represent more than a preliminary feature of the philosophical paradigm, as Plato now construes it. Before justifying this proposal, I turn to some of the details of the *Theaetetus.*

The conversation the *Theaetetus* purports to record is being read to Terpsion by Eucleides. Their encounter takes place some thirty years after Eucleides wrote down a discussion he had heard between Socrates and two mathematicians, the mature Theodorus and the novice *Theaetetus.* In the dialogue's preface Eucleides remarks that Socrates met Theaetetus shortly before Socrates' death. Right at the end of the dialogue proper, Socrates tells Theaetetus that he has to keep an appointment at the lawcourts, in connection with the indictment Meletus has served against him. The dramatic date of the conversation, then, is 399, the year of Socrates' trial and execution. We are alerted to this chronology at the beginning and at the end of the work.

It is possible, presumably, that this dating of the conversation has a historical foundation. Even so, Plato must have other reasons for emphasizing it in this way. The last sentence of the *Theaetetus* is an intertextual allusion to the *Euthyphro*: at the beginning of that dialogue Socrates also tells his interlocutor about the charges Meletus has made against him. Those charges, especially the indictment concerning impiety, are rebutted by Socrates' conversation with Euthyphro. In the *Theaetetus*, as in the *Apology*, Socrates defends his educational mission. In the opening pages of the dialogue proper, Socrates characterizes himself as someone dedicated to investigating the intellectual progress of young men. His preliminary conversation with Theodorus and the young Theaetetus gives the lie to the charge of corrupting the youth. Then, in his declaration of his art as a barren but philosophical midwife, Socrates runs over his career and mission in ways that unmistakably allude to, but (in my opinion) seek to improve on, his account of himself in the *Apology*. He makes it his business to attend to the souls of young men who are pregnant with ideas; he sees it as his job to test the philosophical soundness of these. He is reproached, as he acknowledges, for asking questions and affirming nothing himself. He behaves in this way because he knows himself to have no wisdom. None the less, his work as a philosophical midwife is divinely mandated. With some of his young associates he has been successful, with others not; and these latter have belittled him. In deciding whether to make further efforts with someone, he is guided by his daimonion. He admits that some persons have been infuriated by having their nonsense removed by him. What they fail to realize is that his devotion to truth is always pursued out of pure good will.

These allusions to the *Apology*, situated as they are at an early stage of the discussion, could not be more emphatic. Combined with the dramatic date of the *Theaetetus*, they invite us to include in our reading of the dialogue a strong recognition that Plato is once again defending Socrates and clarifying his significance for philosophy. But this, of course, is what Plato has been doing ever since he first took up his philosophical pen. What is remarkable about the *Theaetetus* is the explicitness of Socrates' defence, its chronology, and its allusions to, and recasting of, the official Apology.

In order to give perspective to this matter, we should recall a selection of the moments in earlier dialogues when Plato signals that he is renewing or correcting his original defence of Socrates. In the *Apology* proper, Socrates, though representing himself as the Athenians' gadfly, minimizes his involvement in political life. Yet in the *Gorgias* he tells Callicles that he may be the only Athenian who is a student of genuine politics and its only proper practitioner. In the same context, to confirm the allusion to the *Apology*, Socrates foresees that he may die for lack of any capacity to pander to the jury. The eschatology at the end of the *Gorgias*, forceful as it is about the soul's afterlife, is a striking departure from Socrates' conditional speculations at the end of the *Apology*. Early in the *Phaedo* Socrates tells those who have joined him in prison: 'Let me try to make a more convincing defence to you [of my unconcern about dying] than I did before my jurors'. A little later he refers to his associates as 'you my jurors', when beginning to explain why a philosopher has no fear of death.

This passage is unusual in the degree of its explicit intertextuality, but my suggestion that Plato continuously rewrites the *Apology* is not, or not primarily, a literary point. What I mean by it is that the Apology is programmatic, in fundamental ways, for most of the works that Plato composed up to the *Theaetetus*. Take this large selection of Plato's major works that probably fall within this time frame *Gorgias*, *Protagoras*, *Meno*, *Phaedo*, *Republic*, *Euthydemus*, *Symposium*, and *Phaedrus*. Each one of these dialogues has its own problematic, its own mise-en-scène, its own distinctive character, including its portrayal of Socrates. Yet, they all share the common concern of justifying philosophy. And they typically seek to justify it by distinguishing it from sophistry, eristic competition, poetry, professional rhetoric, or any other intellectual technç. In saying this, I am restating the principal point which Charles Griswold makes in his article, 'Plato's Metaphilosophy': 'Dialogue after dialogue raises the question "why philosophize?" Plato's dialogues seem obsessed with the fundamental questions concerning the justification of philosophy'.

It needs no argument to assert that the Apology is a justification of philosophy. Whether we regard the dialogue as Plato's defence of Socrates' actual life, or as Plato's first attempt to come to terms with the significance of Socrates' life for philosophy, in either case Plato's purpose in defending Socrates is to show why Socrates' life matters, which is to show in writing why philosophy matters. But to show this is a Herculean labour, for two reasons. First, there are no literary guidelines. No one prior to Plato has written a defence of philosophy; or, rather, no one prior to Plato has articulated philosophy in the way that Plato is beginning to intuit it via his reflections on Socrates. Secondly, as I surmise, Plato was at least as much baffled by the historical Socrates as he was stimulated or educated by him. In saying this, I gratefully acknowledge my indebtedness to a range of observations made by Alexander Nehamas in his recent Sather Lectures at Berkeley on the theme 'Images of Socrates'.

Focusing on the early Socratic dialogues, such as the *Euthyphro*, Nehamas finds Plato unable to make complete sense of the Socrates figure he has created. In Plato's early work, according to Nehamas, he presents us with a Socrates who is an enigma not merely in virtue of Socrates' persistent irony. What chiefly puzzles Plato is Socrates' unaccountability: Socrates has the evident capacity to be perfectly reliable in acting rightly, yet he lacks the knowledge of *aretç*, which, according to himself, is the prerequisite for being the moral exemplar that he is. This opacity of Socrates, as construed by Nehamas, is Plato's challenge to himself to develop thoughts which will provide Socrates with depth and transparency. Dialogues such as the *Gorgias*, *Meno*, and *Symposium* (according to Nehamas) are the beginning of Plato's attempt to understand what enabled Socrates to live the life that Plato confers on him. We should see this as an ongoing process on Plato's part. Which is not to say that Plato is ever satisfied that he has fully or adequately explained the phenomenon of Socrates. The challenge, opacity, and bafflement continue; but in midcareer, however far he departs from anything that Socrates could have thought, Plato is continuing to try to understand what allowed Socrates to live as he did.

I do not intend to commit Nehamas to my own formulation—that Plato keeps rewriting the *Apology*. But what I mean fits his intuitions about Plato's continuous efforts to make philosophical sense of the Socrates which Plato's writings, starting with the *Apology*, have created. I take Stenzel to be making the same point when he writes: 'It is [Plato's intention] to prove that without [the transcendent Good, as Plato came to understand it] there can be no demonstration of the main principle of Socrates' life: that Virtue can be taught, so long as it is not a mere opinion about the Good, but knowledge.'

According to this way of looking at Plato's relation to Socrates, Platonic doctrine or methodology and the Socrates figure resist the bifurcation which Vlastos tried to establish in his great book, *Socrates. Ironist and Moral Philosopher.* What ties Plato to Socrates is not a quasi-historical philosopher, who is succeeded by a thoroughly doctrinal Platonist in disguise. Some of the differences Vlastos signals between the so-called early and middle Socrates are valid, but the 'schizophrenia' that Vlastos took himself to be removing from Plato's Socrates by bifurcating this figure was never at issue. The real separation from Socrates, when it comes, is after the *Theaetetus*. That dialogue was a problem for Vlastos that he never really faced. He includes it in his 'middle' segment, linking it thereby to the *Cratyluss*, *Phaedo*, *Symposium*, *Republic II-X*, *Phaedrus*, and *Parmenides*. Yet, the *Theaetetus* scarcely fits any of his criteria for identifying this Platonic segment: separately existing Forms and the doctrine of recollection, Socrates' search for and confidence in finding demonstrative knowledge, the tripartite *psyche*, Socrates' mastery of mathematics, elaborate political theory, metaphysics of *eros*, and mystical contemplation of Forms. The only one of Vlastos's criteria for his middle Socrates that I find clearly appropriate to the *Theaetetus* is an élitist, as distinct from a populist, conception of philosophy.

It would have suited Vlastos to sever the connection of the *Theaetetus* with his middle Socrates, as indeed he appears to be doing when he writes: 'The metaphysical theory of the preceding dialogues of the middle period is subjected to searching criticism by "Parmenides" and then Socrates, assaying a fresh start, shifts to a new "maieutic" mode of investigation in the *Theaetetus*.' Vlastos says that this Socrates 'has so much in common with early Socrates', and also that the dialogue gives us a glimpse of 'a different, much improved Socrates, who has tried to rest the demon of contentiousness within him' (recall my earlier remarks about Protagoras's exhortations to Socrates to argue fairly, as voiced by Socrates himself). Three specific things, according to Vlastos, justify his assessment of this Socrates as 'Middle' rather than 'Early'. First, a profession of progress at *Theaetetus*187a which is not accompanied by a reassertion of ignorance; second, an increment in Socrates' knowledge at the end of the inquiry (this is Vlastos's inference, and goes against the text, in my opinion); third, Socrates' refutation of a doctrine 'which by no stretch of the imagination could have been fished out of Theaetetus' own belief system'.

I agree with Vlastos that the Socrates of the *Theaetetus* is clearly different from Plato's early Socrates. However, he is also distinctly different from any Socrates in the rest of Vlastos's middle segment of dialogues, whose representations of Socrates in their turn seem to me far less homogeneous than he proposes. The Socrates of the *Phaedrus* in personality, doctrine, and argumentative style is scarcely prepared for by the Socrates of the *Republic*. To be sure, Plato links this pair together by crediting each of them with such substantive points as the tripartite soul, recollection, supra-sensible Forms, and a metaphysically grounded account of dialectic. But it is arbitrary to emphasize these congruities at the expense of ignoring the distinctive interests of the *Phaedrus* Socrates: for instance, the upgrading of rhetoric, the treatment of philosophy as a species of *mania*, collection and division, the philosopher's explicit need to select *logoi* that are peculiarly suited to his interlocutor's soul, and so on. Similar points can be made concerning any two representations of Socrates from the major dialogues.

If Plato's Socrates is as many-sided and variable as I am suggesting, why not treat him as a figure freshly created in each new dialogue, a plastic tool of his author's interests? I have some sympathy for this point of view; but the plasticity of Plato's Socrates, such as it is, confirms, rather than conflicts with, the position I have been sketching up to now. If Socrates were indefinitely plastic, Plato would have no philosophical reason for discarding him in the *Sophist* and *Statesman*. Over many years, he finds no difficulty in making Socrates the vehicle of his own developing thoughts and methodologies. But this plasticity of Socrates, which is also Plato's internal dialogue, has definite limits. I have already mentioned some of these–the frequent reference or allusion to the man who was tried and executed in 399 BC, the defence of philosophy via each representation of Socrates, and Plato's concern (as proposed above) to make his own philosophical findings consistent with, and explanatory of, the life and significance of Socrates. Socrates can be plastic, in the sense that Plato can credit him over time with a range of views about, let us say, the structure of the soul. In a single dialogue, Socrates can be relatively sceptical, relatively doctrinaire, or a combination of these. But he is regularly and firmly contoured in ways that make him recognizably the same throughout: his pursuit of knowledge via interpersonal question and answer, his dedication to this pursuit as his life's purpose, his commitment to consistency between thought and action, his elevation of moral and intellectual goods over everything else. Plato, we feel sure, is always at one with his Socrates about all this.

But these limits to the plasticity, such as they are, cannot disguise a clear tension at times between the Socratic figure with his inimitable style (the challenger of Thrasymachus, the lover in the *Symposium*, the midwife of the *Theaetetus*) and the role of that figure as paradigm or spokesman for philosophy in general. Signs of this tension are particularly evident in the central books of the *Republic*. It is Socrates who characterizes philosophy and the philosopher for his audience there, but he does so in ways that are minimally personal or self-referential. If Plato is now detaching the Socratic figure from the Socratic spokesman, or betraying the tension that exists between them, do we have a clue to the representation of Socrates in the *Theaetetus*?

Let us return to that dialogue. Socrates has renewed his defence of his philosophical activity. He has clarified his peculiar mission as a midwife capable of delivering and testing the thoughts of those who are pregnant with ideas, but who is infertile himself. In the longest stretch of sustained argument in Plato, Socrates explores, refines, and criticizes the thesis, offered to him by Theaetetus, that knowledge is perception. His treatment of Protagoras, though tinged with irony, is immensely searching. Plato has never been as careful as he is here in handling a thesis he intends to refute. Protagoras is given repeated opportunities to make a come-back, and to insist on the strictest standards of dialectical fair play. The linking of the Protagorean thesis to Heracliteanism is not regarded as sufficient to undermine the definition of knowledge as perception. That thesis is finally disposed of only when it is found to conflict with the non-perceptible status of those things–being and not-being, sameness and difference, and so on which must be apprehended as a precondition of grasping any truth.

This manifestation of Socrates' midwifery is interrupted, before it is complete, by his 'digression' to Theodorus. The context of the digression is the question of whether, as Protagoras has been made to claim, the truth of moral judgements is purely relative. Socrates suggests that this position is widely accepted even by those who do not extend relativism to all judgements. The digression starts by distinguishing the impracticality, leisurely discourse, and freedom of the philosopher from the time constraints and servitude of the lawyer or politician. The philosopher is hopelessly inept in practical affairs. Uncertain of what it means to be human, he focuses on questions about precisely that. In this sphere, by contrast, it is the practical man who is inept. Juxtaposing the two types, Socrates rapidly enunciates a series of propositions which clearly recall earlier dialogues, especially the *Republic* and *Phaedo*. They include the need for release from earthly life as soon as possible, the uniform goodness of god, the inter-entailment of wisdom, happiness, and moral excellence, the exposure of sham expertise, the inevitability that a bad pattern of life now will infect the lives someone lives after his present one is over.

These are familiar themes from Plato's earlier Socrates. But in the *Theaetetus* Socrates combines them with other themes that are more novel and foreshadow Plato's latest theology the injunction to resemble god as far as possible, and the conception of god as the paradigm of supreme happiness. In addition, Socrates ends the digression with a homily on the effects of dialectic on a complacent and morally ignorant rhetorician: if such a person has the courage to submit to a private interrogation concerning his contempt for justice, he will lose his conceit and eloquence, and become no different from the child that he really is. Here, if I am not mistaken, Plato recalls the Socrates of the *Gorgias*. Plato also anticipates what I take to be no less 'Socratic' in the *Sophist* the modesty that the elenchus, or the sophistry of golden lineage, engenders by its purgation of persons' 'grand and obstinate opinions concerning themselves'.

Socrates himself calls all this a 'digression', to the disappointment of Theodorus, who finds it 'easier to follow at his age'. What is Plato doing? I think the digression is integral to his farewell to Socrates. It gives a reprise of Socrates which looks far beyond the midwifery role. In doing so, it also reflects the tension I have mentioned concerning Socrates as an inimitable personality and Socrates as the paradigm or spokesman for philosophy. Cast in the role of the barren midwife, Socrates' primary task is the education of the young Theaetetus. But Plato and Plato's readers know that his Socrates cannot be identified so easily, powerful though the midwifery image is. Plato has devoted his literary life to motivating Socrates, giving him convictions and concepts which provide ethical, metaphysical, theological, and psychological underpinning for the dialectic that he practises in the dialogues. Here, on the point of bidding farewell to Socrates, he credits him yet again with a set of such convictions and concepts a final apologia, as it were.

The treatment is brief, because Plato's readers already know that Socrates stands for these things. So why include the passage here, digressive as it is said to be and appears to be? The answer I propose to this question brings me to my main point.

My proposal is that, from the time he began writing the *Parmenides*, Plato had convinced himself that there is more to philosophy and to being a philosopher than even he could attribute to Socrates. The second part of the *Parmenides*, though superficially a dialogue, is really a textbook of disjunctive hypotheses and dialectical exercises. Whatever view we take about Plato's purpose in presenting these, we can scarcely doubt that he is distancing himself from his own Socrates. The training that Parmenides is ostensibly offering to Socrates, the formality of the methodology, the even-handed examination of intensely abstract antinomies as distinct from the beliefs of persons—these are just some of the most obvious indications of this distancing. How far the purpose of the antinomies is constructive rather than gymnastic does not affect this point. I take Plato to be saying that his own Socrates (which includes Plato's philosophy hitherto) has deployed disjunctions between unity and plurality, between being and not being, and between Forms and other things, with insufficient attention to their complexity, ambiguity, and interconnections; a more rigorous logic than any applied before is needed. Though the outcome is also devastating to the historical Parmenides, his contribution to philosophical method and its difference from Socratic conversation will soon be refurbished by the logic of the *Eleatic Stranger.*

Much profit can be had from reading the Theaetetus as a self-contained exploration of attempts to define knowledge and to challenge the reader to work out solutions to the problems it poses. This is largely Myles Burnyeat's approach in his brilliant commentary. For beginning students, who cannot be expected to relate the dialogue to Plato's complete opus, the approach is entirely defensible. But its limitations for interpreting Plato more broadly are evident as soon as we acknowledge, as I think we must, that, to quote Kenneth M. Sayre: ' The Sophist overcomes all the major obstacles set in the Theaetetus to arriving at a credible account of knowledge.' By fully exemplifying collection and division, by distinguishing between negation and difference, by showing how antithetical concepts can be combined without contradiction, by his excursions into grammar, the *Eleatic Stranger* exhibits the philosophical difference between true and false sentences. He shows how true sentences with generic subjects can be hierarchically organized in ways that represent the structure of what is demonstrably knowable. If this is right (leaving aside further details of why and how it is right), it becomes obvious that Plato cannot entrust the exposition to a *Theaetetus* Socrates who advertises his know-nothing stance. Rather than viewing this Socratic disavowal of knowledge as a return to Plato's earlier models, we should interpret it in terms of Plato's current concaption of philosophy.

But Socrates, though silent after the beginning of the *Sophist*, is not omitted from the dialogue's exploration of philosophy. Just about everyone recognizes that the 'sophistry of golden lineage' is an allusion to Socrates' elenctic methodology. What is scarcely noticed, in addition, is Plato's intertextual allusion to the *Theaetetus*. Practitioners of the elenchus, says the *Eleatic Stranger*, are persons who believe that all ignorance is involuntary. They 'interrogate someone on any subject on which he thinks he has something to say, though saying nothing. Then, when such persons are floundering, they readily scrutinize their opinions, and assembling them together by arguments, they confront these opinions with one another', with a view to showing their contradictoriness. The purging effect of this procedure renders its patients 'gentle' in their relationships with others, and also, by convincing them of their own ignorance, it makes them 'modest'. Plato's language here, *'hçmerountai'* and *'aischunç'*, recalls Socrates' verdict on what will happen to Theaetetus if he continues to be barren: 'you will be less oppressive to your associates and gentler (*hçmerôteros*), in your modestly (*sôphronôs*) not thinking that you know things you do not know'.

In the division procedure by which the sophistry of golden lineage is identified, 'education' (*paideutikç*), a species of the sub-genus 'instruction' (*didaskalikç*). We may take this as Plato's sign that there is more to 'instruction' that is, purgation of the soul than is embraced by convincing someone of ignorance. What more there may be to instruction is not explained here. The purpose of this division is still a preliminary stage of sifting the designations of the terms 'philosopher', 'sophist', and 'statesman'. What this division serves to do is both to distinguish the Socratic elenchus from sophistry in that term's other designations and to decline to identify Socrates' educational practice with philosophy in its entirety. As a commentary on the *Theaetetus*, this amounts to saying that the dialogue represents only the necessary beginnings of a philosophical education. A different kind of philosopher, the *Eleatic Stranger*, is needed to guide Theaetetus from the recognition of his ignorance, induced in him by *Socrates*, to reflections which can constitute a genuine understanding of knowledge.

The methodology of the *Sophist* is not compatible with an aporetic and ostensibly barren Socrates. That much is clear. But rather than resolving my main questions, this truism begs them. The Socrates of the *Republic*, tentative though he sometimes is, seems to have much in common with the *Eleatic*

Stranger. In the central books of that dialogue Socrates expounds doctrine after doctrine, albeit by means of images rather than the Eleatic's austere logic and conceptual analysis. There are other procedural differences one could mention, but Socrates' interlocutors in the later books of the *Republic*, like Theaetetus in the *Sophist*, are little more than yes-men. If Socrates' methodology in the *Republic* is significantly different from that of the *Eleatic Stranger*, the difference is not to be measured in terms of the interlocutors' contribution.

By the time he wrote the *Republic*, Plato was quite capable of using the dialogue form as a thin disguise for the exposition of doctrine. He had no compunctions, when it suited him, about playing down Socrates' profession of ignorance. Had he not written the *Theaetetus*, could we imagine him composing a dialogue like the *Sophist* in which Socrates, after being given Eleatic training in the *Parmenides*, plays a role similar to that of the *Eleatic Stranger?* We could imagine this, I submit, only if we forget the limits, wide and sometimes strained though they are, that have encompassed Plato's representations of Socrates—the contours of an enigmatic but historical figure, the search for a philosophy that would explain and motivate that figure, the uniqueness and existential presence of Socrates. *The Eleatic Stranger* is largely void of character and personality. He stands for philosophy, but a philosophy that is formal, mathematical, detached from historical contingency.

The philosophy that he stands for is Plato's philosophy, or rather, Plato's post-Socratic philosophy. At earlier stages in his writing, Plato had begun to develop this kind of philosophy. There are stretches of it in the Meno and the *Phaedo*, and more ambitious excursions of the same in the *Republic*. Socrates' strangeness, his *atopia*, persuaded Plato for a long time that his interpretation of the real man and his passion to understand him were all of a piece with Plato's own philosophy. He could allow Socrates to engage in *ad hominem* argument, and also pursue quite different speculative paths. A philosopher, a Socratic philosopher, could inhabit two worlds simultaneously. He could pass out of the Cave and return to it. As long as Plato retained personal hopes of reforming a society, so I conjecture, he held on to Socrates.

Plato's hopes in this sphere turn sour. There the biographical tradition rings true. At the same time, and independently or not, Plato's logical, mathematical, and empirical interests are developing rapidly. He is heavily engaged in the Academy as distinct from a community at large. Passionately committed, as he always has been, to an ideal of objective knowledge, he finds himself increasingly drawn toward science and away from the predominantly moral concerns of his own Socrates. At some point—I identify this with the composition of the *Parmenides*—he decides that his own intuitions and philosophical techniques have outstripped anything he could plausibly attribute to his own Socrates. He also recognizes that philosophy, as he now conceives of it, is unambiguously élitist as distinct from demotic, academic, and separate from practical life. If these speculations are anywhere near the mark, they go some way to providing an explanation for the farewell to Socrates in the *Theaetetus*—the 'final Apology' as I call it.

Plato had attributed his theory of Forms to Socrates, but, as a theory, it was vulnerable to 'Eleatic' criticism. The *Parmenides* corrects Socrates, tells him that there are things he does not know and needs to learn. That is Plato's first explicit move away from Socrates, his first indication that Socrates does not encapsulate the whole of philosophy. The *Phaedrus*, if it comes next, as I have suggested, gives us a Socrates who is as attractive in his own way as the Socrates of the *Theaetetus*. This Socrates retains clear links with his earlier representations and viewpoints, but he looks forward to the later dialogues where he will be silent. He gives hints rather than full expositions of later Platonic themes—collection and division, cosmic motion, and so on. He is bursting with ideas, but they are ideas which he, like the inspired poets, is scarcely able to control.

In its fecundity the *Phaedrus* is a tremendous compliment to Socrates, but the dialogue has an air of unreality or fantasy. That air, if I am right, is deliberate a sign that Plato is taking his paradigm philosopher out of the city and bidding him farewell. And then, the *Theaetetus*. According to my interpretation, Plato is now asserting, without irony or qualification, that this Socrates who is also the aggregate of every previous Platonic Socrates—is not a philosopher who has the technical equipment and methodology for giving a formal exhibition of what it is to know something. Yet, at the same time, Socrates is superb at conducting the best kind of *ad hominem* argument on this topic, at putting forward proposals for consideration, at helping an interlocutor to discover what the issues are and why solutions to them are so difficult to consolidate. In order to write the *Sophist*, Plato has to let Socrates die, as Socrates is soon to do according to the dialogue's dramatic date. But it is only the Socrates of the *Theaetetus* who can prepare the young man himself for the kind of philosophy he will be taught in the *Sophist*.

The *Theaetetus*, omitting the digression, is a masterpiece of Platonic reticence. It gives the appearance of having an author who has wiped the slate clean, who is deliberately eschewing dependence on everything he has argued up to now concerning knowledge and perception, dialectic and hypothesis, psychology and metaphysics. The midwife Socrates, who gives Theaetetus preliminary lessons in the early Socratic distinction between exemplification and definition, reinforces the impression that Plato has returned to the drawing-board. But with the *Parmenides* already written, the Phaedrus probably written too, and the *Sophist* to be written in the near future, we realize that there is more to the *Theaetetus* than a dazzling essay on the difficulties of doing epistemology. Both the *Phaedrus* and the *Sophist* presuppose that philosophers *have the knowledge* that Socrates in the *Theaetetus* so resolutely disclaims. By anchoring dialectic to collection and division, the former pair of dialogues *exhibits scientific knowledge*, as distinct from seeking, like the *Theaetetus*, to define the psychological conditions satisfied by persons who know concrete individual things, such as 'This is Theaetetus as distinct from Theodorus'.

In getting Socrates to follow this latter track, in having a resolutely know-nothing Socrates unable to assist in producing a definition of empirical knowledge, Plato knowingly runs the epistemological agenda into a blind alley. He deliberately bypasses much that is central to the work of the *Parmenides*, *Phaedrus*, and *Sophist*, while at the same time he adumbrates thoughts about concepts and language that he will develop in sequels to the *Theaetetus*. He gives us a *Theaetetus* Socrates who can refute extreme Heracliteanism, but who finds the exploration of Parmenidean monism too vast a topic for the present inquiry (184 a). Plato does not allow this Socrates to explore the combinations into which Forms can enter without surrendering their individual identity and unity.

I take this strategy to show that the Socratic elenchus (the sophistry of golden lineage) is philosophy's paradigmatic tool of destruction (exposing self-contradiction, etc.). For constructive philosophizing, however, the starting-point of inquiry is no longer to be opinions offered to, or even offered by, Socrates, but conceptual assumptions and formal procedures that are advanced as being objective, independent of personal attachment or personal history. Such I take to be the philosophy Plato is advancing via the *Eleatic Stranger* in the *Sophist* and *Statesman*—a philosophy that Aristotle will take over. Notwithstanding Socrates' role in the *Republic* and his nominal return in the *Philebus*, Plato clearly regarded his Eleatic inheritance as too distant from Socrates, including all of his own Socrates, to be canvassed by that great figure.

Earlier I spoke of limits to the plasticity of Plato's Socrates. I also referred to the tensions within those limits between Plato's defence of the Socrates figure and Plato's defence of philosophy. By focusing on the socalled transitional dialogues, as I have done, I think we can see where and why the tension prevailed over the plasticity. Given Plato's complexity, I hesitate to say more than I have already suggested concerning the philosophical criteria that mark the dropping of Socrates. If it is legitimate to draw inferences from the 'Eleatic' dialogues, the criteria are primarily threefold: the detachment of theoretical from practical inquiry, the depersonalization of dialectic, and a new standard of rigour in the method of doing what we would call logic and metaphysics.

Yet, there is much more to the farewell to Socrates than even this. At the point of explicitly extending his conception of philosophy beyond the Socratic persona, Plato for the last time renews his defence of Socrates, as we have seen, canonizing him with unparalleled brilliance and affection. Nor does he forget the two strands of his earlier Socrates, the elenctic practitioner and the figure with intuitions about the objective grounding of values in the ultimate patterns of reality. We hear about this second strand of Socrates in the digression of the *Theaetetus*. But unlike the Socrates of the *Republic*, his namesake in the *Theaetetus* does not seriously attempt to link epistemology and metaphysics to ethics. More emphatically, and more pessimistically, he draws an apparently unqualified distinction between philosophy and practical politics. This Socrates is much further removed from the city than the Socrates of the *Apology* and *Gorgias*, and still further removed from the philosopher-king. By the same token, he has become still closer to Plato, but just at the moment of severance. The *Theaetetus* is both the final compliment and the indication that philosophy has to include more than the Socratic paradigm Plato has set himself up to now.

There are few facts to settle the relative chronology of Plato's dialogues and the development of Plato's thought. Intuitions about the bearing of one dialogue's doctrinal content upon another's are scarcely avoidable, but more thought needs to be given to the way Plato uses Socrates and other primary spokesmen in dialogues that are not generally regarded as 'Socratic'. Underlying all the speculations of this paper is the Janus face of Socrates in the *Theaetetus*. That Socrates is virtually dropped from Part 2 of the *Parmenides* and from the *Sophist* and *Statesman* is a fact. I have tried to confront this fact by asking how it relates to Plato's apology for Socrates in the *Theaetetus*. The textual evidence for such an apology–the evidence that it too is a fact—seems to me to be overwhelming. This was my starting-point in writing the essay, and it will clamour for explanation whatever credence may or may not be given to any of my other proposals.

Bibliography

AALDERS G. J. D., H. WZN. (1986), *Historische periodisering in de oudheid* (Mededelingen der koninkl. Nederlandse Akad. van Wetenschappen, Afdeling Letterkunde, NR 49. 6; Amsterdam).

ADAM J. (1963), *The Republic of Plato*, 2nd edn. (Cambridge).

ALCOFF L., and POTTER E. (1993) (eds.), *Feminist Epistemologies* (London).

AMES R T. (1983), *The Art of Rulership: A Study in Ancient Chinese Political Thought* (Honolulu).

APPADURAI A. (1986), "Commodities and the Politics of Value" in A. Appadurai (ed.), *The Social Life of Things: Commodities in Cultural Perspective* (Cambridge), 3-63.

AUERBACH E. (1953), *Mimesis: The Representation of Reality in Western Literature* (Princeton; orig. *Mimesis: Dargestellte Wirklichkeit in der abendländischen Literatur* (Berne, 1946)).

BADIAN E. (1981), "The Deification of Alexander the Great", in H. J. Dell (ed.), *Ancient Macedonian Studies in Honor of Charles F. Edson* (Institute for Balkan Studies, 158; Thessaloniki), 27-71.

BINGEN J., CAMBIER G., and NACHTERGAEL G. (1975) (eds.), Le Monde grec: Pensée, littérature, histoire, documents. Hommages à Claire Préaux (Brussels).

BONNECHERE P. (1993), "Les Indices archéologiques du sacrifice humain grec en question: Compléments à une publication récente", Kernos, 6: 23-55.

BOREL M.-J., GRIZE J.-B., and MIÉVILLE D. (1983), *Essai de logique naturelle* (Berne).

BORGEAUD P. (1988), *The Cult of Pan in Ancient Greece (Chicago; orig. Recherches sur le dieu Pan* (Rome, 1979)).

BOUVIER D. (1997), "Mythe ou histoire: Le Choix de Platon", in M. Guglielmo and G. F. Gianotti (eds.), *Filosofia, storia, immaginario mitologico* (Alessandria), 41-64.

CANFORA L. (1995), "Mito e storiografia greca: Minosse, Odisseo, Eraclidi", in M. Rossi Cittadini (ed.), *Presenze classiche nelle letterature occidentali* (Perugia), 109-23.

CARPENTER T. H., and FARAONE C. A. (1993) (eds.), *Masks of Dionysus* (Ithaca, NY).

CARTLEDGE P. (1993), *The Greeks: A Portrait of Self and Others* (Oxford).

CASSIRER E. (1925), *Philosophie der symbolischen Formen; ii: Das mythische Denken* (Berlin).

CULLEN C. (1976), "A Chinese Eratosthenes of the Flat Earth: A Study of a Fragment of a Cosmology in Huai Nan-Tzu", *Bulletin of the School of Oriental and African Studies 39*: 106-27.

DETIENNE M. (1977), *The Gardens of Adonis: Spices in Greek Mythology* (Hassocks; onig. *Les Jardins d'Adonis: La Mythologie des aromates en Grèce* (Paris, 1972)).

DICKIE M. W. (1990), "Talos Bewitched. Magic, Atomic Theory and Paradoxography in Apollonius, Argonautica 4. 1638-88", in F. Cairns and M. Heath (eds.), *Papers of the Leeds International Latin Seminar*, 6 (Leeds), 267-96.

DUNAND F. (1986), "Les Associations dionysiaques au service du pouvoir lagide (IIIe s. av. J.-C.)", in *L'Association dionysiaque dans les sociétés anciennes (Collection de l'École Franqaise de Rome*, 89; Rome), 85-104.

EHRENBERG V. (1931), "Athenische Hymnus auf Demetrius Poliorcetes", *Die Antike*, 7: 279-97 (trans. in Ehrenberg, *Aspects of the Ancient World: Essays and Reviews* (Oxford, 1946), 179-98).

FARAONE C. A. (1992), *Talismans and Trojan Horses:*

Guardian Statues in Ancient Greek Myth and Ritual (Oxford).

FARNELL L. R. (1896), *The Cults of the Greek States*, i (Oxford).

FEHLING D. (1989), *Herodotus and His 'Sources': Citation, Invention and Narrative Art* (Leeds).

FINLEY M. I. (1965), "Myth, Memory and History", *History and Theory*, 4: 281-302 (repr. with revisions in Finley (1975), 11-33).

GEFFCKEN J. (1912), "Euhemerism", in J. Hastings (ed.), *Encyclopaedia of Religion and Ethics* (Edinburgh) v. 572-3.

GERNET L. (1917), *Recherches sur le développement de la pensée juridique et morale en Grèce. (Étude sémantique)* (Paris).

GORDON R. L. (1981) (ed.), *Myth, Religion and Society: Structuralist Essays* by M. Detienne, L. Gernet, J.-P. Vernant and P. Vidal-Naquet; *With an Introduction* by R. G. A. Buxton (Cambridge).

GRUPPE O. (1921), *Geschichte der klassischen Mythologie und Religionsgeschichte während des Mittelalters im Abendland und während der Neuzeit* (= W. H. Roscher, *Ausführliches Lexikon der griechischen und römischen Mythologie*, Suppl. 4; Leipzig).

HARTOG F. (1988), *The Mirror of Herodotus: The Representation of the Other in the Writing of History* (Berkeley and Los Angeles; orig. *Le Miroir d'Hérodote: Essai sur la representation de l'autre*, Paris, 1980; rev. edn. 1991).

JACOB C. (1994), "L'Ordre généalogique entre le mythe et l'histoire", in M. Detienne (ed.), *Transcrire les mythologies: Tradition, écriture, historicté* (Paris), 169-202.

JEFFERY L. H. and MORPURCO-DAVIES A. (1970), "Ðïéíéêáïôáò and ðïéíéêáìæåí: BM 1969.4-2.1, a New Archaic Inscription from Crete", *Kadmos*, 9: 118-54.

JULLIEN F. (1985), *La Valeur allusive: Des catégories originales de l'interprétation poétique dans la tradition chinoise: contribution à une réflexion sur l'altérité interculturelle* (Paris).

KILANI M. (1984), "Les Images de la montagne au passé et au présent: L'Exemple des Alpes valaisannes", *Arch.*

suisses trad. pop. 1: 27-55 (repr. in M. Kilani, *L'Invention de l'autre: Essais sur le discours anthropologique* (Lausanne, 1994), 137-65).

KUHLEMANN F.-M. (1996), "Mentalitätsgeschichte: Theoretische und methodische Überlegungen am Beispiel der Religion im 19. und 20. Jahrhundert", in W. Hardtwig and H.-U. Wehler (eds.), *Kulturgeschichte Heute* (Göttingen), 182-211.

MACK J. E. (1994), *Abduction: Human Encounters with Aliens* (New York).

MALINOWSKI B. (1935), *Coral Gardens and their Magic: A Study of the Methods of Tilling the Soil and of Agricultural Rites in the Trobriand Islands* (New York).

MAZZARINO S. (1947), *Fra oriente e occidente: Ricerche di storia greca arraica* (Florence).

MCGEE M. C. (1980), "The Ideograph: A Link between Rhetoric and Ideology", *Quarterly Journal of Speech*, 66: 1-16.

MEDAGLIA S. M., and CORCELLA A. (1993) (eds.), *Erodoto: Le storie, Libro IV* (Milan).

MEIJER P. A. (1981), "De Pythagoreïsche (leef)regels", *Hermeneus*, 53: 121-37.

MERKELBACH R. (1988), *Die Hirten des Dionysos* (Stuttgart).

MEYERSON I. (1948), *Les Fonctions psychologiques et les œuvres* (Paris).

MOMIGLIANO A. D. (1966), *Studies in Historiography* (London).

NEUMANN J. N. (1995), "La Malformation de l'homme: Son interprétation dans la cosmologie de l'Antiquité et du début du Moyen Age", Ethique, 16: 45-54.

PAILLER J.-M. (1988), Bacchanalia: La Répression de 186 av. J.-C. à Rome et en Italie: Vestiges, images, tradition (Bibliothèque des Écoles Françaises d'Athènes et de Rome, 270; Rome).

RUDHARDT J. (1982), "De l'inceste dans la mythologie

grecque", *Revue française de psychanalyse*, 46: 731-63.

RUSTEN J. S. (1982), *Dionysius Scytobrachion* (Papyrologica Coloniensia, 10; Opladen).

RUTHERFORD R. (1995), *The Art of Plato: Ten Essays in Platonic Interpretation* (London).

SARTON G. (1959), *A History of Science: Hellenistic Science and Culture in the Last Three Centuries B. C.* (Cambridge, Mass.).

SAUNERON S., and YOYOTTE Y. (1959), "La Naissance du monde selon l'Égypte ancienne", in *Sources orientales, i: La Naissance du monde* (Paris), 19-91.

SCHLESIER R. (1992), "Ritual und Mythos: Zur Anthropologie der Antike heute", in R. Faber and B. Kytzler (eds.), *Antike heute* (Würzburg), 93-1090.

SCHLUCHTER W. (1979), *Die Entwicklung des okzidentalen Rationalismus: Eine Analyse von Max Webers Gesellschaftsgeschichte* (Tübingen).

SMITH R. R. R. (1991), "A New Portrait of Pythagoras", in R. R. R. Smith and K. T. Erim (eds.), *Aphrodisias Papers, ii: The Theatre, A Sculptor's Workshop, Philosophers and Coin-types* (Ann Arbor), 159-67.

SNELL B. (1953), *The Discovery of the Mind: The Greek Origins of European Thought* (Oxford; orig. *Die Entdeckung des Geistes: Studien zur Entstehung des europäischen Denkens bei den Griechen* (4th edn.; Göttingen, 1975)).

TOULMIN S., and GOODFIELD J. (1965), *The Discovery of Time* (London).

TRENDALL A. D. (1994), *A Passion for Antiquities: Ancient Art from the Collection of Barbara and Lawrence Fleischmann* (Malibu, Calif.).

TURNBULL C. M. (1961), *The Forest People* (London).

UHLIG S. (1984), "Das äthiopische Henochbuch" (*Jüdische Schriften aus hellenistisch-römischer Zeit, V: Apokalypsen*, 6; Gütersloh).

VALERI M. (1997), "Religion, Discipline, and the Economy in Calvin's Geneva", *The Sixteenth Century Journal*, 28: 123-42.

VAN DER P. W. HORST, and MUSSIES G. (1990), *Studies on the Hellenistic Background of the New Testament* (Utrecht).

VANDERKAM J. C. (1995), *Enoch: A Man for All Generations* (Columbia, SC).

VANDERMEERSCH L. (1980), *Wangdao: ou, la voie royale: Recherches sur l'esprit des institutions de la Chine archaïque* (Paris).

Index